D0325966

PRINCESS *Margaret*

A LIFE OF CONTRASTS

This updated edition published in 2018 by
André Deutsch Ltd
An imprint of the
Carlton Publishing Group
20 Mortimer Street
London W1T 3JW

First published in 2000, second edition in 2002 by André Deutsch Ltd

Text copyright © Christopher Warwick 2002, 2018

The right of Christopher Warwick to be identified as the author of
this work has been asserted by him in accordance with the
Copyright, Designs and Patents Act 1988

All rights reserved. This book is sold subject to the condition that it may
not be reproduced, stored in a retrieval system or transmitted in any form
or by any means, electronic, mechanical, photocopying, recording or
otherwise without the Publisher's prior consent
A catalogue record for this book is available from the British Library

ISBN 978 0 233 00531 7

Printed and bound in the UK

1 3 5 7 9 10 8 6 4 2

The author and publishers are grateful to The Royal Archives for
permission to quote from Princess Elizabeth's essay about the
Coronation of King George VI and Queen Elizabeth as published in
The Royal Encyclopedia (Macmillan 1991); William Heinemann for
permission to quote from Elizabeth: A Biography of Her Majesty The Queen
by Sarah Bradford; and Constable and Robinson Publishing Ltd for
permission to quote from The Diaries of Cynthia Gladwyn, edited by
Miles Jebb. The author and publishers have used their best endeavours
to contact all copyright holders and would be glad to hear from
anyone whose material has been quoted.

PRINCESS
Margaret

A LIFE OF CONTRASTS

CHRISTOPHER WARWICK

ANDRE
DEUTSCH

CONTENTS

CONTENTS

PICTURE CREDITS

The publishers would like to thank the following sources for their kind permission to reproduce the pictures in the book:

Black and white photographs section

Page 1 (top left) Bob Thomas/Popperfoto/Getty Images, (top right) Evening Standard/Getty Images, (bottom left) Central Press/Getty Images, (bottom right) Getty Images
Page 2 (top) Lisa Sheridan/Hulton Archive/Getty Images, (bottom) Paul Popper/Popperfoto/Getty Images
Page 3 (top) Topical Press Agency/Getty Images, (bottom left & right) Keystone-France/Gamma-Rapho via Getty Images
Page 4 all photographs reproduced courtesy of Lady Lowther and by kind permission of H.R.H. The Princess Margaret
Page 5 (top left) Reg Birkett/Keystone/Getty Images, (top right) Bert Hardy/Picture Post/Getty Images, (bottom) Hulton Archive/Getty Images
Page 6 all photographs reproduced courtesy of Miss Marigold Bridgeman and by kind permission of H.R.H. The Princess Margaret
Page 7 Keystone-France-Rapho via Getty Images
Page 8 (top) Ray Howard/AP/REX/Shutterstock, (bottom) Keystone/Hulton Archive/Getty Images

Colour photographs section

Page 1 (top) AP/REX/Shutterstock (bottom) Bettmann/Getty
Page 2 (top) Keystone-France/Gamma-Keystone via Getty
Images, (bottom) Stan Meagher/Daily Express/Hulton
Archive/Getty Images
Page 3 Hulton-Deutsch Collection/CORBIS/Corbis via Getty
Images
Page 4 (top) Getty Images, (bottom) Bettmann/Getty Images
Page 5 (top & bottom) Tim Graham/Getty Images
Page 6 (top left) Julian Parker/UK Press via Getty Images, (top
right) Gamma-Rapho via Getty Images, (bottom) Tim Graham/
Getty Images
Page 7 (top) Tim Graham/Getty Images, (bottom) UK Press/
Liaison/Getty Images
Page 8 REX/Shutterstock

Every effort has been made to acknowledge correctly and
contact the source and/or copyright holder of each picture, and
Carlton Books Limited apologises for any unintentional errors or
omissions which will be corrected in future editions of this book.

ACKNOWLEDGEMENTS

I had the pleasure of knowing Princess Margaret for more than twenty years. We first met in June 1980, when I was working on a publishing assignment with one of her closest friends. Not quite one year later, I found myself making notes for a new book of my own; one that, by virtue of her personal involvement and co-operation, was to become the only authorized biography of the Princess herself.

On one occasion a decade and more later, as we sat talking at Kensington Palace, the Princess asked, 'Do you think you'll ever re-do the biography?' At that time I have to say that I had not considered writing another, but with the eventual approach of her 70th birthday, however, I was persuaded that the time had come to write a new study. I discussed it with Princess Margaret, reminding her of what she had asked several years before. The result was the book you see here, but with one difference. When I wrote this new study to celebrate the Princess's seventieth birthday in August 2000, I did not know that I would be required to update it quite so soon as a memorial tribute to her.

Princess Margaret was always tremendously supportive and interested in the progress of both my biographies of her, before as well as after publication; and though I never once took her co-operation for granted, I was well aware that I could have written neither book without it.

In addition to that of the Princess herself, the assistance of a number of her friends and relations proved invaluable; so too did that of many others who, in various capacities knew or worked with the Princess. For reasons of confidentiality, some asked to remain anonymous and it is for that same reason that it has not always been possible to identify each of my sources. I am, however, deeply indebted to all who gave of their time in so many ways and I therefore offer my thanks to:

Jan Aubertin, Brian Auld, Sara Shackerley-Bennett, Sarah Bradford, Marigold Bridgeman, Colin and Charmian Campbell, Lady Elizabeth Cavendish, the late Lord Charteris of Amisfield, Hubert Chesshyre, Royal College of Arms, Lady Mary Clayton, Ingrid Connell, Cyril Dickman, Sir Anthony Dowell, the late Leslie Edwards, the Hon. Dominic Elliot, Paul Field, Valerie Garner, Lady Caroline Gilmour, Lady Glenconner, Bill Glenton, Warrant Officer Jason Griffiths, Susan Harvey, Maureen Holland, Fraser Jansen, Mrs Derek Lawson, the late Countess of Longford, Lady Lowther, Robin Macwhirter, Alexander McEwen, Sir John and Lady Nutting, Dame Merle Park, Giles Pegram, Lady Penn, Kenneth Rose, the Hon. Mrs Rhodes, Ned Ryan, Lady Elizabeth Shakerley, Juliet Sloggett, Robert Smith, Janie Stevens, Lady Juliet Townsend, Lady Weinberg, Lord and Lady Westbury, and the Hon. Mrs Whitehead.

In connection with this particular edition, I should also like to extend my warmest thanks to Penny Simpson, Susan Atkinson, Emma Bailey, Michele Hirst, Faye Parish and Alastair Gourlay at Carlton/Deutsch for all their assistance, which I very much appreciated.

Christopher Warwick

ONE

For a life that would not be without its share of drama or even tragedy, nature's turbulent performance on the night Princess Margaret was born could scarcely have been more appropriate.

At Glamis, some six miles from the east Scottish town of Forfar, during the evening of Thursday, 21 August 1930, a violent rain storm swept through the lush Vale of Strathmore. As thunder rolled and flashes of lightning silhouetted the turreted, chateau-like form of Glamis Castle, groups of villagers gathered in the driving rain outside the castle's north gate, or came to their front doors, in expectation of news of the birth of a second child to the popular Duke and Duchess of York.

Married seven years earlier in April 1923, Prince Albert, Duke of York, or 'Bertie,' as the second son of King George V and Queen Mary was known, had had no easy task in persuading the former Lady Elizabeth Bowes Lyon, youngest daughter of the 14th Earl of Strathmore and Kinghorne, to marry him. 'You'll be a lucky fellow if she accepts you,'[1] said the King in January of that year, after Bertie had made it known that he intended to propose for a third and final time.

Elizabeth Lyon's reluctance to accept Prince Albert's proposal was at the very least two-fold. First, the prospect of marrying into something that was more institution than family, rigidly constrained by the Victorian protocol that Edward VII had tried to forget, but which his reactionary successor, George V, had long-since embraced, was nothing if not daunting for a pretty, flirtatious and fun-loving 22-year-old. Unlike her royal suitor, she had grown up within a large, unstuffy and, above all, loving family. In later life, she would write to Sir Osbert Sitwell, 'I have nothing but wonderfully happy memories of childhood days at home . . . fun, kindness and a marvellous sense of security.'[2]

Unusually for their time and position, Lady Elizabeth's parents were naturally attentive and communicative. They were warm, ever-present figures in their children's lives. The Countess of Strathmore, in particular, was in many respects ahead of her time. A woman of distinguished mind and character, she possessed a knowledge of French, Latin, German and Italian, was well read, and artistically and musically talented. A handsome woman with what her granddaughter, Lady Mary Clayton, describes as 'the most delicious laugh, really a thing of beauty,' Lady Strathmore was renowned for her brilliance as a hostess and, indeed, as a gifted pianist: literally a leading player in the after-dinner concerts she and her family performed in the imposing Glamis drawing room. In time to come, her youngest daughter Elizabeth, both as Duchess of York and as Queen – and in turn Elizabeth's own daughters, especially Princess Margaret – would keep the family tradition of after-dinner entertainment very much alive.

For his part, the Earl of Strathmore was known to be a judicious magistrate and a considerate laird, a passionate cricketer and an acknowledged expert on forestry. He was for many years Lord Lieutenant of the County of Angus, and, as such, the Crown's representative in that part of Scotland, though neither he nor his wife were much interested in Court life. Indeed, it was Lady Strathmore's dismissive view that, 'some people have to be fed royalty like sea-lions fish.'[3]

Lord Strathmore was of a like mind. For while he certainly had no objection to his sons and daughters enjoying themselves with their equally well-placed friends and contemporaries, he did not want them moving in royal circles. Ironically, as it would transpire, he once said, 'If there is one thing I have determined for my children, it is that they shall never have any post about the court.'

Like his wife, Lord Strathmore also had strong religious beliefs and always prayed as regular as clockwork at a particular hour every day. Lady Mary Clayton recalls that her grandfather, 'always fell asleep in his prayers if he left them till later in the evening, which he thought was an affront to God. So he took to praying earlier, at six o'clock. He always prayed aloud and we thought it was marvellous of him to carry on a conversation with the Almighty like that. I would wait by the doors of his study or the chapel and listen, waiting for him to finish. When he had, my grandmother allowed me to take a cocktail of gin and orange into him.'[4]

By the time Lord Glamis succeeded his father as Earl of Strathmore in 1904, the family houses had echoed for more than twenty years to the sound of an ever-growing number of children at various stages of development – from teenagers to babies. Born almost annually since 1882, they ranged in age from twenty-one-year-old 'May' or, more properly, Mary Frances (later Lady Elphinstone), the eldest surviving child, to four-year-old Elizabeth and her brother David, who was two years younger.*

Alluding to the biblical story of Joseph's favourite brother, Lady Strathmore, who was already thirty-eight when she had Elizabeth and forty when David was born, would always refer to her youngest children as 'my two Benjamins.'

Though the family owned St Paul's Walden Bury, a supremely elegant Georgian mansion in Hertfordshire, as well as town houses in London, first at 20 St James's Square, Pall Mall, and later at 17 Bruton Street, Berkeley Square, Glamis – the oldest inhabited castle in Scotland – was principally regarded as home.

---

* The Strathmore children were: Violet Hyacinth, who died of diphtheria at the age of eleven, born 1882; Mary Frances, who married the 16th Lord Elphinstone, born 1883; Patrick, who became the 15th Earl of Strathmore, born 1884; John Herbert, born 1886; Alexander Francis, born 1887; Fergus, born 1889; Rose Constance, who married William Spencer Leveson-Gower, later 4th Earl Granville, born 1890; Michael Claude, born 1893; Elizabeth Angela Marguerite, who married Prince Albert, Duke of York, later King George VI, born 1900; and David, born 1902.

Steeped in history and legend, as well as tales of ghosts, monsters and secret chambers, St Fergus is said to have lived, preached and died at Glamis during the eighth century; while for several hundred years afterwards, the alleged 'magical properties' of St Fergus's Well made it a site of pilgrimage. But perhaps most famously, it was in one of the oldest and eeriest parts of the castle, known as 'Duncan's Hall', that Shakespeare set the murder of King Duncan I by Macbeth.*

It was here that Lady Elizabeth Bowes Lyon grew up and here – as at St Paul's Walden Bury – in the immediate aftermath of the First World War, that house parties again became a popular feature of family life. Regular guests not only included Elizabeth's closest girl friends, but several young men who readily admitted to falling in love with their hosts' youngest daughter.

Among Lady Elizabeth's admirers at this time were Freddie Dalrymple-Hamilton, a family friend, who had previously fallen in love with Elizabeth's elder sister Rose, later the Countess Granville; the Honourable Bruce Ogilvy, son of the Earl of Airlie, Viscount Gage, Prince Paul of Serbia, and Sir Arthur Penn who, when Lady Elizabeth eventually became Queen Consort, would not only join her Household as Private Secretary and subsequently Treasurer, but would, in time, become one of the greatest cultural influences in the life of her younger daughter.

For now, however, the Honourable James Gray Stuart, son of the 17th Earl of Moray, topped the Elizabeth Bowes Lyon romantic interest league. And here, no doubt, was another reason why, when the young Duke of York first proposed, Lady Elizabeth was in no hurry to sacrifice her freedom.

Three years older than she, Jamie Stuart – who eventually entered politics, became an MP and, from 1951 to 1957, held office as Secretary of State for Scotland – first met the Strathmore family in 1919, through his friendship with Michael Bowes Lyon, a fellow officer in the Royal Scots.

* Historical fact relates that Duncan was killed by Macbeth in battle at Bothnagowan, now Pitgaveny, near Elgin in Morayshire, on 14 August 1040.

Descended from an earlier James Stuart, half-brother of Mary, Queen of Scots, Jamie was, in the words of his daughter, the Honourable Davina Ritchie, 'Drop-down-dead handsome. He never had to make the slightest effort; women just fell at his feet.' Others agreed. In the words of Lady Elizabeth's dresser, Mabel Monty, Jamie Stuart was 'an absolute heart-throb, and [Elizabeth and he] fell for each other in a big way. It was obvious when you saw them together that they were madly in love.'[5]

During the course of 1920, however, events began to lead Elizabeth and Jamie along diverging paths. Through Wing Commander Louis Greig, who for several years had acted as the Duke of York's equerry, and who was now to become his Comptroller, Jamie Stuart was unexpectedly invited to fill the role of replacement equerry.

By this time, Wing Commander Greig had known Prince Albert for more than a decade, since the day in 1909 when the fourteen-year-old cadet had been admitted to the sick bay of the Royal Naval College at Osborne on the Isle of Wight, suffering from whooping cough. Greig was then Assistant Medical Officer at the College and, as a result of the Prince's persistent health problems – ranging from recurring gastric disorders and appendicitis, to an agonizing duodenal ulcer, for which, following repeated requests to his parents, he gladly underwent surgery – their paths had crossed frequently enough in the ensuing years for a warm and trusting friendship to develop.

'My principal contribution,' Greig later said, 'was to put steel into him'; to help him deal with residual traces of immaturity, to overcome moodiness and depression when he encountered 'minor difficulties', and occasionally reprimand him for outbursts of temper when things were not going his way.

In that respect, Greig's task cannot be said to have been an unqualified success. The Prince's alarming temper, or his 'gnashes' as his family would later refer to them, was a characteristic none was able to assuage. Nor was there much anyone could do about his irritability, no doubt caused by his nervous disposition and the frustrations of a stammer which, though evident when he had to speak in public, was rarely as pronounced in private. Greig's influence was nevertheless of paramount importance in the Prince's life, whether in an official capacity, or as a friend with whom he enjoyed a round of golf – the Duke of York was said to have a handicap of six – or a game of tennis. It was, in fact, their expertise in that particular sport, which led to their greatest shared achievement when, in the summer of 1920, they won the finals match in the RAF Doubles Competition at the All England Lawn Tennis Club at Wimbledon.

From a social point of view, if from no other, Louis Greig could have done no better than to think of the gregarious James Stuart as his successor as equerry to the young Duke of York. Already a friend of Greig, Jamie was by no means a stranger to the Duke. At the end of the Great War, Greig had asked him to take a lead in broadening Prince Albert's hitherto restricted social horizons. By enlisting the help of a few friends, parties and dances were specially arranged at which, as Jamie Stuart recalled, the Prince 'had a great deal of fun.'

In later life – and by now the first Viscount Stuart of Findhorn – James published his memoirs in which he claimed to have introduced the Duke of York to Elizabeth Bowes Lyon at a dance at the Ritz in 1921.

Fact tells a different story, however, and traces the very first meeting between the nine-year-old Prince Albert of Wales,* and the five-year-old Lady Elizabeth Bowes Lyon, to a children's party at Montagu House, the London residence of the dukes of Buccleuch, in 1905. On that perhaps not very memorable occasion for either of them, the young Elizabeth is said to have given Bertie the crystallized cherries from the top of her sugar cake.

---

* During his lifetime, the titles of the future King George VI changed several times. Born Prince Albert of York, second son of Prince George and Princess Victoria Mary, Duke and Duchess of York, he briefly became Prince Albert of Cornwall and York, when his father's title changed upon the accession of King Edward VII in January 1901. Ten months later, when his father was granted the title Prince of Wales, 'Bertie' became Prince Albert of Wales. When his father succeeded to the throne as King George V in 1910, he was known as The Prince Albert, and on 3 June 1920, his father elevated him to the Peerage by creating him Duke of York, Earl of Inverness and Baron Killarney. His sixth and last change of title occurred in December 1936, when he succeeded his brother as King George VI.

Fifteen years later, during the summer of 1920, they met again at a small, private dance given by Lord and Lady Farquhar at their house in London's Grosvenor Square. That night, said Bertie, albeit in retrospect, was the night he fell in love. It was hardly surprising. If women fell at the feet of the Honourable James Stuart, the same could just as easily be said of the young men who were unashamedly entranced by Elizabeth Bowes Lyon.

At five foot four (1.62m) with dark brown hair, blue eyes and archetypal peaches-and-cream complexion – all of which was animated by wit, vivacity and a very particular charm – Lady Elizabeth was considered irresistible. In short, her old-fashioned femininity meant that she had no need to be anything but herself. In the words of Mabell, Countess of Airlie, who was not only one of Lady Strathmore's friends, but both a confidante and lady-in-waiting to Queen Mary, Elizabeth 'was very unlike the cocktail-drinking, chain-smoking girls who came to be regarded as typical of the 1920s.'

Two or three months after he and Elizabeth had met at the Farquhars' dance, the Duke of York drove from Balmoral Castle, where his parents were holidaying, to spend a few days with the Strathmores at Glamis. In the words of his official biographer, Sir John Wheeler-Bennett, the Duke's 'enjoyment of his visits to Glamis and St Paul's Walden Bury, can be readily understood. The relations of Lord and Lady Strathmore with their children and the happy badinage and affection of a large and closely knit family were a revelation to him, providing a climate of ideas to which he instantly responded, and in which his own personality throve and blossomed.'[6]

The second son of a second son, Prince Albert, Duke of York, was born into a family whose way of life could not have been chillier or further removed from that which Elizabeth Bowes Lyon knew and valued. A shy, lonely boy, whose left-handed-ness and knock-knees were corrected by force, and whose nervous stammer – developed by the age of seven – was mocked by fellow cadets at the Royal Naval Colleges he attended, Bertie was even born on the most inauspicious date in the royal calendar.

At the time of his birth, his great-grandmother, Queen Victoria, had occupied the throne for fifty-eight years of her eventual sixty-four year reign. This fact was not lost on the Queen's middle-aged son and heir, Albert Edward, Prince of Wales – the future Edward VII – who is said to have remarked after one church service, 'It is one thing to pray to an Eternal Father, but quite another to have an eternal mother.'

Married in 1863 to the beautiful Princess Alexandra of Denmark, the eponymous 'Sea King's Daughter' of Tennyson's famous poem, Albert Edward, an earlier 'Bertie', and 'Alix' became the acknowledged leaders of high society, presiding over a glittering, if somewhat philistine and certainly self-indulgent alternative court known (after their official London residence) as the 'Marlborough House Set.' During the first six years of their marriage, the Prince and Princess of Wales were to have five children. It is a kind fate, however, that has a way of disposing of the Crown's most unsuitable heirs. And just as it would remove a new and unsuitable king from the throne almost fifty years later, so in January 1892, it disposed of a prince who stood closer to the crown than many considered desirable.

Prince Albert Victor, Duke of Clarence and Avondale, was the Wales's first-born. Known to his family as 'Eddy', and to the popular Press as 'Collars and Cuffs', derived from his dandified, high-collared, deep-cuffed shirts, Eddy was a slothful young man of highly dubious character.

Capable of falling in and out of love almost at will, he once proposed to his first cousin, Alix of Hesse, and fell in love with the Comte de Paris' daughter, Princess Hélène d'Orléans.

Far less seemly than falling in and out of love with pretty princesses was the pleasure Eddy allegedly sought with prostitutes of both sexes. Until he became involved in a major scandal that centred on a male brothel at 19 Cleveland Street, in London's West End, his penchant for the low life might have remained a relatively closely guarded secret. Still more sinister, though, were the rumours that Albert Victor, Duke of Clarence, was in some way associated with Jack the Ripper, who in 1888 mutilated five East-End prostitutes.

It was while staying with his family at Sandringham, in January 1892, that Prince Eddy caught the influenza virus that had swept through the house, sending his sister 'Toria', Princess Victoria, and members of the royal household, to their beds. Yet while they recovered, Eddy did not. Within a week he had died of pneumonia. Among those at his bedside, comforting the griev-ing Prince and Princess of Wales, was Queen Victoria's cousin, Princess Mary Adelaide, Duchess of Teck.

The youngest child of Adolphus, Duke of Cambridge, seventh son of King George III and Queen Charlotte, Mary Adelaide or 'Fat Mary', as this jovial eighteen- or possibly twenty-stone princess was affectionately known, was an immensely popular figure with the Victorian public. It was her only daughter, Victoria Mary, otherwise known as 'May', who had been carefully selected as the most suitable bride for the Duke of Clarence. In fact, no more than five weeks had passed since Eddy had proposed during a ball at Luton Hoo, in Bedfordshire.

At the moment of Eddy's death, his younger brother, the twenty-seven-year-old Prince George, assumed the mantle of heir to his father's eventual inheritance. Royal continuity was further maintained sixteen months later, when Queen Victoria gave her blessing to the engagement of Prince George, recently created Duke of York, to his late brother's fiancée, whom she considered to be 'a superior girl . . . so quiet & yet cheerful & so v[er]y carefully brought up & so sensible . . .'

Balanced against the far from charitable views of an otherwise status-conscious royal family, it was as well that Queen Victoria could not have been less concerned about the morganatic blood that ran through May's veins. As James Pope-Hennessy pointed out, it was a stigma which in other circumstances, would have rendered her 'too Royal to marry an ordinary English gentleman, and not Royal enough to marry a Royalty.'*

At the Chapel Royal, St James's Palace, on 6 July 1893, May's sense of inferiority may have been counter-balanced by a certain quiet satisfaction. For on that morning she not only married a 'royalty' but, by becoming Duchess of York, was elevated from the station of a mere Serene Highness to the superior rank and style of *Royal* Highness.

The first of Georgie and May's six children, a son who would one day become King Edward VIII and afterwards Duke of Windsor, was born on Midsummer's Eve the following year. When news of the birth reached the baby prince's grandfather during the Ascot Week ball he was hosting at the Fishing Temple, a royal folly on the edge of Virginia Water in Windsor Great Park, he stopped the music to announce, 'It is with the greatest pleasure that I am able to inform you of the birth of a son to the Duke and Duchess of York. I propose a toast to the young prince.'

At Windsor Castle, a few miles away on the far side of the Great Park, Queen Victoria was no less delighted. Writing to her daughter Vicky, she enthused, '. . . it seems that it has never happened in this Country that there shd. be three direct Heirs as well as the Sovereign alive.'

If the birth of Prince Edward of York, who would always be known to his family as 'David', the last of his seven Christian names, was greeted by popping champagne corks, loyal toasts, gun salutes and pealing bells, the atmosphere surrounding the arrival of his brother Bertie, on 14 December 1895, could not have been more restrained, nor his family more contrite. Their apprehension was founded entirely on a question of timing. For

---

* Morganatic blood in the nineteenth and early twentieth centuries carried with it an often insurmountable social stigmatism. In the case of the future Queen Mary's lineage, her paternal grandfather, Alexander, Duke of Württemberg, had contracted a morganatic marriage in 1835 with the Hungarian Countess Claudine Rhèdey who, only six years later, was thrown from her horse at a military review and trampled to death by a squadron of cavalry. But for this 'misalliance,' Princess May's father, Prince (later Duke) Franz of Teck, might one day have inherited the throne of the small kingdom of Württemberg, sandwiched between Baden and Bavaria to the south of Prussia.

each December the fourteenth marked the death in 1861 of Queen Victoria's beloved husband Albert, the Prince Consort, who had died of typhoid at the age of forty-two, and of their second daughter, the thirty-five-year-old Princess Alice, Grand Duchess of Hesse, who had succumbed to diphtheria in 1878. Amid apologetic messages and expressions of regret that events had intruded on so profound an anniversary, Queen Victoria was, it transpired, less put out than her family had feared. 'I have a feeling it may be a blessing for the dear little boy and may be looked upon as a gift from God', she noted in her diary. Shortly afterwards, while insisting that she was 'all impatience to see the new one', the Queen gladly accepted Prince George and Princess May's invitation to stand as godmother to their son, and naturally approved that he 'shd. have the dear name of *Albert* . . . which is the byeword for all that is great & good.'

Contrary to what anyone might reasonably have expected, the York children did not have much of a start in life. Royal though they might have been, Bertie, his elder brother, to whom he was devoted, and soon their only sister Mary,* were entrusted to the care of nurses who proved disastrous. The career of the first head nurse soon came to an end when she was dismissed for insolence to the Duchess of York's mother, Princess Mary Adelaide. The second, more seriously, was eventually sacked for cruelty and physical violence. Having developed a jealous, almost obsessive preference for the elder prince, the unnamed nurse would pinch or twist his arms immediately before taking him to see his parents. The result was that, having been unable to mollify their sobbing child, the nurse would be instructed to take him back to the nursery. It was her perverse way of demonstrating a control over the royal children that the Duke and Duchess did not have.

* The six children of the Duke and Duchess of York, later Prince and Princess of Wales and ultimately King George V and Queen Mary, were Edward Albert Christian George Andrew Patrick David, later King Edward VIII and Duke of Windsor, 1894-1972; Albert Frederick Arthur George, Duke of York and King George VI, 1895-1952; Victoria Alexandra Alice Mary, known as Mary, Princess Royal, 1897-1965; Henry William Frederick Albert, Duke of Gloucester, 1900-1974; George Edward Alexander Edmund, Duke of Kent, 1902-1942; and John Charles Francis, 1905-1919.

Prince Albert, meanwhile, was ignored to the point of negligence. 'So completely did [the nurse] disregard his wants and comforts', wrote Sir John Wheeler-Bennett, 'that he was frequently given his afternoon bottle while driving in a C-sprung Victoria, a process not dissimilar to a rough Channel crossing – and with corresponding results. It is not surprising that the baby developed chronic stomach trouble, which may have laid the foundation for the gastric complaint from which he was later to suffer so acutely.'

The children also suffered beatings at the hands of the same head nurse who, according to the reminiscences of the maternity nurse at Sandringham, would 'hit them with a big rod for no reason and never cared for them at all. They weren't even properly fed. She was particularly cruel to Prince Albert because he had a stutter and had temper tantrums; but the more she hit him with the rod, the more difficult he became . . . when she vented her anger on him . . . he would just cower away and hide.'[7]

That the nurse's sadistic rule should have lasted quite as long as it did was partly due to the fact that the Duke and Duchess of York were distant parents. Like most of their royal and aristocratic contemporaries, they knew little about raising children simply because they were not expected to know. Though in the Yorks' case the system had worked miserably until the kindly Mrs Bill, known as 'Lalla', took control, the prevailing view was that the responsibility of looking after children belonged to the nursery staff. Yet even if they saw relatively little of their children when they were small, over and above the usual morning and evening 'presentations', the Duke and Duchess still considered themselves to be anxious, loving and responsible parents. In their own way, so they were.

Their greatest – and saddest – disadvantage lay in their inability to communicate. Throughout their married life, even words of love and affection had to be expressed by letter. On one occasion, for instance, Georgie wrote to his wife, 'We suit each other admirably & I thank God every day that he should have brought us together, especially under the tragic circumstances of dear Eddy's death, & people said I married you out of pity and sympathy. That shows how little the world really knows what it is talking about.'[8]

If the Yorks could not communicate on an intimate level with one another, they had even less chance of forming a loving, interactive relationship with their children. With nothing more than 'the limited education of a nineteenth century naval officer', to inform his ways, the Duke relied too heavily on criticism and ridicule to temper the pride he took – but could never show – in his children. And though Bertie turned out to be the son he respected most – 'he has more guts than the rest of them put together', he once said – he clearly did not have a clue about the psychological harm he caused by shouting, 'Get it out', when Bertie nervously stumbled and stuttered.

Just as harmful was their mother's inability to protect them from their father's intimidating onslaughts. During their early years, it is not too great an exaggeration to say that the closest she came to her children on a regular basis was in captioning the countless photographs of them that she had carefully pasted into her scarlet-bound photograph albums. Later on, rather than speak up for them or take their part if the occasion demanded, she would simply defer to her husband's superior position. 'I have always to remember', she would say, 'that their father is also their king.'

It was this curiously detached and suppressed world that Lady Elizabeth Bowes Lyon had such doubts about entering when Prince Bertie, Duke of York, first proposed to her in 1921. Mabell, Lady Airlie, who not only knew them both well but had also acted as confidante to both sides, told Lady Strathmore that when Elizabeth rejected him, the Duke had 'looked so disconsolate. I do hope he will find a nice wife who will make him happy.' In reply, Elizabeth's mother had been equally sympathetic. 'I like him so much', she said, adding percipiently, 'he is a man who will be made or marred by his wife.'

By the start of 1922, the pattern of things to come had already started to take shape. Undaunted by Lady Elizabeth's initial refusal, Bertie continued to pay court with quiet but resolute determination. James Stuart, who up to this point had still been a feature in Lady Elizabeth's life, was no longer considered the best of suitors after all and was packed off to the Oklahoma oil fields, where he was to work as a rigger for the next year. By the time he returned, Elizabeth was about to become Duchess of York, while his own engagement to Lady Rachel Cavendish, a younger daughter of the Duchess of Devonshire, Mistress of the Robes to Queen Mary, had been carefully arranged.

Barely had James Stuart said his farewells that New Year of 1922, than Elizabeth Bowes Lyon was given a foretaste of the kind of royal ceremonial that would soon become part of her life. Through her involvement with the Girl Guide movement Lady Elizabeth, who was District Commissioner for Glamis and Eassie Parish, had established a friendship with Bertie's sister, Princess Mary, who was President of the Girl Guide Association. It was a friendship that would last until the Princess's death more than forty years later in 1965.

At the age of twenty-four, Princess Mary had become engaged to Henry, Viscount Lascelles, later 6th Earl of Harewood, a tall, gaunt-looking, but vastly wealthy forty-year-old whom Queen Mary had lined up for the hand of her only daughter. As Lady Elizabeth already knew, and the Queen subsequently discovered to her evident fury, Princess Mary was in love with the Earl of Dalkeith, son and heir of the 7th Duke of Buccleuch and brother of Lady Alice Montagu Douglas Scott, the future Duchess of Gloucester.[9]

From the Queen's point of view, and it must be assumed from the King's also, the die was cast. Harry Lascelles, far richer than Lord Dalkeith and the Buccleuchs, had already been chosen for their daughter and would, so far as they were concerned, have no rivals. Thus, on 28 February 1922, as Elizabeth Bowes Lyon stood behind her, one of a group of eight veiled bridesmaids, Princess Mary was married at Westminster Abbey, amid all the colour, pomp and splendour of a state occasion.

That September, Bertie, who had become a frequent guest of the Strathmore family, was back at Glamis to join a shooting party and, for a second time, to propose to the Lady Elizabeth. Though he received a second gentle refusal, Lady Strathmore had noticed that her daughter was beginning to worry about the Duke of York's attention. 'I think', she said, 'that she was torn between her longing to make Bertie happy and her reluctance to take on the responsibilities which this marriage must bring.'

During the first weekend of the New Year, while Lady Elizabeth was staying with another of her friends and admirers, George, Viscount Gage, at his house in Sussex, a report appeared in the *Daily News* which speculated on the imminent engagement between Bertie's brother, David, Prince of Wales, then the 'golden boy' of Empire, and 'a noble Scottish lady.' It was this kind of press speculation, now striking a little too close to home, that may have persuaded Bertie to propose one more time. This he did while he and Elizabeth were walking in the woods at St Paul's Walden Bury on 13 January 1923.

To his undisguised delight, she finally accepted. Writing to his mother two days later, Bertie said, 'I am very happy & I can only hope that Elizabeth feels the same as I do. I know I am very lucky to have won her over at last.'

The formal betrothal was announced in the Court Circular on 16 January. 'I was so startled and almost fell out of bed . . .' wrote Chips Channon.* 'We have all hoped, waited so long for this romance to prosper, that we had begun to despair that she would ever accept him . . . He is the luckiest of men, and there's not a man in England today that doesn't envy him. The clubs are in gloom.'

---

* Sir Henry Channon (1897-1958). In his memoirs, *Palimpsest*, Gore Vidal wrote of Channon, 'He came from Chicago; drove an ambulance in the First War; married a Guinness, by whom he had a son; became British and a Conservative member of Parliament. In the process, he shed the wife, but kept her fortune. He lived splendidly in Belgrave Square and also at a country house near Plymouth. Sexually, he preferred men to women and royalty to either.'

Public reaction to the couple's engagement was also one of pleasure, not least because the bride was *British*. Not since James II married Anne Hyde as his first wife in 1659 had a prince of the British royal house legitimately taken a British bride. Queen Mary's bloodline was almost exclusively German; Queen Alexandra had had a Danish father, King Christian IX of Denmark, and a German mother, Louise of Hesse-Cassel; while Queen Victoria's father, Edward, Duke of Kent, had married Victoria of Saxe-Coburg-Saalfeld, the young widow of the second Prince of Leiningen. Before that, each of the four Hanoverian Georges had married princesses of Zelle, Brandenburg-Anspach, Mecklenburg-Strelitz, and Brunswick Wolfenbuttel; while even earlier the Stuart princes – James I, Charles I, Charles II and ultimately James II – had looked respectively to Denmark, France, Portugal and Italy for their consorts.

Bertie and Elizabeth were married at Westminster Abbey on the morning of Thursday, 26 April 1923, a typical spring day of rain and sunshine. Although the King had decreed that the wedding of his second son should be 'of as simple a character as possible', involving 'no unnecessary expense', it was a sparkling occasion that certainly equalled Princess Mary's wedding in terms of colour and splendour, pomp and circumstance.

That morning outside 17 Bruton Street, Lord and Lady Strathmore's Mayfair town house, an estimated crowd of between 5,000 and 6,000 well-wishers gathered at windows, on balconies and in the street itself as, drawn by four grey horses, Edward VII's crimson and gold 1902 State Landau, escorted by four mounted police officers, arrived to convey the bride and her father to the Abbey. Until George V's cousin 'Patsy', Princess Patricia of Connaught, had chosen to marry there in February 1919, family weddings were more usually celebrated at Windsor. Already long-established as the Coronation church of Britain's sovereigns, Westminster Abbey – or the Collegiate Church of St Peter in Westminster – was now to become the setting for most twentieth century royal weddings.

During the ceremony as the bridal couple stood before him

– the Duke of York wearing the blue-grey ceremonial uniform of a Group Captain in the Royal Air Force and Lady Elizabeth in ivory silk crêpe and antique lace – the Archbishop of York took the opportunity to remind the congregation of the bridegroom's dedicated work for Industrial Welfare, and the annual summer camps that he had personally established and in which he would, even when he came to the throne, enjoy taking part. These camps were designed to encourage a better cultural understanding between boys of differing class and background.

'You, sir,' said the Archbishop, 'have given many proofs of your care for the welfare of our working people. You have made yourself at home in the mines and shipyards and factories. You have brought the boys of the workshop and the public school together in free and frank companionship. You have done much to increase the public sense of the honour and dignity of labour.'

Listening to the Archbishop as she stood at the steps of the Sacrarium, under the watchful gaze of the entire bejewelled and beribboned royal family, including Queen Victoria's four surviving offspring as well as the Dowager Empress of Russia, mother of the murdered Tsar Nicholas II, the new Duchess of York may perhaps have spared a thought for the carefree life she had left behind her and the responsibilities of the position she had just assumed.

After a five-week honeymoon that began at Polesden Lacey, the Surrey estate of society hostess Mrs Ronald Greville, continued at Glamis Castle, where the bride contracted whooping cough – 'So unromantic on your honeymoon', as the Duke wrote home to Queen Mary – and concluded at Frogmore House in the Home Park at Windsor, the Duke and Duchess of York began their married life in what proved to be the most inconvenient of houses.

Put at their disposal by George V, who wanted to 'keep it in the family', White Lodge in Richmond Park was a three-storey, Palladian-style mansion of white Portland stone that had originally been designed as a hunting lodge for George II. More than a century later, after various other royalties had come and gone, Queen Victoria gave the house to her cousin Mary Adelaide, Duchess of Teck, and her family. It was here, in fact, that the future Queen Mary, then herself Duchess of York, had given birth to her first child in June 1894 and here, not long after-wards, that both her parents died, Princess Mary Adelaide in 1897 and the Duke of Teck two years later.*

While Bertie and Elizabeth turned the undeniably elegant house into an attractive and comfortably furnished home, neces-sary comforts such as heat, sanitation and light seemed to have changed little, if at all, since Victorian times. Added to which – as their niece Princess Alexandra was to discover forty years later, when she and her husband moved into Thatched House Lodge on the far side of Richmond Park – was the inconvenience of the location. Not far enough from London to keep inquisitive day-trippers at bay, it was for the Yorks, with official duties to perform, just a little too far from the centre for it to be viable. Other very real considerations such as the expense of running and staffing such a large establishment meant that it wasn't long before the royal couple were looking for somewhere else to live.

Surprisingly, perhaps, there was no easy answer to finding alternative accommodation for Bertie and Elizabeth of York until Princess Mary and Viscount Lascelles came to the rescue and offered the use of Chesterfield House, their own London residence not far from Buckingham Palace. It was here that they stayed while looking for something of their own.

It was not until 1927 that they finally found what they were looking for and took a lease on number 145 Piccadilly. No more than a stone's throw from Hyde Park Corner and only four doors away from Apsley House, the Adam mansion acquired by the first Duke of Wellington in 1817, two years after Waterloo, No. 145 was a solid five-storey, semi-detached building faced with grey stone that had stood empty for several years. For some

---

* Over thirty-five years later, Princess Margaret, as President of the Royal Ballet, would come to know White Lodge as the home of the Royal Ballet School.

unknown reason it had proved impossible to let, and at one stage the Crown Estate Commissioners had considered a proposal that it should be converted into several flats.

As a complete residential unit it had been available to let since the autumn of 1921, when it was advertised as an 'important mansion . . . containing entrance hall, principal staircase hall, a secondary staircase with electric passenger lift, drawing room, dining room, ballroom, study, library, about twenty-five bedrooms, conservatory, etc . . .'

By the time the Duke and Duchess of York moved into these spacious rooms, newly decorated in Elizabeth's favourite pastel colours of misty blue, fawn and pink, a pastel-coloured nursery was also a necessity. For the first two years of their marriage, motherhood for the 'Smiling' or 'Little' Duchess, as she was popularly called, seemed to have been put on hold, presumably while she became acclimatized to her new and inevitably very public way of life.

Among Elizabeth's earliest public engagements were those connected with the patronages and presidencies she assumed as successor to her husband's great-aunt Helena, Princess Christian of Schleswig-Holstein, the third of Queen Victoria's five daughters, who died in June 1923. Included among the organizations which now benefited from the Duchess's interest were the Young Women's Christian Association, and the National Society for the Prevention of Cruelty to Children, the NSPCC, of which, in time, Princess Margaret would become a demonstrably committed President.

In addition to public functions at home, there were visits to Northern Ireland and the Balkans, as well as an extended semi-official tour of East Africa and the Sudan, which the Yorks undertook during the winter of 1924–25. It was towards the end of that summer that the Duchess of York discovered she was pregnant.

The following spring, only twelve days before the start of the General Strike – precipitated by a long and bitter dispute in the coalfields of England – the birth of Princess Elizabeth Alexandra Mary of York was seen as a cause for public celebration at a time of intense public disquiet. So great was the excitement, in fact, that crowds gathered outside 17 Bruton Street, where the Yorks had been staying, to cheer the comings and goings of all who called, from messenger boys to royalty.

For the Duchess, who endured long and painful hours of labour, the birth of her first child was a considerable ordeal. Found to be a breech baby, the attendant doctors took the only course open to them and delivered the future Queen Elizabeth II by Caesarean section at 2.40am on 21 April 1926.

'Such a relief and joy', noted Queen Mary in her diary.* Twelve hours later, after she and the King had visited their son and daughter-in-law, the Queen described her first grand-daughter as 'a little darling with a lovely complexion & pretty fair hair.'

The birth of Princess Elizabeth, who immediately occupied third place in the line of succession, automatically displacing her father's younger brothers, was a reminder, if one were needed, that the heir to the throne, now thirty-two and still a bachelor, showed no inclination to marry and secure the succession with children of his own. Unbeknown to the public at large, however, the charismatic and phenomenally popular Prince of Wales enjoyed a particular penchant for married women.

At the time of his niece's birth, the Prince, who was later to claim that his life had been an emotional void until he met and married the American Wallis Simpson, was already eight years into his sixteen-year relationship with Mrs Freda Dudley Ward, then the wife of the Liberal Member of Parliament for Southampton and Vice-Chamberlain of the Royal Household.

After the Prince of Wales tired of her and ended their affair by the simple, if dishonourable, expedient of refusing her telephone calls, he moved on to Thelma, Lady Furness. The American-born wife of the shipping magnate, Viscount Furness,

* Having received the news of the birth of her first granddaughter, Queen Mary lunched that day with the King's cousin, Alice, Princess Andrew of Battenberg. Twenty-one years later, in November 1947, the Princess's youngest child and only son, Philip, then aged five, would marry the newly-born princess.

and twin sister of Gloria Vanderbilt, Thelma soon went the way of her predecessor after she had introduced the Prince – or 'the Little Man', as she called him – to Mrs Ernest Simpson.

It was this weakness for other men's wives that would not only lead to his downfall, but would force his brother into a position he would never have sought and certainly did not want.

During the spring of 1926, however, there was little reason to believe that David would not have a family of his own; thus allowing the Yorks, who were very much the focus of popular attention, to maintain a lower profile.

Until the birth of her sister just over four years later, Princess Elizabeth or 'the World's Best Known Baby', as an insatiable press described her, was to feature in the world's newspapers and magazines with almost obsessive regularity. At the age of three, 'Lilibet', as she styled herself in an early attempt to pronounce her name, even appeared on the cover of *Time* as an unwitting trend-setter in children's fashion, while all around mushroomed small Lilibet lookalikes in dainty dresses, coats and bonnets in white or yellow.

'It almost frightens me that the people should love her so much', the Duchess of York confided to Queen Mary who, perhaps a little surprisingly, in view of the fact that she found it difficult to bond with other women, was always the most affectionate and supportive of mothers-in-law.[10]

Quite apart from boosting the profits of newspaper publishers, tailors, dressmakers and anyone else with a commercial interest in her, the fair-haired, three-year-old Princess Elizabeth was an endless source of delight to the ageing King George V. As adoring a grandfather as he had been a brusque, often insensitive father, the King once astounded his friend, Dr Gordon Cosmo Lang, then Archbishop of Canterbury, when he came across his Sovereign down on all fours. At that moment, he was no longer the revered King-Emperor, but a horse being led round the paddock by an infant 'groom', with a firm hold on the royal beard.

Lilibet's privileged status as only child was soon to change –

and media interest to intensify still further – when, during the spring of 1930, the Duchess of York's doctors were able to confirm that she was again pregnant.

TWO

At the end of each summer season, High Society ritually migrated from London to their country houses or family estates the length and breadth of Britain. Towards the end of July 1930, as George V and Queen Mary retired to Sandringham, 'the place I love better than anywhere else in the world', as the King liked to describe his Norfolk home, the Duke and Duchess of York, with the little Princess Elizabeth, travelled north to Glamis, where the Duchess wanted to give birth to her second child.

Following not long behind was Mr John R. Clynes, a former Lord Privy Seal, and now Home Secretary in Ramsay MacDonald's second Labour Government. With him was Mr Harry Boyd, his Ceremonial counterpart at the Home Office.

In a custom that was established after the so-called 'Warming Pan Incident' of 1688, when Mary of Modena, the second wife of King James II, was accused of substituting a changeling, smuggled in in a warming-pan, as heir to the throne, a Minister of the Crown was required to attend all royal births as an independent and incorruptible witness to the due processes of nature.

Though neither the Home Secretary nor Mr Boyd would witness the actual birth, their presence was still a reminder of days gone by when ministers and courtiers alike were permitted to observe some of royalty's most intimate moments, childbirth among them. In the fulfilment of a duty that would be abolished at the time of the present Prince of Wales's birth in 1948, the Home Secretary was kept waiting on this occasion for more than two weeks. Miscalculation rather than an overdue birth was to blame for this, however. While he had been advised that his presence would be required at Glamis in early August, the over-eager Home Secretary chose not to wait until he received more specific information. Instead, he and his small, 'anxious-looking' companion, Mr Boyd, made arrangements to travel to Scotland on the fifth.

Since it was said that Lord Strathmore's own political allegiances would not permit him to accommodate a Labour minister beneath his roof, and the Ceremonial Secretary was anxious not to have to take rooms in an hotel too far away, it was arranged that both Mr Clynes and Mr Boyd should stay with Mabell, Lady Airlie, at Airlie Castle, at that time her family's Dower House, some eight miles from Glamis.

'Before I left London', she was later to recall in her autobiography, *Thatched With Gold*, 'Mr Boyd came twice to see me . . . He was obsessed with the fear that because the Duchess of York had decided to have her baby at Glamis there might be some impression that the affair was going to be conducted in "an irregular, hole and corner way", as he put it . . . In his agitation he sprang out of his chair and paced up and down my sitting room. "This child will be in direct succession to the throne and if its birth is not properly witnessed its legal right might be questioned." I told him that he need not worry as Airlie was quite near enough to Glamis to prevent such a calamity.'

Two days after arriving at Airlie Castle, the Home Secretary drove to Glamis to lunch with the Duke and Duchess of York and Lord and Lady Strathmore. On the tenth he made a brief return visit to the expectant parents before leaving for Dundee to discuss industrial relations with the Lord Provost. By the sixteenth, when he looked in on a local flower show, and was heard to say, 'I am here in relation to a pending happy event which is naturally attracting the attention not only of the United Kingdom but of people throughout the Empire,'[1] Secretary

Clynes had obviously realized that, unlike the royal baby – or 'the little Scottish Princess', as the Marquess of Aberdeen and Temair, Lord Lieutenant of Aberdeenshire, would refer to her – his own arrival in Scotland had been much too premature.

Even the Duke of York was beginning to find the Home Secretary's presence something of an embarrassment. 'I feel so sorry for Mr Clynes having to be here for so long', he wrote to Queen Mary. 'I always wanted him to come up when he was sent for, which would have been so much simpler.'[2] To fill his days, as Lady Mary Clayton recalls, members of the Strathmore family and some of the estate staff entertained the minister by taking him on drives around the surrounding countryside and to places of local interest.

At last, on the evening of 21 August, sixteen days after they had left their Whitehall offices in expectation of a brief absence, the Home Secretary and his still anxious colleague, Mr Boyd, received the long-awaited summons to Glamis. Publishing the report of its on-the-spot special correspondent, the *Evening Times* told its readers, 'Shortly after nine o'clock . . . there came the piercing rays of a fast limousine turning the bend in the Kirriemuir Road and along the straight stretch towards the Castle. The lodge keeper threw the gates open and the car passed into the broad avenue.'

Arriving at the main door, Mr Clynes and Mr Boyd were immediately shown into the drawing room. Sixty feet long with a high arched ceiling of embellished white stucco, a massive fireplace above which the royal arms were flanked by caryatids, and walls at eight feet thick hung with imposing family portraits, this vast chamber had once been the 3rd Earl's Great Hall. It was here, while events elsewhere in the Castle took their course, that the Home Secretary had only a little longer to wait before he and Mr Boyd could fulfil their traditional roles.

Meanwhile, in the bedroom of her first-floor suite of rooms, the Duchess of York had been in labour for some time and consideration had again been given to a Caesarean section. At 9.22pm, however, the baby, weighing 6lbs 11 ounces, was delivered naturally. Two hours later, a brief formal statement that was not only transmitted to emissaries and news agencies around the world, but was also read to the villagers who had braved the stinging rain at the Castle's north gate, was issued. It read:

> Her Royal Highness The Duchess of York gave birth to a daughter this evening. Both Her Royal Highness and the infant Princess are making very satisfactory progress.

The bulletin was signed by the Duchess's three doctors, Sir Henry Simson, Obstetric Surgeon to the West London Hospital, Dr Frank Neon Reynolds, Senior Obstetric House Physician and Resident Accoucher at St Thomas's Hospital in London, and Dr David Myles, the Strathmore family's local GP.

As the exhausted mother rested in her room, Nurse Beevors, a cockney midwife with rattling false teeth, who had attended most of the family's births, carried the newest member of the Royal House of Windsor to her cot in the next room. Even at that extraordinarily early stage, there was, as the Duchess's sister, Lady Rose Leveson-Gower observed, already a suggestion of the strong-willed personality that was to develop. For as fast as Nurse Beevors took the newly-born princess's hand away from her mouth to stop her sucking her thumb, the more insistent the infant seemed to become.[3]

Less than an hour later, Sir Henry Simson accompanied the Home Secretary to the former Tapestry Room where, surrounded by the Duke of York, Lord and Lady Strathmore and Lady Rose, he saw 'a fine chubby faced little girl lying wide awake.'

At around midnight, having formally conveyed the news of the birth to the Lord Mayor of London, to the Governors-General of the Dominions and the Governors of the Crown Colonies, Mr Clynes left Glamis to return to Airlie Castle. As he drove away, local people who had heard the news were already hanging flags from their windows and doors, the church bells of the neighbourhood were being rung in celebration for the first time since peace was declared at the end of the Great War; while in the distance, searchlights were seen flashing across the night sky as a sign of good news.[4]

The following day, as the Royal Horse Artillery fired 41-gun salutes from both Hyde Park and the Tower of London, as the bells of St Paul's Cathedral and Westminster Abbey pealed out across the capital, and all Mayfair 'was gay with flags on the clubs and shops', villagers and townspeople in and around Glamis were preparing for their own celebrations. On nearby Hunter's Hill, where King Malcolm II was mortally wounded in battle in 1034 (he later died at Glamis), a brushwood beacon piled 600-feet high (almost 200m), towered over the village.

That night, no fewer than 4,000 people, including estate workers, children and visitors from as far away as Edinburgh and Aberdeen, gathered in the village square before the Glamis Pipe Band, playing the specially composed *Duke of York's Welcome*, *Highland Laddie* and *The Earl of Strathmore's Welcome*, led them to the summit of the Hill. Once there, the fire was set ablaze by two young villagers, Huldah Roy and Rita Duncan. Pupils at the local school, they used the same torches, now tied with pink ribbon, that had lit the beacon to celebrate the marriage of the Duke and Duchess of York seven years before.

As the blaze took hold and barrels of beer provided by Lord Strathmore were opened, revellers began dancing reels 'with proper Scottish zest', as one observer put it. At the same time, hundreds more watched 'the dazzling sight' from vantage points in the district. 'Groups could be seen silhouetted against the sky on the crests of hillocks and on sloping fields in the Valley of Strathmore.'[5]

Another young observer, who had evidently been allowed to stay up well past her usual bedtime so that she could watch the lighting of the beacon from a window in one of the castle's towers, was Princess Elizabeth. Having been taken to see her baby sister on the morning after her birth and, at her persistent request, two or three times the following day, Lilibet was reportedly discovered kneeling in front of her toy cupboard. Beside her were some of her favourite playthings, a blue velvet frog, a woolly rabbit or two, a pair of prized dancing dolls and two or three picture books. 'I'm getting them ready for the baby to play with,' she explained.

Such was Princess Elizabeth's fascination and delight with her sister, that she talked endlessly about little else. Almost a week after the birth when Lady Strathmore took her to visit Hayston, a farm on the Glamis estate, the Princess told the wife of James White, the oldest tenant and one of the best known cattle breeders in Scotland, 'I have got a new little baby sister. She is so lovely, and I am very, very happy to have her.'[6]

As yet, the infant – who was the first member of the royal house to have been born in Scotland since Queen Victoria's granddaughter, Victoria Eugenie of Battenberg in 1887, and, still more significantly, the future King Charles I in 1600 – was without a name.

It has been said that the delay in naming the baby was due to the fact that the Duke and Duchess of York had hoped that their second child might be a boy; in other words, a prince to strengthen the royal line. Such claims, however, are without foundation. Not since the death in childbirth in 1817 of Princess Charlotte of Wales, the only child of and heiress presumptive to the future George IV, had the succession been a matter for concern. Certainly in 1930, the line was as secure as it needed to be. And despite the fact that the Prince of Wales was still no nearer to marrying, there was as yet no suggestion of the train of events that would lead to the Abdication crisis six years hence.

Moreover, as the Prince of Wales pointed out when arguing to be allowed to go the Front during the Great War, he had three brothers to succeed him; Albert, 'Bertie', the Duke of York, Henry, 'Harry', the Duke of Gloucester, and Prince George, the future Duke of Kent. Beyond that, although they were not strictly royal, the male line was further secured by Princess Mary's two sons, George and Gerald Lascelles.

In addition, though princes usually took precedence over

princesses – for example, the present Queen's younger sons take precedence over their sister, even though she is older – gender has never been an obstacle to a princess assuming the throne in her own right.

When the matter of naming the newest Princess of York was considered, her mother wrote to Queen Mary, 'I am very anxious to call her Ann Margaret, as I think that Ann of York sounds pretty, & Elizabeth and Ann go so well together. I wonder what you think? Lots of people have suggested Margaret, but it has no family links really on either side.'

There may have been no immediate family links, but even overlooking the fact that Marguerite was one of her own names, the Duchess could hardly have forgotten that her sister, May, Lady Elphinstone, had named her second daughter Margaret; or that the King's first cousin 'Daisy', who married the Crown Prince of Sweden, had been born Princess Margaret of Connaught. Nor, for that matter, was it to be overlooked from an historical point of view, that of the seventeen princesses in British history who were named Margaret, seven had links of the highest distinction with Scotland. They included St Margaret (1046–93), the second consort of Malcolm Canmore, King of Scots; Margaret of England (1240–75), daughter of Henry III, first wife of the Scottish king Alexander III; Margaret, Queen of Scots (1283–90), the granddaughter of Alexander III; and Margaret Tudor (1489–1541), consort of James IV, King of Scots, and daughter of Henry VII, King of England. Another medieval princess, this time the sister of Edward IV, was the very first Margaret of York. Born in 1446, the sixth child of Richard Plantagenet, 3rd Duke of York, she became at the age of twenty-two the third wife of Charles 'the Bold', Duke of Burgundy. Like her namesake six centuries later, the princess gained a reputation for her patronage of the arts.

The casting vote in this discussion of names, however, lay with the King. And he did not like the name Ann. Resigned but determined, the Duchess of York wrote again to her mother-in-law, 'Bertie & I have decided now to call our little daughter

"Margaret Rose", instead of M. Ann, as Papa does not like Ann. I hope that you like it. I think that it is very pretty together.'

This time, George V made no objection, but was nevertheless keen to meet the new granddaughter he was hearing so much about. In the event, it was more than a week before he and the Queen did so. Curiously, the delay was caused by the Duke of York himself who, only three days after his daughter's birth, had left Glamis for Balmoral, where he spent the next six days with his parents and younger brother Harry.

On Saturday, 30 August, the Duke returned to Glamis, bringing the King and Queen with him. If, as seems likely, George V was invited by the Earl of Strathmore to toast the health of the infant princess, he would have been offered 'The Lion of Glamis' for the purpose. A huge sixteenth-century silver goblet in the shape of a lion sitting on its haunches, the cup holds a pint of wine. Put to use only on the most special of occasions, the last time it had been used was more than four years earlier to toast the health of the Princess Elizabeth.

Although the King's impressions of the newest princess appear not to be on record, Queen Mary noted in her diary that day, 'E. looking very well and the baby a darling.'

While the Scottish press expressed the hope that the christening of Princess Margaret Rose might take place in Scotland – St Giles' Cathedral in Edinburgh was much mooted as a more than suitable setting – it wasn't long before it was announced that the ceremony would be a family occasion and, like that of Princess Elizabeth, would be celebrated in the private chapel at Buckingham Palace. It was, in fact, one of the last occasions of its kind to take place in the chapel before it was destroyed during the Blitz of 1940.

At her christening on 30 October, the Princess was carried to the lily-shaped font containing water from the River Jordan, wearing the cascading robe of cream satin and Honiton lace that had first been worn by Queen Victoria's eldest child, Vicky, the Princess Royal, and which, by tradition, has been worn at their christenings by all royal babies up to the present day.

Included in the christening party were three of the Princess's five godparents, or 'sponsors' as they are known in Court parlance. They were her great-aunt, Princess Victoria, the unmarried daughter of Edward VII and Queen Alexandra, who was always said to be George V's favourite sister, Lady Rose Leveson-Gower, later the Countess Granville,* the Duchess of York's older sister, in honour of whom the infant received her second name, and the Duchess's younger brother, the Honourable David Bowes Lyon.

Not there in person but represented by family members were the baby's remaining godparents, the Prince of Wales, for whom his brother Prince George stood proxy, and Princess Ingrid of Sweden, later Queen of Denmark, who was represented by her aunt, Lady Patricia Ramsay (the former Princess Patricia of Connaught). The ceremony itself was conducted by the Archbishop of Canterbury, Dr Lang, who, when visiting the Duke and Duchess of York at home in later years, usually managed to embarrass the young Princess Margaret by placing his hand firmly on her head and solemnly pronouncing, 'Bless you my child.'[7]

Not so many years later, when frustrated by the media's insistence on referring to her as though her names were hyphenated, the Princess complained bitterly to her mother, 'You gave Lilibet three names. Why didn't you give *me* three instead of only two? *Margaret Rose!*'[8] Later still, while her parents and sister invariably called her 'Margaret', Prince Charles's childhood adaptation of her name to 'Margot' was subsequently adopted by her niece Anne and later by her younger nephews Andrew and Edward.**

Though it was always possible that the Duke and Duchess of York, who were still only thirty-five and thirty respectively, might have more children, the public perception of them as a family

---

* Lady Mary Clayton, the daughter of Lady Rose and her husband, 'Wisp', otherwise William Spencer Leveson-Gower, later Vice-Admiral the 4th Earl Granville, has said that after Princess Margaret's birth, it became something of a tradition for girls in the Leveson-Gower family, to be given 'Rose' as one of their Christian names.

** Charles, Prince of Wales, born 1948; Anne, The Princess Royal, born 1950; Andrew, Duke of York, born 1960; Edward, Earl of Wessex, born 1964, children of HM Queen Elizabeth II & HRH The Prince Philip, Duke of Edinburgh.

was in every way complete. More than ever they were the true personification of an ideal.

An attractive, perfectly symmetrical unit on which people throughout the imperial world could project their dreams and fantasies, the Yorks represented the distillation of everything that was good and virtuous. They were middle England at its best and most comfortable. They were unpretentious, unostentatious and above all, as Lady Mary Clayton put it, they were 'free and easy and very happy. They were almost a naval family.'[9]

A sense of 'ordinariness' was something that must also have impressed itself on the unassuming Duke of York somewhere along the way, for he is known to have said on at least one occasion, 'I am only a very ordinary person when they let me be one.' He was mistaken, of course. Royalty – and the Yorks were very much a case in point – may be *natural*, but by definition they can never be ordinary. The restrictive framework of protocol and Court etiquette, offset by the *quid pro quo* of wealth, privilege and 'other worldliness', does not permit it.

Nevertheless, for six years after the birth of Princess Margaret, 'we four', as the Duke would affectionately, even protectively, refer to his family after the Abdication had robbed them of their lives, evicted them from 145 Piccadilly, and thrust them on to centre stage, were able to enjoy an approximation to that unattainable state of anonymity.

Following the birth of Lilibet in 1926, the Duke and Duchess of York had employed a family retainer, the redoubtable Clara Cooper Knight, otherwise known as 'Allah' (pronounced 'Ah-la'), as nanny to the baby princess. Originally taken on by Lady Strathmore in September 1900, as nanny to her month-old daughter Elizabeth, Allah, whose father and brother were among the Strathmore's tenant farmers, stayed with the family until the eldest daughter, Lady May Bowes Lyon, married Lord Elphinstone.

When they in turn produced a family, Allah joined them as nanny to their own daughters Jean and Margaret. 'Allah', remembered Jean, 'was quite strict but very, very loving . . . We were terribly upset when she left to look after Princess Elizabeth.'[10]

To help in the nursery at 145 Piccadilly, the Yorks, who already employed a butler, an under-butler, a housekeeper, two footmen, a cook, three kitchen maids, a valet, a dresser, an odd-job man, a night-watchman, a telephonist, a chauffeur, and an RAF orderly, most of whom lived in, also engaged a young nursery maid to help Allah.

The daughter of a Black Isle railway worker, Margaret MacDonald, or 'Bobo' as Lilibet would call her, was twenty-two when she joined the York household. As Princess Elizabeth grew up, so the devoted and increasingly influential Bobo went on to become her dresser and confidante. With the birth of Princess Margaret, Bobo's younger sister, the sixteen-year-old Ruby, was recruited to the nursery staff. She too was to remain in royal service for more than thirty years and, following her sister's example, became dresser to the younger princess.

Beyond the warm, safe environment of the nursery at 145 Piccadilly, the nature of world events had become far graver than they were at the time of the General Strike, when Princess Elizabeth had been born.

In August 1929, the first signs that America's prolonged economic boom was coming to an end could be detected in the gentle decline of share values, which only two months later led to the dramatic Wall Street Crash of 18 October. As nearly a third of the country's businesses failed and production fell by ten per cent per year, twelve million men found themselves without work.

The knock-on effect not only led to political and economic unrest in Latin America but gave rise to extreme financial distress as far away as Australia. Moreover, in May 1931, the collapse of the Kreditanstalt Bank in Vienna caused unprecedented economic eruptions throughout Europe. The effect in Britain, where industrial output declined by ten per cent between 1929 and 1933, meant an alarming increase in unemployment from seven to more than sixteen per cent, while in the regions where it was already highest, in the coal mines, iron foundries and shipyards of north east England, Scotland and Wales, it rose from thirteen to twenty-eight per cent.

On 21 September 1931, Britain went off the Gold Standard and the value of sterling was decreased by almost a third – a development which cut the cost of British exports and led to the economy's gradual, if long-term, recovery. After Ramsay MacDonald's Labour administration resigned because of its inability to meet the financial emergency, George V invited him to form a National Government and acknowledged the inevitability of retrenchment by voluntarily surrendering £50,000, or fifty per cent of the annual Civil List income he received from the Government.* He also intended 'to give up shooting in Windsor Park, as I can't afford it . . .'

As a corresponding measure, the King instructed the fast-living Prince of Wales to give up £50,000 from the revenues which, as heir to the throne, he received from the Duchy of Cornwall. Though the Prince, who received his father's instructions while entertaining his mistress Thelma Furness in a Biarritz night club, was far from happy at this enforced economy, he was aware that his brother, the Duke of York, had also been required to tighten his belt. In so doing, Bertie reluctantly gave up hunting and, even more reluctantly, given that he had built up his stable with care and discernment, had put his six hunting horses up for auction.

'It has come as a great shock to me that with the economy cuts I have had to make my hunting should have been one of the things I must do without', he wrote to the Master of the Pytchley Hunt, Ronald Tree. 'And I must sell my horses too. This is the worst part of it all, and the parting with them will be terrible.'[11]

It was ironic that as the long-term result of one particular hunting party, the Duke of York would ultimately sacrifice more

---

* In 1760 upon his accession to the throne, King George III surrendered the revenues from the Crown Lands to Parliament in return for an annual income, known as the Civil List. A similar surrender has been made by all successive sovereigns.

than his love of chasing foxes around the country. At Burrough Court, Viscount Furness's country house in Melton Mowbray during the autumn of 1930 or 1931,* depending on which version of events is the most accurate, the Prince of Wales first met Mrs Ernest Simpson, a not unattractive, stylishly-dressed American in her mid-thirties. As the Prince later recalled:

'Mrs Simpson did not ride and obviously had no interest in horses, hounds, or hunting in general . . . Since a Prince is by custom expected to take the lead in conversing with strangers, and having been informed that she was an American, I was prompted to observe that she must miss central heating, of which there was a lamentable lack in my country and an abundance in hers.

'The affirmative answer that, in the circumstances, any Briton had reason to expect would then have cleared the way for a casual discussion of the variety of physical comforts available in America, and the conversation would have been safely anchored on firm ground. But instead, a verbal chasm opened under my feet. Mrs Simpson did not miss the great boon that her country had conferred on the world. On the contrary, she liked our cold houses. A mocking look came into her eyes. "I am sorry, Sir," she said, "but you have disappointed me."

"In what way?"

"Every American woman who comes to your country is always asked that same question. I had hoped for something more original from the Prince of Wales." '[12]

Little could they have imagined that autumn weekend, what Wallis Simpson's hopes for 'something more original from the Prince of Wales', would lead to.

If the Great Depression was no time for extravagance, the prospect of economic recovery at least permitted the Duke and Duchess of York to plan the renovation of a house which King

---

* In his memoirs, *A King's Story*, published in 1951, the Duke of Windsor claims to have met Mrs Simpson in the autumn of 1931. When she published her autobiography, *The Heart Has its Reasons*, in 1956, Mrs Simpson, by now Duchess of Windsor, insisted the Duke was wrong; and stated that their first meeting had occurred at Melton Mowbray in the autumn of 1930.

George V had offered them as an out-of-town residence. Situated in the centre of Windsor Great Park, about three miles from Windsor Castle, the Royal Lodge was in a dilapidated condition when the King asked the Duke and Duchess to have a look at it and decide if they would like to take it on.

Having visited the house in September 1931, the Duke wrote to his father, 'It is too kind of you to have offered us Royal Lodge & now having seen it I think it will suit us admirably.'

Built by the Prince Regent on the site of an earlier house known as the Lower Lodge, Royal Lodge was a rather more flamboyant *cottage ornée*, built to the designs of John Nash and Jeffry Wyatt. With George IV's death in June 1830, his brother and far less imaginative successor, William IV, demolished most of the Royal Lodge. Apart from the Chapel of All Saints, just over a hundred yards away to the north-east, where members of the royal family and estate workers still worship, the Great Saloon, though minus a roof, was the only part of the house to be spared.

Subsequently occupied by a succession of private secretaries, equerries and lords-in-waiting, the Great Saloon was eventually partitioned into five ill-proportioned rooms that were used first by Sir Arthur Ellis, Comptroller of the Lord Chamberlain's Office and equerry to King Edward VII, and afterwards by other senior members of the Royal Household.

It was this once magnificent room, measuring 48 feet long, 29 feet wide and 20 feet high (14.6 x 8.8 x 6m), that the Duke and Duchess of York restored to its former neo-gothic glory. Painting the panelled walls a cool Regency green, they gave pride of place to a portrait of George IV, which hangs over the fireplace to this day. In addition, the Yorks built a new family wing, with ground-floor principal bedrooms, to accommodate themselves and their two young daughters. Begun with the assistance of the Crown Lands Department at Windsor in May 1932, and using the Duke's own plans, estimates and builders, the new wing was completed in October of that year and first occupied by the family the following month. When the two-storey, mansion-like Royal Lodge, with its fine views over Windsor Great Park was complete, its exterior walls were given a distinctive rose-pink wash, which was later picked up in the external finish of several gate-houses and lodges in the Park.

Through the years, renovations were undertaken at the house from time to time and on one occasion led to an unexpected discovery. During the early 1980s, by which time Royal Lodge had been the widowed Queen Mother's country home for more than thirty years, a basement kitchen was rediscovered. An old Windsorian who was carrying out repairs, said at the time, 'It was as if somebody had finished work, closed the door and left everything as it was; lovely copper pans and all. Just sealed it all up.'[13]

One of the pleasures in the lives of both the Duke and Duchess of York was a shared passion for gardening; something they had in common with the Prince of Wales. In April 1930, when George V permitted his eldest son to take over Fort Belvedere, an eighteenth-century castellated 'folly' on the edge of Windsor Great Park, near Virginia Water, the prince enthusiastically took on the task of clearing acres of tangled yew and laurel. At Royal Lodge, the Duke of York was no less dedicated to transforming sixteen acres of rampant undergrowth into an informal woodland garden of vistas, glades and walks, planted with flowering shrubs, azaleas and rhododendrons, on the subject of which he became an acknowledged connoisseur.

Entering this rural idyll during the spring of 1932 was the newest member of the York household. Miss Marion Crawford, or 'Crawfie', as Princess Elizabeth would call her, was a twenty-two-year-old graduate of the Moray House [Teacher] Training College in Edinburgh who, at the instigation of the Duchess's sister, Lady Rose Leveson-Gower, joined the family as governess first to Lilibet, who was then almost six years old, and later, when she was old enough, to her sister as well.

A Scot, as so many royal household staff tended to be, Crawfie had been born in Ayrshire and brought up in Dunfermline after her widowed mother had remarried. Later, while studying to be a teacher – as opposed to a governess, a distinction Crawfie herself was keen to make – she witnessed poverty and malnourishment on a scale that, in her own words, fired her 'crusading spirit', and reinforced in her a need 'to do something about the misery and unhappiness I saw all around me.'[14]

Little by little, chance was to take Crawfie further away from the poverty that had so inspired her – and, for that matter, her altruistic ideals – than she could ever have imagined. Home from Edinburgh, she received a letter from the Countess of Elgin, asking if she would consider teaching history to her seven-year-old son, Andrew. No sooner had she embarked on what she regarded as 'a pleasant interlude, a temporary arrangement to fill in the time between one course of study and another', than Crawfie found herself teaching the Elgins' other children, Martha, Jean and Jamie.

It was about this time that Vice-Admiral William Leveson-Gower, his wife Lady Rose, and their daughter Mary (later Lady Mary Clayton), moved to Admiralty House at nearby Rosyth. Once again, fate stepped in when Crawfie was asked if she would accept young Mary as a part-time pupil. Looking back on those long-distant days, Lady Mary remembers Crawfie as 'a lovely country girl, who was a good teacher, except when it came to mathematics, which she really wasn't very good at.'[15]

In much the same way that the Yorks had purloined Allah Knight from the nursery of the Elphinstone household, so Crawfie, albeit at Lady Rose's recommendation, was prevailed upon to accept the post of royal governess. For the next fifteen years, until in 1947 at the age of thirty-eight, she finally left the royal household to marry a fellow Scot by the name of George Buthlay – and subsequently embarked on a brief, but lucrative 'writing' career – Crawfie was to act as teacher, mentor and companion to the Princesses Elizabeth and Margaret.

Three years after her marriage, however, 'doing a Crawfie', entered the royal vocabulary as an expression of disdain for anything the royal family regarded as a betrayal of trust. And betrayal, so far as they were concerned, was precisely what Crawfie was guilty of, when she published a book about her life with the King and his family. Though *The Little Princesses* was written in the adoring tone of contemporary women's magazines, by an unidentified ghost-writer specializing in saccharine prose, there was clearly no malice in Crawfie's ambitions. And while it may not be unbiased or indeed accurate in every detail, her book still provides a valuable insight into the family life of George VI and, more particularly, into the personalities and development of his daughters.

It is also perhaps worth adding that Crawfie's book assumes still more significance, when it is realized that Queen Elizabeth The Queen Mother has never kept a diary;[16] that those of the present Queen will not be made accessible until such time as her official biographer is appointed during the reign of her successor; and that the early part of her own life is not something Princess Margaret finds sufficiently interesting to discuss in any detail.

Where Crawfie was at fault, and she undoubtedly lived to regret it, was in believing she could publish without royal approval and get away with it. In March 1949, not long after she had married and retired to Nottingham Cottage, one of the attractive grace-and-favour properties at Kensington Palace, the Queen heard that Crawfie had written, or was currently in the process of writing, a book that dealt primarily with the lives of the two princesses. Writing directly to the former governess, the Queen asked her not to pursue the idea, reasoning that it would be an invasion of her family's privacy. Crawfie evidently responded that she would respect Her Majesty's wishes and would not proceed.

Later that year, however, Crawfie's duplicity was finally laid bare when Nancy, Lady Astor, was sent proofs of her book from America, where it was about to be serialized in the magazine *Ladies Home Journal*. The whole episode, which today seems so trivial, had become quite a drama within royal circles.

Writing to Nancy Astor, the Queen said that what their 'late and completely trusted governess' had done had been 'a great shock for us', not least because she had given her written promise not to write about the princesses. Hard on the heels of the Queen's letter came another from her Private Secretary, Major Tom Harvey, in which he, too, referred to Her Majesty's 'shocked and distressed' state that so trusted a member of the household should publish personal reminiscences.

'Such a thing', he told Lady Astor, 'is utterly alien to the spirit and custom of Their Majesties' households and staff and great regret is felt by all those who care for the sanctity of their family life at this unhappy breach of decency and good taste . . .'

In America, Bruce and Beatrice Gould, the editors of *Ladies Home Journal* and friends of Nancy Astor, were understandably mystified by the near hysterical reaction of the royal family and those around them. 'I realize', said Bruce Gould, 'that the whole idea of royalty is a kind of conspiratorial ballet which depends upon everyone's unquestioning acceptance of the agreed-upon steps', but how – when royalty from within was pretty much a closed shop – could anyone object to something which, in today's jargon, was a royalty-friendly, public relations coup?

Though Crawfie's fall from grace was immediate and complete, there were those who thought the governess 'no longer seemed her old self.' Among them was the kindly Lady Mary Clayton, who in retrospect said, 'I think life at Court must have turned her head. She wasn't the sort to be a mischief.' Then she added, albeit in understatement, 'I can only think she fell under a bad influence and was beguiled into writing that book.'

George Buthlay, the man Crawfie married, was that 'bad' beguiling influence, and it was he who was responsible for wanting to capitalize on his besotted wife's connections. Apart from a misguided notion that the royal family might be persuaded to abandon Coutts, their traditional bankers, for Drummonds, where he was employed, Buthlay was undoubtedly the driving force behind some of Crawfie's more persistent requests to her former employers. Among them was the idea that she might be appointed lady-in-waiting to one of the princesses; and repeated requests for money to be paid into her husband's bank account.

The latter was almost certainly born of opportunism, rather than any question of financial hardship. For the Buthlays would certainly have received healthy percentages of fees and royalties from the sale of rights in *The Little Princesses*. The British publishers George Newnes, for instance, had paid £30,000 for world rights, while Crawfie had received a tax-free sum of more than $6,000 from *Ladies Home Journal*. There was more to come. John Gordon, editor and chief columnist of the *Sunday Express*, and for almost twenty years the 'scourge' of the royal family – a period in which Princess Margaret is adamant the *Express* deliberately singled her out for criticism – employed Crawfie as the so-called 'social editor' of *Woman's Own*. Now, for the magazine that had been the first to publish extracts from *The Little Princesses* in Britain, Crawfie was to churn out 'insider' articles, as well as a weekly column, about the royal family.

Journalism, however, was to be a short-lived career. In 1955, Crawfie's literary exploits left her high and dry when, early that summer, she not only wrote of 'The bearing and dignity of the Queen at the Trooping of [*sic*] the Colour ceremony . . .' but followed it up with a glowing description of Royal Ascot. Sadly for Crawfie, a rail strike that year had ensured that neither event took place.

Ostracized by the staff and residents of other grace-and-favour apartments at Kensington Palace, and pushed by an ambitious husband and demanding publisher to the brink of a nervous breakdown, Crawfie fled to Aberdeen, where she lived until her death in February 1988, an embittered, all but friendless widow, ignored by the royal family.

When she arrived at Royal Lodge, Windsor, early in 1932, however, Marion Crawford's tragic dénouement still lay many years distant. In fact, her long-term prospects at that time had yet to be decided. Having written to the Duchess of York, 'saying how honoured I was to have been asked to undertake the education of the Princesses . . . I suggested that I should take up the work for a trial period during which I would be able to determine whether it would be easy for me to become reconciled to the idea of leaving Scotland and my intended career, and living permanently with other people.'

The Duchess's response was to invite her to '. . . come for a month and see how you like us and how we like you.'

Crawfie, of course, stayed on.

THREE

Unlike her sister at the same age, public interest in Princess Margaret during the first three or four years of her life, was only partially satisfied. Glimpses of her while out driving with Allah Knight in Hyde Park, or the publication of appealing, if carefully-posed photographs, commissioned – with or without Lilibet by her side – from the studios of photographers such as Marcus Adams, Bertram Park and Lisa Sheridan, were virtually all people ever saw of her.

It was this apparent reluctance to allow the Princess to be seen more generally in public that led to speculation that she was being held back for a reason. That in turn gave rise to the widespread rumour that she was deaf and dumb. The simple truth of the matter was that Allah, with no baby in the house, was determined to hold on to her younger charge for as long as she could; even if it meant that she was 'penned in a pram long after she pined to run [with her sister] in the gardens, and was fed by hand when in reality she had done with such childish things.'[1]

Before long, the deaf and dumb story died a natural death, helped on its way by the Princess's grandfather, George V. In November 1934, the first family wedding since the Yorks' own eleven years earlier, was celebrated between the King and Queen's youngest surviving son, the debonair, artistic and some-what dissolute Prince George, Duke of Kent, and the elegant and statuesque Princess Marina of Greece and Denmark, much of whose life had been spent with her family in Parisian exile.*

It was when the royal family appeared on the balcony at Buckingham Palace after George and Marina's marriage ceremonies – first at Westminster Abbey and immediately afterwards, according to the rites of the Greek Orthodox church, in the private chapel at Buckingham Palace – that the King suddenly bent down and whisked the four-year-old Princess Margaret off her feet. Standing her on the balcony's balustrade, he held her there for a minute of two, so that she could be seen by the cheering crowds below.

As Lady Mary Clayton explained, 'The King loved the Yorks and he was very angry about the rumour that Princess Margaret was deaf and dumb. That is why he lifted her up like that. It was his way of saying, "Here is my granddaughter and there is nothing wrong with her." '2

Princess Margaret's own memories of George V, despite the fact that he far preferred his York granddaughters to his Lascelles grandsons, are of a gruff, shadowy figure of whom Allah for one, was more than a little afraid. It was, said the Princess, one of the reasons why their visits to Buckingham Palace tended to be infrequent.

Nevertheless, being swept off her feet by the King and held on the edge of the balcony with such a considerable drop to the forecourt below, was something she never forgot. 'It was', said the Princess, who freely admitted she has no head for heights, 'a *terrifying* experience.'3

From her earliest years, there was no doubting the fact that Princess Margaret was her father's daughter. She was in every way totally devoted to him. Even as a toddler she would make

* The third and youngest daughter of Prince Nicholas of Greece and his Russian wife, the Grand Duchess Helen Vladimirovna, a first cousin of Tsar Nicholas II, Princess Marina's maternal grandparents were the Grand Duke Vladimir, and the highly-influential, German-born, Grand Duchess Marie Pavlovna, acknowledged doyenne of Russian society and, after the Empress Alexandra and Dowager Empress Marie Feodorovna, third lady in the land.

straight for his side when, having been given her own lunch in the nursery, she would come down to the dining room to join her parents towards the end of their own meal. Having pushed 'her small fat face' round the door, she would climb up on to her father's knee to sip soda or 'windy' water, as she called it, take a handful of the barley-sugar crystals her parents stirred into their coffee and, when asked, regale them with graphic descriptions of the 'hooshmi' – as the Duke of York[4] called any spoon-fed mixture, especially of meat, vegetables and gravy – that had been prepared for her.

Of the love that existed between the Duke of York and his younger daughter, Crawfie was to say that Princess Margaret brought 'delight' into his life. 'She was a plaything', she wrote, 'warm and demonstrative, made to be cuddled and played with. At one time he would be almost embarrassed, yet at the same time most touched and pleased, when she wound her arms round his neck, nestled against him and cuddled and caressed him.'

Beyond the special bond she would share with her father until his death in 1952, the next most important relationship was the one she established with her sister. Though in character they would always be as different as chalk and cheese – the elder more reserved and self-assured, the younger less confident, but more extrovert – an unquestionable devotion developed between them almost from the moment Princess Margaret was born. As protector, a role she would invariably play in one way or another throughout their lives, Lilibet kept a watchful, and at times concerned, eye on her younger, more precocious, sibling.

On one occasion, when Princess Elizabeth was no more than five years old and her sister only eighteen months, the then chaplain of the Chapel of All Saints at Royal Lodge visited the Duke and Duchess of York. Mesmerized by his prominent buck teeth, the Princess could scarcely take her eyes off him. When the conversation finally turned to the baby of the family, the chaplain looked at Lilibet and asked, 'May I see your little sister?' Slowly and very solemnly, while looking him straight in the eye, she shook her head. 'No,' she replied, 'I think your teeth would frighten her.'[5]

This sense of 'big sisterly' responsibility, of attempting to protect the young Margaret if not from the world, then at times from herself, often became manifest as they were growing up. It also served to highlight the differences in the Princesses' characters. 'Unlike Lilibet, to whom one could always explain things', said one who was aware of the younger Princess's shortcomings, 'Margaret would not listen to reason. She was lively, high spirited, a great mimic, and wayward. But because she also had an entrancing charm, she always got away with it.'[6]

Another who knew them well was to say, 'As a child, Princess Margaret was impish and mischievous. The problem was that she was never admonished, and that really can't be a good thing for any child. But her naughtiness made her parents laugh and she got that down to a fine art. She always managed to wind people round her little finger and, of course, she liked to get her own way, which she was extremely good at. In fact, she was *exactly* like the little girl in the nursery rhyme that went something like:

> There was a little girl who had a little curl
> in the middle of her forehead;
> When she was nice, she was *very, very* nice,
> but when she was bad she was horrid.[7]

The childhood characteristics that would shape Princess Margaret's life as an adult were soon a source of concern to the young and, if Crawfie is to be believed, remarkably astute Princess Elizabeth who sensed they would lead to trouble. 'In her own intuitive fashion', wrote the children's governess, 'she saw . . . how later on Margaret was bound to be misrepresented and misunderstood. How often . . . I heard her cry in real anguish, "Stop her, Mummie. Oh, please stop her", when Margaret was being more than usually preposterous and amusing and outrageous. Though Lilibet, with the rest of us, laughed at Margaret's antics – and indeed it was impossible not to – I think they often made her uneasy and filled her with fore-boding.'

Perhaps the only other member of the royal family to express concern about the way in which Princess Margaret's character was developing was Queen Mary. In the spring of 1940, when the Princess was still only nine, Lady Cynthia Colville, one of Queen Mary's ladies-in-waiting, was instructed to write to Miss Crawford, 'Her Majesty is rather sorry to hear that Princess Margaret is so spoilt, though perhaps it is hardly surprising. I dare say, too, she has a more complicated and difficult character, and one that will require a great deal of skill and insight in dealing with . . .'[8]

As the years passed, however, any representation on the part of Queen Mary would, so far as Princess Margaret was concerned, fall on deaf ears. As an adult she would rarely disguise the fact that, in her own words, she 'couldn't stand' her grandmother. On one occasion, she went even further, telling a friend in particularly vehement terms, 'I detested Queen Mary. She was rude to all of us except Lilibet, who was going to be queen. Of course, she had an inferiority complex. We were royal, and she was not.'[9]*

If, as one former courtier put it, 'The royal family aren't just bad at communicating with each other, they are *terrible* at it',[10] then Queen Mary can never have known how alienating her stiff, upright manner was, or the unintentional effect it had on her granddaughter. 'How small you are! When are you going to grow up?' was one early, if insensitive, remark that deeply offended the Princess. At just over five feet (1.5m) tall, she would never cease to be conscious of her lack of height and in an unnecessary attempt to make up for it, would wear platform shoes long after they had ceased to be fashionable.

On another occasion, when she came across the young Princess Margaret playing with the cords of a window blind,

---

* This was clearly a reference to Queen Mary's morganatic inheritance, discussed in Chapter One, and to the fact that, unlike her granddaughters, she had been born a 'Serene' and not a 'Royal' Highness.

Queen Mary launched into what was no doubt a well-intentioned – but ill-received – history lesson on the fate of King George of Hanover, who lost his sight after hitting himself in the face with a chain purse he had been swinging.

According to Crawfie, it was she who first involved the matriarchal Queen Mary, with her keen appreciation of history and her unshakeable belief in personal responsibility, duty and the high ideals of monarchy, in her plans for the Princesses' education.

Having devised a traditional programme of lessons based on the three Rs, reading, writing and arithmetic, which in turn was complemented by tuition in French, singing, dancing, drawing, and music – no less traditional subjects in those days for a private education – Crawfie sent a copy of her proposed timetable to Queen Mary, who responded with questions and suggestions of her own.

She wondered if, for example, given her granddaughters' position, two-and-a-half hours of history a week was really sufficient. In order that more time might be devoted to that all-important subject and, indeed, to the study of 'genealogies, historical and dynastic', would it not be possible to drop one or two periods of arithmetic? After all, the Queen reasoned, it was highly unlikely that either child would ever have to keep her own household accounts.

Tuition in the 'physical geography' of the British Empire – India and the Dominions – was also a subject that Queen Mary believed should be taught in some detail. In addition, there was the matter of Bible studies, to which she felt Crawfie had allocated too little time. And what, she asked, of poetry? Though the notion might be old-fashioned, learning poems by heart was an excellent way of training the memory.

Other reading matter, the Queen suggested, should consist only of 'the best type of children's books', such as classics by Jane Austen, Robert Louis Stevenson and Kipling. A. A. Milne's *Winnie the Pooh*, and *When We Were Very Young*, which the Princesses received as gifts from their uncle David, the Prince of

Wales, were added to the collection, along with *Lamb's Tales from Shakespeare,* Hugh Lofting's *Dr Doolittle* stories, and Thackeray's *The Rose and the Ring.*

Black Beauty, which instantly appealed to their inherent love of horses, was a firm favourite, while Princess Margaret was said to be so fond of *The Little Red Hen* that she was able to recite it by heart. Neither princess ever cared for Lewis Carroll's *Alice in Wonderland,* however, which they thought 'rather stupid'. Years later, Princess Margaret would tell the writer and historian, Kenneth Rose, that she had never forgotten the story's 'nightmare ingredients: claustrophobia [from which she suffers], falling down unseen holes, grotesque animals that talk'.[11]

In order to take a more active part in Crawfie's revised schedule, Queen Mary assumed responsibility for organizing 'instructive amusements' for her granddaughters. On the itinerary were outings to places of interest such as the British and Victoria and Albert Museums, the Tower of London and the Royal Mint.

Though her feelings towards her grandmother may very well have coloured her view, Princess Margaret maintains that Crawfie's hymn of praise to Queen Mary and her contribution to their curriculum not only diminished her parents' interest in that aspect of their lives, but assumed an unmerited importance.[12]

Nevertheless, all the indications were that the Duke and Duchess of York did not appear to put too great an emphasis on their daughters' education, and certainly did not wish either one of them to be regarded as intellectual. Now and then, the press alluded to private discussions about public school education for the Princesses, though most of it amounted to nothing more than speculation.

At one point, however, there was some reason to believe that the Duchess of York – who, as a girl had spent two terms at a Chelsea day school – would have liked Princess Elizabeth, and in turn Princess Margaret, to have gone to school 'like any normal girl.' Society photographer Lisa Sheridan supported this contention in her memoirs *From Cabbages to Kings,* when she recalled the Duchess telling her that 'she regretted her own daughters would not be able to go to school.'[13]

In this, as with the choice of names for Princess Margaret just a few years earlier, the Yorks had had to defer to the King, whose almost pathological loathing of change would never have permitted his granddaughters anything more revolutionary than the private education they received, albeit under the direction of a governess whom both he and the Queen originally considered to be much too young.*

George V's intransigence and the Duchess of York's presumed disappointment may explain why Randolph Churchill, although he was writing after the Second World War, claimed that the Duchess 'never aimed at bringing her daughters up to be more than nicely behaved young ladies.'[14]

Whatever the truth about schools, public or private, the level of Queen Mary's involvement in the Princesses' education, or the Yorks' aspirations – or lack of them – for their daughters, the King's only anxiety seems to have revolved around a question of calligraphy.

'For goodness' sake, teach Margaret and Lilibet to write a decent hand . . .' was his one and only directive to Miss Crawford. 'Not one of my children can write properly. They all do it exactly the same way. I like a hand with some character in it.'

If, however, the Duke of York's attitude towards his daughters' education was one of 'genial casualness, undisturbed in the early years by any premonition of what lay ahead',[15] his chief desire was for Lilibet and Margaret to remember their childhood as a 'golden age,' something that was denied him but which his children could look back upon with affection. 'As a

---

* Although George V's eldest grandchildren, George (Earl of Harewood) and Gerald Lascelles, were educated at Eton, the present Duke of Kent and his sister Princess Alexandra, children of Prince George and Princess Marina, Duke and Duchess of Kent, were the first *royal* offspring to go to school. In 1943, the Duke started at Ludgrove Preparatory, followed by Eton, and Le Rosey in Switzerland; while in 1947, at the age of eleven, Princess Alexandra became a boarder at Heathfield School, Ascot.

father', Lady Mary Clayton recalled, '[the Duke] was very loving. Always happy and at ease with his children and very observant. He noticed everything they did.'[16]

From their earliest days, first with Princess Elizabeth and later when Princess Margaret was born, the pleasure the Duke took in his wife and children meant spending as much time together as possible. The Princesses began every day with fun and games, or 'high jinks,' in their parents' bedroom, while the bedtime ritual every evening involved further fun at bath time, when both the Duke and Duchess often came in for a soaking. Finally handed over to Allah and the nursery maids Bobo and Ruby, the princesses' calls of 'Goodnight Mummie', 'Goodnight Papa', would echo round the stairwell at 145 Piccadilly, as the children wound their way to bed and the Yorks themselves went downstairs to dress for dinner.

Although in the royal pecking order the Duke of York, as the King's second son, ranked as a senior member of the royal family, his official life – and that of the Duchess – was much less onerous at this time than it would soon become or, for that matter, would be today. But it did at least mean that the Duke was often free to join his daughters for their mid-morning games in the private communal garden that lay behind the row of houses to which number 145 Piccadilly belonged. Known as Hamilton Gardens, its immaculately kept lawns were crisscrossed by gravel footpaths, dotted with trees, shrubs and bushes and girded by iron railings beyond which lay the 360-acre expanse of Hyde Park. In the centre of Hamilton Gardens stood a statue of Lord Byron, which served as 'home base' for the Princesses – as well as their father – in their races and in their games of tag and hide-and-seek which, according to Princess Margaret, they particularly enjoyed. Other games that were played, with or without the necessity of clambering through the bushes, were hopscotch, at which the Duke himself was especially adept, Cowboys and Indians, and a variation of Sardines.

The Princesses also ran a horse market, a game that involved some of their collection of thirty-odd toy horses. Of varying sizes and descriptions, with or without wheels, but all with saddles and bridles that the Princesses themselves were expected to polish and maintain, they were stabled beneath the glass dome on the top floor nursery landing of number 145. As Princess Margaret recalled, those horses 'had to be groomed, fed and watered all day!'[17] Before long, toy horses would give way to the real thing when the princesses were taught to ride first by their parents and then by Horace Smith, the riding instructor who, in royal folklore seems to have been eclipsed by the popular Mr Owen, the Windsor groom with whom the Princesses would often go out riding in the Great Park.

This preoccupation with horses that would all but dominate their childhood and would continue to be the elder Princess's most passionate on- and off-duty interest throughout her adulthood, was also shared in true country style with dogs. In fact, one of the most enduring and popular images of the Yorks as a family, seen in newspapers, magazines and newsreels, is that of the Duke and Duchess – he in jacket and tie; she most often in hat, pearls and heels – together with their more casual, but similarly-dressed daughters, cuddling, stroking, chasing, playing with or otherwise surrounded by dogs.

Of its kind, one particularly successful picture book, *Our Princesses and their Dogs*, with photographs by Lisa Sheridan (which in 1936–37 sold for two shillings and sixpence, 12½ pence in today's currency), portrayed the Yorks on the terrace of their London house, on the lawn at the Royal Lodge, Windsor and outside *Y Bwthyn Bach*, ('The Little House'), a two-thirds life-size thatched cottage which the people of Wales had presented to Princess Elizabeth on her sixth birthday. With them were two Pembrokeshire Corgis Jane and Dookie, three yellow Labradors, Mimsy and her offspring Stiffy and Scrummy, Choo-Choo a long-haired, grey and white Tibetan Lion Dog, a Golden Retriever called Judy and a black Cocker Spaniel known as Ben.

This appealing family image wasn't all that it seemed, however, for though the Duke and Duchess and their elder daughter were genuinely fond of and deeply interested in dogs and horses, Princess Margaret was never totally enamoured of either. While she was certainly no admirer of corgis, the breed so beloved of her mother and sister, the dogs she, herself, would own were few in number. Those who spring to mind were Johnnie, a Sealyham terrier who from the late 1940s to the mid-1950s was very probably the Princess's favourite, Rowley, a King Charles spaniel, whose moment of fame came when he appeared in some of his mistress's engagement photographs at Royal Lodge in 1960 and, most recently, Pippin, a Windsor-based, long-haired dachsund who, in surprise partnership with one of the present Queen's corgis, was responsible for siring a new cross-breed known as a 'dorgi'.

It was her near indifference to dogs that led Princess Margaret at the age of nineteen, to decline an invitation to become Patron of the Canine Defence League. To have accepted, she said at the time, would have been an act of 'the greatest hypocrisy.'[18]

It is not, of course, beyond the realms of possibility that, without realizing it herself, the Princess was a juvenile advocate of the theatrical maxim never to work 'with children or animals.' For here was a highly imaginative child with much too lively a character to want to share the spotlight with, much less find herself upstaged by, any Dookie and Jane, Mimsy, Stiffy and Scrummy of the canine world.

Always a strong performer in her own right, there would be those who were of the opinion that had she not been born royal, or had come along much later on, she might, like her youngest nephew Edward, have pursued a career of some description in the Arts or Theatre.

Be that as it may, her sense of the theatrical – whether she was appearing in wartime pantomimes at Windsor, playing charades with her family or at house parties given by friends, mimicking 'types' of people in the style of Joyce Grenfell, singing and playing the piano after dinner, or simply as a regular theatre-goer – was certainly awakened at an early stage in her life.

When, as an enthralled five- or six-year-old, she returned home with her parents and sister from seeing a Christmas pantomime, which was always considered a great treat, she would cast her family in various roles and with them re-enact her own version of the show they had just seen.[19]

To the amusement of her parents – and the occasional exasperation of her governess – Princess Margaret would also create imaginary friends, such as Cousin Halifax, whom Crawfie remembered but in later years the Princess did not, and Inderbombanks, whom the Princess remembered and Crawfie evidently did not. Of indeterminate gender – 'I suppose he must have been male,' said the Princess – the tales, conversations and adventures she relayed to her parents about Inderbombanks meant that he became the Duke and Duchess of York's favourite character.[20]

Nor was Princess Margaret's inventiveness restricted merely to her waking hours. Her dreams, said Crawfie, were appalling, 'and the telling of them was one of her ways of postponing the start of an unpopular lesson, or some chore she disliked. Just as . . . she had used the handy "Cousin Halifax", it was now, "Crawfie, I *must* tell you an amazing dream I had last night", and Lilibet would listen with me, enthralled, as the account of green horses, wild-elephant stampedes, talking cats, and other remarkable manifestations went into two or three instalments.'[21]

Though in quite another way, something Princess Margaret once said to Sir James Barrie, the Scots dramatist best remembered as the creator of *Peter Pan*, earned immortality in his play, *The Boy David*. Invited to a Glamis tea party, held on what the Princess believed was her fifth birthday, Barrie noted, 'Some of her presents were on the table, simple things that might have come from the sixpenny shops, but she was in a frenzy of glee over them, especially one to which she had given the place of honour by her plate. I said to her as one astounded, "Is that really your very own?" and she saw how I envied and immediately placed it between us with the words, "It is yours and mine." '

For using those few words in his play, Sir James promised the Princess a penny for every performance, but by the time *The Boy David* was staged two years later, that promise had slipped the playwright's mind. The Duke of York (by now King) on the other hand, had not forgotten, and he sent a message saying that, on pain of hearing from the royal solicitors, Sir James should at once remit his daughter's outstanding royalties. The amused, but contrite dramatist immediately prepared a mock-solemn agreement, which he had engrossed on parchment. It was, in fact, the last thing he wrote and after his death in 1937, it fell to Lady Cynthia Asquith, who had been his secretary for some years, to deliver his dues to the Princess.

Ranging in scope and breadth from church, choral and classical to show tunes, jazz, blues, and country and western, music would always be a constant in Princess Margaret's life. As a pianist – though in her own words, 'Not a very good one; I have no "left hand" '[22] – it was as natural for her to sight-read music as it was easy to pick up tunes by ear. At the age of three, said her cousin, the late Jean Wills, Princess Margaret knew all the words to the Easter hymn, *There is a Green Hill Far Away*.

An even earlier example of her alert musical ear, though two or three versions of the same story have been published through the years, was recalled by Lady Mary Clayton. At the time of Princess Margaret's first birthday in August 1931, the Countess of Strathmore and Allah who was carrying the infant Princess in her arms, were walking up a mossy bank on their way to join a family shooting lunch at Hayston Hill, one of the Lower Sidlaw Hills close to Glamis Castle. To her grandmother's astonishment, the Princess began humming the entire waltz from *The Merry Widow*. 'It's a true story,' said Lady Mary, 'and because she was only a year old, it was thought delightful. But then my grandmother [Lady Strathmore] was intensely musical and Glamis was always full of music. That's no doubt how Princess Margaret heard it.'[23]

But for the fact that it has been verified by an unimpeachable source, this story, and others like it, might easily be regarded as apocryphal; just one of the ways in which royalty, especially in those less cynical, more respectful, pre-war years, were seen as different, untouchable and other-worldly. The truth was, of course, that as they were growing up, so both Princesses became increasingly curious about the outside world. For a short while, these children whose lives would soon have to fall in line with the predictable 'seasons' of the royal calendar, were able to glimpse something of the everyday lives of everyday people.

Crossing over from Hamilton Gardens with Crawfie at their side, they were able to explore Hyde Park several times unrecognized and on foot, instead of driving through as passengers in a car or carriage. They were able to wander round the Serpentine, watching people swimming or enjoying themselves in rowing-boats; and walk as far as the Round Pond in Kensington Gardens where they watched other children – who, said Crawfie, 'had an enormous fascination, like mystic beings from a different world' – sailing toy yachts. On the far side of the Round Pond lay Kensington Palace, or the 'Aunt Heap', as their Uncle David referred to the stately red-brick complex which housed several of his elderly relations. It was here in the house that Wren had been commissioned to build for them that William and Mary came to escape the fogs of Whitehall, where both Queen Victoria and Queen Mary had been born, and where, one day, Princess Margaret herself would come to live.

In response to Princess Elizabeth's 'wistful' remark that it must be 'fun' to travel on the London underground, what was intended as a private visit was arranged to the headquarters of the YWCA in Great Russell Street. Dressed in their matching velvet-collared tweed coats and dark berets, they took the tube that all but ran beneath 145 Piccadilly from Hyde Park Corner to Tottenham Court Road, from where, still unrecognized, they walked the few hundred yards to the YWCA building. There, just like everyone else, they bought tea in the canteen, though when the elder Princess, unaccustomed to serving herself, forgot to pick up the tea pot, the woman behind the counter bawled out, 'If you want it you must come and fetch it.' Perhaps not too surprisingly, the visit did not end without somebody recognizing them and, as a crowd began to gather, they had to return home in one of their father's hastily-summoned, chauffeur-driven limousines.

Of all the impressions Crawfie created, one of the most misleading was that the Princesses lived in isolation from other children. Although it is true that they belonged to a pretty select group drawn from family and friends, they saw a good deal of their favourite cousins Jean and Margaret Elphinstone, Lord and Lady Louis Mountbatten's two daughters Patricia and Pamela, the immensely popular Patrick Plunket (who would one day become Deputy Master of the Royal Household), and Elizabeth Cavendish, daughter of the 10th Duke of Devonshire, who not only remained a life-long friend, but was to become one of Princess Margaret's earliest ladies-in-waiting. There were other friendships, too, with the children of courtiers such as Alexander Hardinge, and Joey Legh,* and the youngsters with whom they played in Hamilton Gardens. Among them were Nicky Beaumont, younger son of Lord and Lady Allendale, who lived next door to the Yorks at 144 Piccadilly, and his friend, Colin Campbell. Nowadays a film maker, and half-brother of the interior decorator Nina Campbell, he clearly remembers the very first time he and Princess Margaret met.

Although they were both only six years old, he recalls that it was not an occasion he 'had anything to be proud of,' because he deliberately upset the toy pram into which the Princess had been happily piling autumn leaves. While a friendship which continues to the present day was established some years later, Campbell said, 'I don't mind admitting that I was severely reprimanded by my nanny, Miss Newcombe, who was a friend of

---

* Sir Alexander Hardinge (2nd Baron Hardinge of Penshurst), the son of a former Viceroy of India, became an Assistant Private Secretary to King George V in 1920, and Private Secretary to both King Edward VIII (in 1936) and King George VI from 1936 to 1943. Lt-Colonel the Hon. Sir Piers Legh, known as 'Joey', was an Equerry to the Prince of Wales from 1919 to 1936; Equerry to King George VI from 1936 to 1946 and simultaneously Master of the Household from 1941 to 1952.

Allah Knight, the Princesses' nanny, not so much because the little girl was Princess Margaret, but because I should not have done such a thing in the first place.'[24]

If it did not lead to their establishing friendships as such, the two Princesses also had the opportunity to mix with other children when they took swimming lessons at the Bath Club. Under the instruction of Miss Amy Daly and watched by an anxious Allah who, according to the ever-present Crawfie, hovered 'at the water's edge like a distressed hen that has mothered a couple of ducks', the Princesses first learned the movements of breast-stroke by lying on a wooden bench. Shorter and at that stage plumper than her sister, Princess Margaret's first 'wobbling' attempts at making the letters *Y, I, T* and *X*, with her arms and legs, were a source of amusement to Lilibet. 'You look like an aeroplane about to conk out', she laughed. 'Keep steady, Margaret.'

Having ultimately progressed to earning their life saving certificates, their admiring father said, 'I don't know how they do it. We were always so terribly shy and self-conscious as children. These two don't seem to care.' They did, of course, but both as children and as adults, the Princesses' apparent confidence, particularly in public, was largely attributable to what one of Princess Margaret's friends was to call their 'enamelled self-assurance; it is thinner than you think and very easily chipped.'[25]

1935, the year in which the Imperial world celebrated the Silver Jubilee of the reign of its King-Emperor, George V, was also to prove the very last year of freedom, relatively speaking, for the Duke and Duchess of York and their two young daughters. For the past year or two, the Prince of Wales's relationship with Wallis Simpson had been a source of increasing unease within the royal family and the cause of concern to the King and Queen in particular.

Of all his sons, the King's most difficult relationship had always been with the man who would succeed him. For although

David had proved himself – as much to his father as, on his exhaustive overseas tours, to the world at large – a spectacularly popular and effective Prince of Wales, he was also a man whose love of all things fashionable and modern represented a potential threat to tradition and, it was feared, to the future of the monarchy itself. In short, he was the representative of everything with which the King felt most ill at ease.

'The things that my father found wrong with the "Brave New World" would have made a long list', wrote the Prince, as Duke of Windsor. 'He disapproved of Soviet Russia, painted fingernails, women who smoked in public, cocktails, frivolous hats, American jazz and the growing habit of going away for weekends.'[26] To that, the Prince might also have added that his father disapproved of infidelity quite as strongly as he disapproved of the twice-married woman with whom the heir to his throne had become so inextricably involved.

Although, as the wife of a British citizen, Wallis Simpson had in June 1931 been presented at Court, wearing borrowed train, feathers and fan; and, in what she described as a 'magnificent set-piece of pageantry', had made her curtsy before the enthroned Sovereigns, she had never actually met the King and Queen.

When she did so, it was at the pre-wedding ball given at Buckingham Palace in November 1934, in honour of Prince George and Princess Marina. Mrs Simpson recalled that the evening had been 'rendered truly memorable . . . for the reason that it was the only time I ever met David's father and mother. It was the briefest encounters, a few words of perfunctory greeting . . . [but] I was impressed with Their Majesties' great gift for making everyone they met . . . feel at ease in their presence.'[27]

It was an indication of royalty's professionalism that Wallis Simpson could never have guessed that, far from being pleased to meet her, the King was outraged by her presence. 'That woman in my own house', he had fumed. If Wallis and her husband Ernest Simpson had been present at the Kents' wedding at Westminster Abbey two days later, there was no invitation to the Jubilee Thanksgiving Service at St Paul's Cathedral the following Spring.

Such were the feelings of loyalty, reverence and even affection for the King, now approaching his seventieth birthday, that the twenty-fifth anniversary of his accession to the throne was seen as an occasion for celebration across the Empire.

From London to Bombay, where even the façade and tower of the Victoria Terminus of the Great Indian Peninsular Railway was floodlit in tribute to the King-Emperor, celebratory parties and carnivals, receptions and balls, culminated in the spectacular Jubilee pageant which honoured both the King and Queen Mary at St Paul's on 6 May 1935.

That morning, George V, wearing the ceremonial uniform of a Field Marshal, his scarlet tunic dressed with the full insignia of the Order of the Garter, the Star of the Thistle and the Royal Victorian Chain, left Buckingham Palace in the 1902 State Landau for the drive to the Cathedral. Beside him, as upright and stately a figure as ever, dressed in silver tissue, white fox fur and diamonds, sat Queen Mary, 'glittering in the sun like the Jungfrau', as one witty observer put it.

Riding in the carriage procession that preceded that of the King and Queen, were other members of the royal family. 'First came the Duke and Duchess of York . . .' ran one contemporary newspaper report. 'Opposite them, sat their two little girls, Princess Elizabeth and Princess Margaret, both dressed in salmon pink frocks with pink bonnets.

'The Princesses captured the hearts of the multitude instantly. The dignified self-possession of Princess Elizabeth and the laughing happiness of her little sister sent the crowds into raptures. While the children waved their hands with an entire lack of self-consciousness the crowd roared with delight.'

That evening, having broadcast his thanks, and those of Queen Mary, to his 'very, very dear people for all the loyalty and . . . love, with which this day and always you have surrounded us', the King wrote in his journal, 'The greatest number of people in the streets I have ever seen in my life.

The enthusiasm was indeed most touching . . . I am beginning to think they must really like me for myself.'

That autumn, as a recurrence of the bronchial trouble from which he suffered began to undermine his health yet again, George V attended what would be the last ceremonial occasion of his life. On 6 November, his thirty-five-year-old (third) son Harry – Prince Henry, Duke of Gloucester – married Lady Alice Scott, third daughter of the 7th Duke of Buccleuch. Celebrated not at Westminster Abbey as originally intended but, due to the death of the bride's father only three weeks earlier, in the private chapel at Buckingham Palace, it was the first time that Princess Margaret had acted as a bridesmaid.

Dressed like her sister and Lady Alice's two other child attendants, Mary Cambridge and Anne Hawkins, in a frilly dress trimmed with rosebuds, the King had requested the designer, Norman Hartnell, to keep the skirts short because he wanted 'to see their pretty little knees.'

Four weeks later, the King was dealt a blow that hastened his own final decline. On the morning of 3 December, he received news that his favourite sister, the sixty-seven-year-old Princess Victoria, had died at 'Coppins', her house in Iver, Buckinghamshire, during the early hours. Devastated by the news and, as his doctor, Lord Dawson of Penn had already told Prime Minister, Stanley Baldwin, 'packing up his luggage and getting ready to depart', the King cancelled the State Opening of Parliament, which was to have taken place that morning. It was very probably the only time in his life that he had permitted his sense of duty to falter.

The life and reign of King George V came to an end at Sandringham on 20 January 1936. That afternoon, piloting his own aircraft, the Prince of Wales accompanied by the Duke of York – the Duchess was at Royal Lodge, recovering from pneumonia – flew up to Norfolk from Windsor. Later that day, as Queen Mary noted in her diary, the King 'became weaker during the evening . . . and we realized the end was approaching . . . at 5 to 12 [helped, it was eventually revealed, by a fatal dose of morphine and cocaine which Lord Dawson had administered] my darling husband passed peacefully away . . .'[28]

It was the start of what would become known as 'The Year of the Three Kings'.

FOUR

Was it simply an inspired guess or a more profound sense of foreboding that had led King George V to say that, as Sovereign, David would 'ruin himself within a year'; adding that he prayed nothing would 'come between Bertie and Lilibet and the Throne'?

Those who looked for portents – for the intervening hand of the same fate that had removed George V's elder brother from the succession – needed no further indication of impending disaster than an incident that occurred as the late King's body was borne to Westminster Hall, where it was to lie in state. Brought to London by train, the coffin was draped with the crimson, gold and blue Royal Standard on top of which, along with Queen Mary's flowers, rested the Imperial State Crown. Placed on a gun-carriage and escorted by a bearer-party of Grenadier Guards, the cortège left King's Cross Station followed on foot by the new King, Edward VIII, his brothers, the Dukes of York, Gloucester and Kent, his brother-in-law, Lord Harewood, and an entourage of private secretaries, assistant private secretaries, equerries and other members of the Royal Household.

As it passed through streets packed to capacity with silent crowds, the Maltese cross – set with a sapphire said to have belonged to Edward the Confessor, eight medium-sized diamonds and 192 smaller diamonds – inexplicably fell from its place at the very top of the Crown. Having caught a 'flash of light dancing along the pavement', the new King's instinct was to pick it up until, as he wrote, 'a sense of dignity restrained me.'

'Fortunately,' he went on, 'the Company Sergeant-Major bringing up the rear of the two files of Grenadiers . . . had also seen the accident. Quick as a flash, with scarcely a missed step, he . . . scooped up the cross with his hand, and dropped it into his pocket. It seemed', said the King, 'a strange thing to happen; and, although not superstitious, I wondered whether it was a bad omen.'[1]

At this juncture, the events that would soon begin to unfold with such dramatic consequences still lay around the corner. For the moment, the obsequies attendant upon the death of a Sovereign took precedence over everything else.

At Royal Lodge, Windsor, where the Duchess of York thought it best her daughters should remain for the present, Crawfie was advised, 'Don't let all this depress them more than is absolutely necessary. They are so young.' At five years old, Princess Margaret understood little or nothing about what was going on, even though she was intrigued by the fact that every now and then, Allah would burst into tears. It was a different matter for the nine-year-old Princess Elizabeth, however. Not only did her mother take her to witness her grandfather's lying-in-state – at an hour when her father and three uncles, each wearing full dress uniform, stood at the four corners of the catafalque, their heads bowed over reversed swords – but was also taken to the State Funeral at St George's Chapel, Windsor.

As the first effects of grief and mourning within the royal family subsided, the new and undeniably popular King embraced his duties with an enthusiasm that impressed many, not least Mrs Simpson, and concerned others, particularly those members of George V's Household who were used to and comfortable with the old and familiar ways.

If the King's official life had changed, however, little or nothing in his private life had. The weekends at Fort Belvedere with Wallis and friends that had been an inalienable part of his life for the past five or six years could now continue without any sense of disapproval emanating from Windsor Castle.

It was, in fact, during one of his weekend house parties at the Fort during the spring of 1936, that the King suggested driving over to visit his brother and sister-in-law in the Great Park. Not long before, he had bought a new American station wagon which Wallis, as Duchess of Windsor, explained in her autobiography, was a type of car then almost unknown in Great Britain. 'One afternoon, David said, "Let's drive over to Royal Lodge. I want to show Bertie the car."

'Turning into the entrance of Royal Lodge, he made a complete swing around the circular driveway and drew up to the front door with a flourish. The Duke and Duchess of York met David at the door. David insisted that they inspect the station wagon. It was amusing to observe the contrast between the two brothers – David all enthusiasm and volubility . . . the Duke of York quiet, shy, obviously dubious of this newfangled American contrivance. It was not until David pointed out its advantages as a shooting brake that his younger brother showed any real interest. "Come on, Bertie", David urged, "let's drive around a little, I'll show you how easy it is to handle."

'After a few minutes they returned and . . . we [went into] the house for tea, which was served in the drawing room. In a few moments the two little Princesses joined us. Princess Elizabeth . . . was then ten, and Princess Margaret Rose was nearly six. They were both so blonde, so beautifully mannered, so brightly scrubbed, that they might have stepped straight from the pages of a picture book.

'It was a pleasant hour; but I left with a distinct impression that while the Duke of York was sold on the American station wagon, the Duchess was not sold on David's other American interest.'[2]

Wallis Simpson was, of course, absolutely right to believe that the Duchess of York disliked her. Though a life-long vendetta was denied years after Wallis's death in April 1986, there can be very little doubt that the Duchess of York's hostility towards her –

both before the Abdication and during the half-century that followed – scarcely ever diminished; even to the point where she helped 'put the bullets in the gun', as one of her ladies-in-waiting once put it.[3]

During her brother-in-law's brief reign, the Duchess of York particularly disliked Mrs Simpson's increasing influence, as much as the proprietorial manner she adopted in the King's houses. Even more understandably, as they began to see much less of him than before, both she and the Duke were concerned that, despite the fact that he was now his heir, the King made little attempt to take his brother into his confidence or consult him about the changes he had in mind for the royal estates. When, for example, he asked the Duke of York to look into how savings might be made at Sandringham, he apparently did not tell him that he already had plans to sell the estate.

Still more disconcerting was the way in which the King's attitude to his position and its responsibilities was beginning to change. Indeed, little by little, what Edward VIII called 'the relentless grind of the King's daily life' began to betray his growing distaste for many aspects of his new role. State papers, contained in the famous red leather dispatch boxes delivered to the Sovereign every day of the week, were at first attended to expediently. Then days, sometimes even weeks, would drift by before they were returned, often without any evidence that the King had looked at them, or stained by the bases of whisky glasses. There was concern, too, that confidential documents were left unattended at the Fort. Alarmed by his evident negligence, the Foreign Office even took the unprecedented step of screening all documents before they were sent to the King at Fort Belvedere.

To those around him, it had become abundantly clear that the only thing that interested him was his relationship with Wallis Simpson. Everything else was irksome and intrusive. 'It was she who filled his thoughts at all times', wrote Alexander Hardinge, the King's Assistant Private Secretary; 'she alone who mattered, before her the affairs of State sank into insignificance.'

Affairs of State were not alone in suffering from the King's lack of consideration. Friends of his were summarily dropped in favour of Wallis's, while members of the new Royal Household grew increasingly angry at the unsociable hours at which the King might decide their services were required. At Buckingham Palace, servants were outraged when their 'beer money' was cut and in his attempt to make the royal houses more cost-effective, domestic staff were suddenly made redundant, without regard to either length of service or future prospects.

Mean-spirited and gratuitous acts such as these served to highlight mounting criticism of the King's arrogance and conceit, while the savings made from his so-called economies were as nothing when compared to the sums he blithely spent on the jewels from Cartier and Van Cleef & Arpels, in Paris and New York, that he lavished on Mrs Simpson.

That summer, as usual, the Duke and Duchess of York took the Princesses to Birkhall, the eighteenth-century house on the Balmoral estate that had always been put at their disposal for the holidays. The King and Mrs Simpson had also been up at Balmoral, staying at the Castle itself. Then at the beginning of August, in keeping with his usual practice of spending part of the summer holidays abroad, David (as he was still known to those closest to him), together with Wallis and a group of friends, set off on what was to become – at least in the foreign press (the British press maintained its silence until early December) – a highly-publicized 'royal progress' along the Dalmatian coast.

The Yorks themselves returned to London in the middle of October to be told by the King's Assistant Private Secretary that Mrs Simpson's divorce petition was to be heard at Ipswich Assizes (chosen on the grounds that a London hearing would attract too much Press attention), on 27 October. It was, perhaps, the first time anyone had thought to warn the Duke – no matter what his and the Duchess's personal anxieties may or may not have been – that he could be called upon to succeed his brother.

As the crisis developed and the Yorks watched mute yet fearful from the sidelines, the King told the prime minister, Stanley Baldwin, on 16 November, that he intended to marry Wallis Simpson. 'If I could marry her as King, well and good . . . But if, on the other hand, the Government [and, it would transpire, those of the Dominions of Canada, Australia, New Zealand, South Africa, Newfoundland, and the Irish Free State] opposed the marriage, as the prime minister had given me reason to believe it would, *then I was prepared to go.*'

It was the first time abdication had been mentioned, and it was the King – not his prime minister – who had introduced it. The thought of surrendering his royal position had, in fact, crossed David's mind even before the death of King George V, with whom, or so he claimed in his memoirs, he intended to discuss his dream of marrying Wallis Simpson.

Now, at quite another time and in quite different circumstances, the question of renouncing his birthright – his 'duty' as his mother, Queen Mary, saw it – was again an option. And again, he could take 'comfort from the fact that my brother Bertie, to whom the succession would pass, was in outlook and temperament very much like my father . . . Strongly rooted each in his own existence, they tended to be withdrawn from the hurly-burly of life that I relished. Both were devoted family men, a quality that goes a long way for a King in a constitutional monarchy.'[4]

Perhaps because royalty often appear to think of themselves before anyone else, there was on Edward VIII's part no real concern about what effect his abdication would have on his younger brother. Although nobody's fool, the Duke of York was nevertheless, in the words of Sir Edward Ford, his last Assistant Private Secretary, 'a highly strung, neurotic man, who was not, by nature, self-confident . . .' and who, more to the point, had very definitely not been raised to be King.

As events unfolded and tension mounted, the Yorks, like the Gloucesters, Kents, Harewoods and other more peripheral members of the royal family, attempted to carry on with their lives as normal. But, as the Duke and Duchess of York were to discover, gossip and speculation were everywhere, even among those with whom they stayed at grand country house parties. 'It was terrible', the Duchess was to say many years later, 'because the conversation always stopped as soon as we entered a room. It was perfectly obvious from the sudden silence that they had all been talking about us.'[5]

Finally recognizing the fact that he faced formidable opposition to his proposed marriage from the Governments of Britain and the Dominions, as well as the Church of England, of which the Sovereign is Temporal Governor, Edward VIII accepted his Prime Minister's ultimatum: he had either to give up Wallis Simpson or the Throne. He, of course, chose the latter.

From the beginning of December, the Duke of York kept his own chronicle of the events that led to his brother's abdication and his own accession. In it, on 7 December, he noted that he had arrived to see the King at Fort Belvedere at seven in the evening. 'The awful & ghastly suspense of waiting was over', he wrote. 'I found him pacing up & down the room, & he told me his decision that he would go. I went back to Royal Lodge for dinner & returned to the Fort later.' Then he added, with far greater kindness and consideration than he had lately been shown, 'As he is my eldest brother I had to be there to try & help him in his hour of need.'[6]

Two days later, as the immensity of what was happening began to sink in, the Duke of York drove up to London to see his mother at Marlborough House, her official residence next to St James's Palace. Such was the depth of the Duke's despair and sense of isolation that when he told Queen Mary, normally the last person whose shoulder he would have sought for comfort, 'what had happened', he 'broke down & sobbed like a child.'

Later, when talking to his cousin, Lord Louis (later Earl) Mountbatten, he said, 'Dickie, this is absolutely terrible. I never wanted this to happen; I'm quite unprepared for it. David has been trained for this all his life ... I'm only a Naval Officer, it's the only thing I know about.'

Mountbatten replied, 'This is a very curious coincidence. My father once told me that, when the Duke of Clarence [George V's brother] died, your father came to him and said almost the same things that you have said to me now, and my father answered: "George, you're wrong. There is no more fitting preparation for a King than to have been trained in the Navy." '

In 1952, when the man who was later described as 'the most unsung monarch of the twentieth century'[7] died, Lord Mountbatten took Princess Margaret aside and in tribute said, 'Your father was made of integrity, and that is something your Uncle David never had. *That* is why your father was such a smashing success as King.'[8]

At ten o'clock on the morning of Thursday, 10 December 1936, in the octagonal drawing room at Fort Belvedere, the Dukes of York, Gloucester and Kent watched their brother sign the formal Instrument of Abdication that would take effect the following day, and added their own signatures, as witnesses. It was David's last act as King and Emperor.

That evening, after dining at Royal Lodge, the man who was about to become King George VI returned to London and as he arrived at 145 Piccadilly, where the Duchess of York was in bed suffering from what was variously described as a 'chill', a 'cold' or 'flu', the Duke found a large crowd 'cheering madly.' At the end of what had been a day of turbulent emotions, the Duke said simply, 'I was overwhelmed.'

Though they had watched the comings and goings of the great and the good from the well of the glass dome, the Princesses, if Crawfie is to be believed, were told nothing of the momentous events that were about to change their lives, until such time as their father had already become King and their uncle was on the point of leaving Britain for a lifetime in exile. In common with most six-year-olds, it is unlikely that Princess Margaret would have understood more than the simplest of explanations. But at not far off eleven, Princess Elizabeth was old enough and bright enough to have grasped the essentials of what had been happening.

When the Abdication was finally raised, and again if Crawfie isn't embellishing the truth, it was she, not the new King and Queen, who had 'to make the two little girls realize that . . . great changes would take place.' She began by telling them that they would shortly be moving from 145 Piccadilly. 'When I broke the news to Margaret and Lilibet that they were going to live in Buckingham Palace', she wrote, 'they looked at me in horror. "What!" Lilibet said. "You mean for ever?"' Just as plaintive was the remark of the younger Princess. Having only recently learned to write her name in full, she said unhappily, 'I used to be Margaret of York and now I'm nothing.'

It is highly likely, however, that Princess Elizabeth grasped more – and probably rather sooner – than her governess chose to reveal, for as Princess Margaret was to recall, 'I remember my sister telling me, "Uncle David is going away and isn't coming back, and Papa is to be King." I said, "Does that mean you are going to be *Queen*?"' [9]

It did mean she was going to be Queen, at least one day. But it also meant a more immediate change in the nature of the Princesses' relationship to each other; not so much on a personal level as sisters, that would always remain sacrosanct, but rather, as daughters of the King, one of whom was now heiress presumptive to her father's throne. What the Abdication had done, in effect, though the young Princesses could not have realized it at the time, was rob them of lives and identities that would almost certainly have been very different had their uncle chosen to put duty before personal ambition. One immediately noticeable change in their lives, however, no doubt under Crawfie's influence, was the way in which the Princesses no longer referred to 'Mummie' and 'Papa' when speaking of their parents to outsiders. Now formal, though quite correct, it was 'The King' and 'The Queen'.

The Duke of York, or King George VI, as he chose to be known, ascended the throne four days before his forty-first birthday. With the exception of his brother, he was the youngest prince to succeed since his great-great-great-grandfather King George III succeeded his grandfather in 1760, at the age of twenty-two.

On the day his reign began with the same seamless continuity that marks the accession of every British monarch, the new King visited his brother at the Fort to tell him that, at his Accession Council the next morning, his first act as Sovereign would be to bestow a dukedom on him. The King asked, 'How about the family name of Windsor?' 'Duke of Windsor', David murmured approvingly and, 'liking the sound of it', nodded in agreement.

That evening, however, having been formally introduced by Sir John Reith, Director of the BBC, it was as 'His Royal Highness The Prince Edward', that the former King-Emperor broadcast to the nation from Windsor Castle. Returning to Royal Lodge, where he had dined with his family, the Prince said his farewells and at about midnight, as he bowed to the new King, their youngest brother Georgie, the Duke of Kent, shook his head in disbelief and cried, 'It isn't possible! It isn't happening!'

A few minutes later, David drove off through the night, across the Hartford Bridge Flats to Portsmouth where, unescorted, the destroyer HMS *Fury* waited to take him across the Channel. Having given Commander Howe, the destroyer's captain, leave to sail, the former king went below. It was then, as he realized 'the drawbridges were going up behind [him]', that the magnitude of all that had happened may have started to dawn on him. Alone, save for Major Ulick Alexander, his former Keeper of the Privy Purse, who accompanied him across to France, and Slipper, Wallis's beloved Cairn Terrier, the exiled king spent the night drinking heavily and, in a state of high agitation, constantly paced up and down the officers' mess. At one point, Major Alexander, who was almost on his knees with exhaustion, asked the Captain to take a turn at keeping his royal passenger company.[10]

David's eventual destination on this first part of his journey into an uncertain and, as it turned out, completely aimless future was Austria. There, until Wallis's divorce was made absolute the following April, he would not only have to live without everything he had taken so much for granted in England, but for the next four months, without the reassuring presence of the woman for whom he had given it all up.

It may have been for that reason, or perhaps a sudden sense of isolation, that the former Edward VIII sought an urgent answer to an almost desperate question. Arriving in Vienna on 14 December, he was greeted at the railway station by Sir Walford Selby, Britain's Ambassador to Austria. It was then, as if searching for an identity, or at least for reassurance that he still had one, that he asked, 'What is my name?'

Somewhat surprised, Sir Walford replied, 'Sir, you are His Royal Highness The Duke of Windsor.'[11]

Christmas at Sandringham less than two weeks later was undoubtedly a time of reflection and even consolidation, for a family that had been traumatized by the events of a year that had begun in mourning for one king and had all but ended with the shocking departure of another.

George VI himself, though in a state of near nervous collapse, was nevertheless determined to stabilize what he called 'this rocking throne', and to that end he wrote to Prime Minister Baldwin, 'I am new to the job, but I hope that time will be allowed to me to make amends for what has happened.' In a more general message to Parliament, he said, 'It will be my constant endeavour, with God's help, and supported as I shall be by my dear wife, to uphold the Honour of the Realm and promote the Happiness of my peoples.'

For members of the royal family themselves, a timely and wholly appropriate note of happiness was introduced with the birth on Christmas morning of a second child and only daughter to the Duke and Duchess of Kent. Born at Prince George and Princess Marina's London residence in Belgrave Square, to the sound of a lone street musician playing Christmas carols somewhere nearby, the arrival of Princess Alexandra – a niece for King George and Queen Elizabeth, an only female royal cousin for the Princesses Elizabeth and Margaret – was celebrated in traditional manner the following day. Then, forty-one-gun salutes were fired simultaneously at the Tower of London and by the Royal Horse Artillery in Hyde Park.

Early in the New Year, the King and his family left 145 Piccadilly for Buckingham Palace in two deliberate and carefully planned stages. The King and Queen were the first to take up residence in the house George III had originally acquired from the Duke of Buckingham in 1761. Although transformed by King George IV, the greatest of our royal master builders, into a palace or, in the aftermath of the Napoleonic Wars, 'a symbol of national greatness', it was the eighteen-year-old Queen Victoria who was the first Sovereign to live at Buckingham Palace, moving in on 13 July 1837, only three weeks after her accession to the throne.

Like his illustrious great-grandmother, George VI had been King for only a matter of weeks when he and Queen Elizabeth moved into the ground-floor pink and gold Belgian Suite, so called in honour of Queen Victoria's beloved uncle Leopold, King of the Belgians, and his French-born second wife, Queen Louise. 'Life in a palace rather resembles camping in a museum,' said Crawfie, but while the King and Queen had to 'camp out' in the Belgian Suite until their private apartments on the first floor, formerly occupied by George V and Queen Mary, were redecorated, rooms for the two Princesses were chosen and painted before they moved in. There were bedrooms for each overlooking the Mall, Princess Elizabeth's shared with Bobo, Princess Margaret's with Allah; while the day and night nurseries were bright, cheerful rooms, a world removed from those the King remembered from his own childhood.

In fact, selecting a schoolroom for his daughters clearly brought back less than fond memories. Opening the door to 'one of the darkest and most gloomy rooms in the place, in the middle of the top floor of the palace', the King stood in the doorway and paused for a moment or two. No doubt recalling his own lessons there, his legs in braces to correct his knock-knees and, despite a natural inclination to write with his left hand, being forced to use his right, he looked around him and slowly turned away. 'No,' he said closing the door, 'that won't do.' A far brighter room overlooking the garden was chosen instead.

So that the Princesses could become acclimatized to living at Buckingham Palace, a house they did not actually know particularly well, they were brought across from number 145 on regular 'visits' to their parents. The day when the last furniture van drew away from the front door of the house in Piccadilly was not long in coming, however, and on 17 February 1937, the King and Queen called to collect their daughters and, perhaps, to take a last look at the house that had been their home for the past ten years.

The strategy of allowing the Princesses to become gradually accustomed to the idea of moving to Buckingham Palace was a complete success. So much so, in fact, that Princess Margaret's lasting impression of that day has nothing to do with sentimental attachment to her old home, but of 'battling through enormous, loving crowds' as the car in which she, her parents and sister were travelling, approached the Palace gates.[12]

Once installed in their new rooms, outside which all along the nursery corridor their toy horses were inevitably lined up, the Princesses began exploring the rooms and endless corridors of the principal floor and beyond. Built on four floors around a central quadrangle Buckingham House, as it was originally known, was later renamed The Queen's House in honour of George III's bride, Charlotte of Mecklenburg–Strelitz. Only afterwards did it gradually start to evolve into the palace we know today. Not simply the home of the immediate royal family, as indeed it has been since the days of Victoria and Albert and their nine children, Buckingham Palace is also the administrative headquarters of the monarchy, with no fewer than 92 offices catering for its needs. In addition, there are 19 State Rooms, 52 royal and guest bedrooms, 188 staff bedrooms and 78 bathrooms and lavatories. Adding to the total are the suites of private royal apartments on the north and east sides and, way down below, an extensive basement. As a girl, Princess Margaret once claimed to have seen most of the rooms in the palace by following the clock-winder on his seemingly interminable rounds.

When they first moved in, however, Princess Margaret, if not running after her sister with the familiar cry, 'Wait for me Lilibet, wait for *me*', would hurtle along in her kiddy-car, a form of tricycle; or both would race off 'laughing and shouting as usual' to join their parents for their morning 'high jinks', for lunch, or – the King's and Queen's new and increasingly demanding schedules permitting – for the time they always spent together at the end of the day.

For outside recreation, instead of having to share Hamilton Gardens with other residents, to say nothing of onlookers who always peered through the railings to watch the Princesses at play, the private 40-acre Buckingham Palace garden, enclosed behind high brick walls, was now at their disposal. Here they could row on the lake, 'rather green and dirty' as Princess Margaret remembered it, into which Princess Elizabeth fell on one occasion while looking for ducks' nests, to emerge covered in slime. There was also the hillock near the monumental Waterloo Vase that had been carved for the Prince Regent from a single block of marble, from which the Princesses could see over the perimeter wall and watch the world go by.

As Crawfie pointed out, however, it was not to be thought that 'all was sweetness and light' between the royal sisters at all times. Fights broke out as they do between all children and frequently for the smallest of reasons. At other times, snapping the elastic on one another's hats, which they hated wearing, was sufficient provocation. By all accounts, Princess Elizabeth had a formidable 'left hook', while Princess Margaret went in for a closer approach, not above biting or delivering the odd kick.

Of the Princesses' presence at Buckingham Palace, where the natural behaviour and spontaneity of children is unlikely to have been encouraged since the early years of Queen Victoria's reign, one member of the Household told Miss Crawford, 'It was as though the place had been dead for years and had suddenly come alive.'

To the King who had always been at his happiest in his work when no 'damned red carpet' got in the way, the longest red carpet of them all, hypothetically speaking, loomed before him as the inescapable ritual of his coronation approached.

Edward VIII was to have been crowned at Westminster Abbey on Wednesday, 12 May 1937, observing the unwritten rule that while a new reign began at the moment of the preceding Sovereign's death, the coronation of his or her successor was not observed for at least a year. This not only took into account the official period of Court Mourning, but also allowed time for the ceremonial arrangements necessary to a royal enthronement to be made.

In these unparalleled circumstances, however, it had been decided that since no useful purpose would be served by delaying or re-scheduling the ceremony, the coronation of King George VI and Queen Elizabeth should proceed on the date originally set.

As the day itself approached, friends and relations, ambassadors and emissaries of foreign heads of state began to arrive in London. Among them were Prince and Princess Chichibu of Japan, representing Emperor Hirohito, Crown Princess Juliana of the Netherlands and Prince Bernhard, representing Queen Wilhelmina; and the Crown Princes and Princesses of Norway, Sweden, Denmark, and Greece.

The royal family's old friend, Prince Paul of Yugoslavia, now Regent, together with his wife Princess Olga, eldest sister of the Duchess of Kent, the Grand Duchess of Luxembourg, and the Prince of Monaco, the exotically-named Grand Voevod of Alba Julia, and the Prince of Preslav were formally received, as were the representatives of the Kings of Egypt, Saudi Arabia, the Yemen, Iraq, Siam, Italy, Romania, and the Albanians, the Emperors of Ethiopia and Iran, and the ambassadors of the

United States of America, the Soviet Union, and the German Reich.

Inside Westminster Abbey, which had been closed to the public since the beginning of the year, tiered galleries where these guests and thousands more would sit, were built on either side of the Nave. In front of the High Altar, a raised coronation 'theatre' was constructed on which a dais would support the Chairs of Estate of both the King and the Queen, as well as the ancient Coronation Chair itself.

From the Royal Gallery, constructed above the tomb of Anne of Cleves, the fourth wife of Henry VIII, Queen Mary would watch the coronation of her son and daughter-in-law with her granddaughters Elizabeth and Margaret, her daughter Mary, the Princess Royal, her daughters-in-law the Duchesses of Gloucester and Kent, and her sisters-in-law Queen Maud of Norway and Princess Alice, Countess of Athlone. Here, too, seats were reserved for Lord and Lady Strathmore who, when they watched their daughter marry the Duke of York in the very same place, can scarcely have imagined that they would return fourteen years later to see her crowned Queen.

Though it was undoubtedly intended to be seen as a public act of support and solidarity, Queen Mary's decision to attend the coronation of her second son was also a deliberate break with tradition. Until now, Queens Dowager did not attend the coronations of their successors.

For weeks on end, royal dressmakers Madame Handley-Seymour, who had designed the Duchess of York's wedding dress and would now make the Queen's coronation gown of gold-embroidered ivory satin, and the thirty-six-year-old Norman Hartnell, whose star was very firmly in the ascendant, had shuttled backwards and forwards between palace, salon and workroom, occupied with the business of preparing watercolour dress designs, selecting fabrics (or 'stuff' as Princess Margaret calls any kind of material, dressmaking or otherwise), and endless fittings.

For the first time in their lives, the young Princesses would wear long dresses though, as usual, they would be almost identical. Of white lace trimmed with silver bows, they would be worn with the family Orders of their father and grandfather (oval miniature portraits set in gold or platinum, surrounded by diamonds and attached to bows of watered silk), their first pearl necklaces, elbow-length white fingerless gloves and silver pumps with which were glimpsed white ankle-socks.

If everything about the design of their outfits had met with youthful royal approval, including the lightweight gilt coronets the King had specially commissioned for them, one detail did throw Princess Margaret into a tantrum. For while both she and Princess Elizabeth were to wear purple velvet mantles edged with ermine, the younger Princess's train was cut slightly shorter than her sister's. It wasn't right, she is said to have complained, it wasn't fair, and promptly threw herself to the floor. Only when it was carefully explained to her that the trains had been designed in direct proportion to height – Lilibet was nearly four inches taller – was Princess Margaret placated.

Through all this, the King prepared himself for the very considerable ordeal ahead, not least in consultation with his speech therapist, Lionel Logue. When at home or in private, the stammer that had plagued George VI since boyhood was hardly noticeable. But public speaking, which was anathema to him, or stressful situations of any kind frequently rendered him all but speechless.

If the British press were sufficiently tactful not to refer to it, certain sections of the American press were painfully derisive. Suspicious that nationality alone had disqualified Wallis Simpson from marrying Edward VIII, they struck back by referring to the new King as 'the stuttering Duke of York.'

On 12 May, Coronation Day itself, George VI and Queen Elizabeth were woken at 3am by loudspeakers being tested on Constitution Hill. 'One of them might have been in our room', the King wrote. At 5am, the Princesses were woken by the band of the Royal Marines, 'striking up just outside my window' as

Lilibet noted later that day. As the morning wore on and the level of activity increased, both inside Buckingham Palace and in the streets outside, the Princesses in their lace dresses and velvet robes went along to their parents' bedroom. There they found the Queen 'putting on her dress', while 'Papa', as Princess Elizabeth noted afterwards, 'was dressed in a white shirt, breeches and stockings, and over this he wore a crimson satin coat.'

As the spectacular fleet of state and semi-state carriages in which the royal family were to drive to Westminster Abbey arrived from the Royal Mews, crossing the Quadrangle to the Grand Entrance in a cacophony of horses' hooves, jingling harnesses and coach wheels on gravel, the Princesses kissed their parents, 'wished them good-luck' and made their way down to the Grand Hall.

Watching her younger sister, Princess Elizabeth expressed the hope that she would not 'disgrace us all by falling asleep in the middle' of the ceremony, adding with typical concern, 'after all, she is *very* young for a coronation, isn't she?'

Having ridden with their aunt Mary and cousin George Lascelles in the Irish State Coach, the Princesses awaited the arrival of Queen Mary, who they thought 'looked too beautiful in a gold dress patterned with golden flowers', before processing along the length of the nave to their places in the Royal Gallery.

Recalling her impressions afterwards, in a commemorative essay for her parents, Princess Elizabeth wrote:

> I thought it all <u>very</u>, <u>very</u> wonderful and I expect the Abbey did, too. The arches and beams at the top were covered with a sort of haze of wonder as Papa was crowned, at least I thought so.
>
> When Mummy was crowned and all the peeresses put on their coronets it looked wonderful to see arms and coronets hovering in the air and then the arms disappear as if by magic. Also the music was lovely and the band, the orchestra and the new organ all played beautifully.

What struck me as being rather odd was that Grannie did
not remember much of her own coronation. I should have
thought that it would have stayed in her mind for ever.[13]

On the long and circuitous return journey to Buckingham
Palace, as the King and Queen rode in the magnificent four-ton
State Coach built for George III in 1762, the Princesses drove
back with Queen Mary in the much less cumbersome Queen
Alexandra's State Coach, or 'the Alix' as it is colloquially known.
According to the results of an experiment conducted with a
decibel counter rigged up on the roof of a public building somewhere along the processional route, sound levels produced by
cheers and applause as the King and Queen passed by registered
eighty-three decibels; only fractionally lower than the eighty-five
decibels recorded minutes earlier at the sight of the two young
Princesses and their grandmother.

When they finally arrived back at the Palace, tired but exhila-
rated, Crawfie's first question to Lilibet was, 'Well, did Margaret
behave nicely?' To which she replied, 'She was wonderful . . . I
only had to nudge her once or twice when she played with the
prayer books too loudly.' Well behaved though she was, the six-
year-old princess had, in fact, watched much of the ceremonial
in awed bemusement. It had evidently not occurred to anybody
to explain the meaning and significance of the various stages of
the coronation of her father and her mother, and since both her
grandmother and her aunt Mary were, as she put it, 'preoccu-
pied with their tears', she realized little or no explanation would
come from either direction. Instead, the little Princess kept
quiet and watched patiently until the final fanfares rang through
the Abbey, heralding the fact that it was now time to go home.

Later that day, after the Princesses had appeared with their
parents on the balcony several times – '*millions* of people were
waiting below', said Lilibet – and had posed for official
photographs 'in front of those awful lights', the King sat down
at his desk to record his own sometimes amusing impressions of
the coronation. If to the uninitiated or less observant, the cere-

mony seemed to have passed off faultlessly, the central figure in the pageant knew otherwise.

The Lord Great Chamberlain shook so much, said the King, that he had to fasten the sword-belt himself; St Edward's Crown was very nearly put on the royal head the wrong way round; and one of the attendant bishops trod on the King's robes, almost pulling him down. 'I had to tell him to get off it pretty sharply', he wrote, much to the subsequent amusement of his family.

The coronation had, not surprisingly, touched Queen Mary very deeply. She, too, put pen to paper. 'I sat between Maud [Queen of Norway, wife and consort of Haakon VII, and youngest of George V's three sisters] and Lilibet, and Margaret came next, they looked too sweet in their lace dresses and robes, especially when they put on their coronets. Bertie & E looked so well . . . & did it all too beautifully', she wrote. 'The service was wonderful & impressive – we were all much moved . . . A wonderful day.'

Nobody was happier or more relieved that the King had played his part so well and with such gravitas, than the King himself. It was even said that he suddenly seemed to 'look taller.' Not long afterwards, while fulfilling an official engagement King George, in the words of one observer, seemed to be 'growing in stature as the months go by – it is as though the charisma of the Coronation had effected a deepening and enlightening of the inner man . . .'[14]

An echo of the same sentiments came from a source much closer to the royal family. Queen Elizabeth's niece, Lady Mary Clayton, was to say that the King, 'blossomed during the first year of his reign. He seemed so much more assured, as though he had found himself.'[15]

FIVE

At a château in the Loire Valley on 3 June, three weeks after the coronation, a much simpler and entirely private ceremony that merited no greater acknowledgement than a 55-word statement in the BBC's regular news bulletins, took place. At the Château de Candé, a fine old castle set in the middle of its own private park, in Touraine, near Tours, the Duke of Windsor married Wallis Simpson or, since she had by then dispensed with her married name and, by deed-poll, reverted to her maiden name, Wallis Warfield.

In her diary on what would have been George V's seventy-second birthday – a coincidence not lost on the royal family – Queen Mary wrote, 'Alas! The wedding day . . . of David & Mrs Warfield. We all telegraphed to him.' The King also wrote. In his letter, which was hand delivered to the Duke of Windsor by Walter Monckton, a trusted go-between, George VI told his brother that while he was entitled to enjoy the rank and style of 'Royal Highness', which was in any event his birthright, the same distinction would not be extended to his wife. The Duke was outraged. 'This is a nice wedding present,' he told Monckton. 'Why in God's name would they do this to me at this time!'

The denial of royal status to the Duchess of Windsor immediately gave rise to an unbridgeable gulf between the royal brothers and a rift between Queen Elizabeth and Wallis that would never heal. It would, in fact, be thirty years before the Queen (by then Queen Mother) and the Duchess met again. The occasion, in June 1967, was the unveiling by Elizabeth II of a memorial plaque to Queen Mary on the garden wall of Marlborough House.* They would not meet again until the Duke of Windsor's death brought his widow back to England in June 1972 for his funeral at Windsor.

Princess Margaret also met the Duchess on that occasion for the first time since her childhood. She would meet her once more when she paid a courtesy call on the Duchess at the Waldorf Astoria in New York, during a visit to America in 1974; but in 1986, the Princess refused to attend the funeral of, in her own words, 'the woman who ruined my uncle.'[1]

At the time of their parents' coronation, Princess Margaret and her sister would have known little or nothing of family politics and Court intrigues. What they had heard of their uncle's marriage would almost certainly have been picked up more or less *en passant*. As they grew older, however, the Princesses' attitude towards the Duke and Duchess was shaped by the collateral influences to which, in their enclosed world, they were inevitably susceptible.

What was surprising for someone with so intelligent and enquiring a mind as Princess Margaret was that throughout her life, she would always be influenced – some say too easily – by the opinions of others, to whom she listened too closely, though not always wisely. 'She is virulent in her dislikes', said one friend. 'If she doesn't like one or finds you have acted reprehensibly, that's it. Verdict – "No appeal!" '[2]

---

* The present Queen (Elizabeth II) met the Windsors for the first time since her childhood in 1965, when the Duke was recovering in the London Clinic from surgery to save the sight of his right eye. They met again on 7 June 1967 at the ceremony to honour Queen Mary referred to, and again in May 1972, during the State Visit Her Majesty and Prince Philip, accompanied by the Prince of Wales, made to Paris. When the Duke died at the end of that month, the Duchess of Windsor accepted the Queen's invitation to stay at Buckingham Palace until after the Duke's funeral on 5 June. Although they did not meet again, the Queen attended the 89-year-old Duchess's funeral service at St George's Chapel, Windsor, followed by her burial at Frogmore on 29 April 1986. Queen Elizabeth The Queen Mother attended the funeral service, but did not accompany the Queen to Frogmore.

One example of this was evident following the death in 1982 of Lord Rupert Nevill, a long-standing friend of the royal family and Private Secretary to Prince Philip. When told that his widow, the former Camilla Wallop, known as Micky, had decided, against her family's wishes, to sell a part of her husband's estate, though it was indisputably hers to do with as she wished, Princess Margaret sided with the family and refused to see or speak to Micky again. Save for the most cursory of 'hello's some fifteen years later, when their paths crossed at Windsor, where Lady Rupert was staying as a guest of the Queen for the annual Horse Show, that, to her utter incomprehension, was the end of an extremely close friendship that had begun forty years earlier with the formation of an exclusive company of Girl Guides.[3]

It was in an attempt to bring a sense of ordinariness, or at least community, into the Princesses' lives that, not long after the coronation, the 1st Buckingham Palace Girl Guide Company and Brownie Pack was set up under the captaincy of Miss Violet Synge, who later became Guide Commissioner for all England. Happy though both parents were at the idea, the King had only one reservation. 'I'll stand anything', he said, 'but I won't have them wear those hideous long black stockings. Reminds me too much of my youth.' They wore knee-length beige socks instead.

The four year difference in their ages meant that Princess Elizabeth joined the Guides as second-in-command to Patricia Mountbatten, in the Kingfisher Patrol, while Princess Margaret joined the Leprechaun Six of the Brownies.

When she was old enough, and having passed her Golden Hand (First Class) Test, the Princess 'flew up,' as it was put, to the Bullfinch Patrol of the Guides in which, following a firmly structured process, she earned proficiency badges in such things as Morse code, first aid and cooking. Finally, to her immense delight, she was awarded the much coveted 'All-round Cords.' It was at about this time that the celebrated portrait photographer Dorothy Wilding, who had already taken formal studies of the royal family, including the official coronation portraits, was commissioned to photograph the Princesses in their uniforms. One of the studies was subsequently adapted for two New Zealand Health Issue postage stamps.

At fifteen, Princess Margaret followed her sister into the Sea Rangers, whose sleeker, more flattering uniform of dark skirt, white shirt, kerchief and lanyard she particularly liked. Three years later, when she was eighteen and her sister was about to become a mother for the first time, Princess Margaret was invited to succeed Princess Elizabeth as Commodore.

Though they were days the Princess was to remember fondly, any idea that the Buckingham Palace Company was at all typical of Guiding across the country was misleading. To begin with, while it might conform to the principles of kinship and public service, there was nothing very democratic about it. The fourteen Brownies and twenty Guides were still drawn from the elite world of noble families, courtiers and palace employees and despite Miss Synge's early advice that 'Guides must all treat one another like sisters', they were still expected to curtsy to the Princesses. Unlike other Guides and Brownies, they were personally enrolled at a special ceremony by the Princess Royal, whom Princess Margaret would eventually succeed as President of the Girl Guides Association, while George V's summer house in the garden at Buckingham Palace became their headquarters.

All the same, both Princesses took the more normal Guiding activities – tracking, bird-watching, trekking, cooking sausages over a campfire – very seriously. So seriously, in fact, that one of the earliest fictions to appear in the popular press about Princess Margaret, by now a fifteen-year-old Sea Ranger, still rankled more than forty years later.

In her own words, 'I was with some of my fellow Sea Rangers in a boat on the lake at Frogmore, and *what* do you think appeared in the newspapers? They said I had pulled the bung from the bottom of the boat! That made me frightfully cross. I was part of a *team* and very proud of it I might tell you. I would never have dreamt of doing something so irresponsible.'[4]

Princess Margaret Rose of York at the age of three.

Princess Margaret with her mother and elder sister arriving at Crathie Church Hall near Balmoral, with the Duchess of Gloucester, 1936.

The two Princesses with Crawfie about to take their first ride on the London underground. Princess Margaret holds the tickets.

Princess Margaret in the schoolroom at Windsor Castle in June 1940.

Dressed alike, the royal sisters with Labradors and Corgis in the garden of The Royal Lodge, Windsor Great Park, 1936.

The King and Princess Margaret watch as Princess Elizabeth plants a tree at the Royal Naval College, Dartmouth, July 1939.

Princess Margaret with Sunny Blandford, Colin Tennant and friends at a ball held at the British Medical Association in December 1948.

Princess Margaret with Group Captain Peter Townsend seated behind at an RAF display at Farnborough in July 1950.

Princess Margaret at the wedding of her friend Elizabeth Carew Pole on 31 October 1953.

Royal Master Class:
the nineteen-year-old
Princess Margaret
impersonating 'types'
with the celebrated
mimic and comic actress
Joyce Grenfell.

(Top left) At the Badminton Horse Trials, a now-famous photograph of Group Captain Peter Townsend (standing on left) with Princess Margaret, The Queen, the Princess Royal and the Duke of Gloucester (left).

(Top right) Princess Margaret at the Edinburgh wedding of Johnny Dalkeith and Jane McNeill, January 1953.

Returning to Buckingham Palace after The Queen's Coronation, Princess Margaret steps down from the Irish State Coach, 2 June 1953.

With Jonathan Lewis at the wheel of a vintage Rolls-Royce, Princess Margaret is seen with members of her prayer group, including Marigold Bridgeman (in plaid shawl) and Elizabeth Elphinstone (seated on left).

The Princess relaxing in a friend's swimming pool.

Princess Margaret and Antony Armstrong-Jones in the Throne Room at Buckingham Palace after their wedding at Westminster Abbey on 6 May 1960.

Princess Margaret and Tony Snowdon look intently at a Henry Moore scultpure, 1965.

As President of the Royal Ballet, Princess Margaret attends a reception with Rudolf Nureyev and Dame Margot Fonteyn circa 1968.

*

The start of the Spanish Civil War in 1936, during which Hitler's Germany was actively on the side of the fascists, meant that George VI had scarcely ascended the throne before his reign was overshadowed by the prospect of international conflict. During the same year, Hitler had marched into the Rhineland, signed agreements with Italy and Japan and, with his eye on Czechoslovakia, was preparing to annexe Austria.

It was against this increasingly ominous background of fascist aggression that the Government began making plans for the first foreign visit of the new reign. Originally arranged to begin on 28 June 1938 (one month after Hitler's much-trumpeted visit to Mussolini in Rome), the King and Queen's State Visit to Paris was not only designed to re-affirm the solidarity of the British and French democracies but also, as the distinguished writer and historian Elizabeth Longford put it, 'to demonstrate the strength of Britain in her new Sovereigns.'

On 23 June, however, just five days before they were to leave, the Queen's mother, Cecilia Strathmore, died at Glamis, and the visit to Paris was put back, at the suggestion of President Lebrun, by three weeks. Of her mother's death, Queen Elizabeth told the Prime Minister, Neville Chamberlain, 'I have been dreading this moment ever since I was a little child and now that it has come, one can hardly believe it. She was a true "Rock of Defence" for us, her children, & Thank God, her influence and wonderful example will remain with us all our lives.'[5]

In just under three weeks, Norman Hartnell – who had originally been asked by the King to take Franz Xavier Winterhalter's romantic portraits of the nineteenth-century Empresses Eugénie of France and Elisabeth of Austria, as his inspiration when designing for his wife – recreated the Queen's entire wardrobe – hats, coats, dresses, evening gowns, wraps, even parasols – in white; the alternative shade for royal and, appropriately, French mourning. From the sparkling crinolines she wore for the very first time, to the trailing full-skirted dress of cobweb lace worn with a hat of ostrich feathers at a garden party at the Bagatelle, the effect was stunning and even 'evoked transports of admiration in the newspapers.'

It was, in fact, one of the most successful of State Visits, as much from a personal as a diplomatic perspective; and it was one that had got off to a tumultuous start. Describing the royal couple's arrival in Paris on 19 July, Lady Diana Cooper wrote, 'We saw the King and Queen from a window coming down the Champs Elysées with roofs, windows and pavements roaring exultantly, the Queen', she added, as if on cue, 'a radiant Winterhalter.'

Though the programme for the three-day visit was a crowded one, the emphasis at every turn was placed squarely on friendship and, above all, on world peace. On the last day of the visit, the King and Queen attended a review of 50,000 troops at Versailles during which, 'The grim mechanical devices of modern armour, the dash and elan of the Moroccan cavalry recalling the warfare of a bygone age, mingled in a great pageant which inspired both awe and confidence.'[6] It was, of course, as illusory as the 'fairy-like magnificence' of the great salons and 'lantern-decked gardens' of the French Foreign Ministry on the Quai d'Orsay for the farewell fête, but nobody was to realize it just yet.

Returning home, the King and Queen brought back gifts for the Princesses that had been presented to them on behalf of the children of France. To Princess Margaret's horror, however, they had been sent dolls. Called *France* and *Marianne*, they were not only beautifully made and beautifully dressed, but they also came with a remarkable wardrobe of clothes that had been specially made by some of France's most distinguished couturiers, Dior, Worth and Balenciaga among them.

Dolls, however, were most decidedly not for Princess Margaret, who said that she had always hated them because, 'they're like dead babies.'[7] Even when she herself became a mother, she loathed the fact that, no matter how kindly, people automatically thought of presenting her with dolls as gifts for her daughter. 'I would see them coming', said the Princess, 'and so, fortunately, would my ladies [in waiting], who would swiftly intercept them and take them away.'[8]

Two months after George VI and Queen Elizabeth returned in triumph from their Parisian State Visit, intelligence reports indicated that Hitler was planning to go into Czechoslovakia. The King, who was at Balmoral with his family, returned to London only to discover that the Prime Minister was already en route to Germany to see Hitler at Berchtesgaden. As tension mounted, it seemed that the Führer had drawn back from the brink. Chamberlain flew out to Munich and came back with the famous 'piece of paper' that, he proudly boasted, represented 'peace with honour.'

What the world did not know was that Hitler was already preparing to invade the Sudetenland, and on 15 March 1939, his troops marched into Prague. It was then that Hitler proclaimed that 'Czechoslovakia had ceased to exist.' That May, as a second world war hung in the balance, the King and Queen sailed for North America, first to Canada – which they crossed from east to west and very nearly back again – and then on their second, and most important State Visit, to the United States as the personal guests of President and Mrs Franklin Delano Roosevelt.

Once again, a diplomatic mission that it was hoped would be of benefit to Britain should there be a war, proved triumphant. A friendship was immediately forged with the Roosevelts themselves, and the response they received from the estimated 3,500,000 people who, according to the police, turned out to see them in New York, was overwhelming. On Capitol Hill, one Senator ecstatically congratulated the King, 'My, you're a great Queen-picker', and the eight-year-old daughter of Harry Hopkins, a great friend of the President, turned to her father after the be-gowned and be-jewelled Queen had spoken to her and said breathlessly, 'Daddy, oh Daddy, I have seen the Fairy Queen.'

The tour which the King had said with obvious pleasure 'has

made us', and which, in his own mind, had done much to secure his reign, was greeted with equal satisfaction at home. Upon their return on 22 June 1939, the Princesses had sailed out from Southampton aboard a destroyer to join their parents on the *Empress of Britain*, in mid-Channel. It was a joyful reunion in which mother, father and daughters hugged and kissed each other again and again, and Princess Margaret clung to her mother's hand and said, 'Look, Mummie, I am quite a good shape now, not like the football I used to be.'

In London, huge crowds lined the route from Waterloo Station to Buckingham Palace where another 50,000, all in fine voice, waited to welcome them home. Even the House of Commons interrupted its session so that MPs could join in the cheering. Describing the scene outside Parliament, Harold Nicolson wrote, 'They went very slowly . . . the King and Queen and the two princesses. We lost all our dignity and yelled and yelled. The King wore a happy schoolboy grin. The Queen was superb. She really does manage to convey to each individual in the crowd that he or she has had a personal greeting.'

Although the European situation had deteriorated no further during King George and Queen Elizabeth's six-week absence, there was still a sense of anticipation, of expectation. In July, before they went up to Scotland for what was to be their last holiday at Balmoral for six years, the King with the Queen and the Princesses visited the Royal Naval College at Dartmouth. Coupled with his wish to inspect the College he had last seen as a youth was the King's interest in seeing how the naval cadets were shaping up at a particularly crucial time.

Sailing on board the then royal yacht *Victoria and Albert*, the Princesses took their lessons in what Crawfie called 'a very pretty little schoolroom' or up on deck, took lunch and dinner in the dining saloon where, to their fascination, the yacht's main mast came out and through one end of the dining table, and were taught to dance the *Lambeth Walk* and *Palais Glide* by some of the young officers.

With them as the yacht dropped anchor in the River Dart on

22 July, was the King's cousin Lord Louis Mountbatten. Otherwise known for some inexplicable reason as 'Dickie', he was good-looking, charming, and vastly ambitious, not least when it came to capitalizing on his royal connections and promoting the interests of his family name.

The second son of Prince Louis of Battenberg, who in 1917, when George V adopted the name of 'Windsor' for the Royal House and anglicized all other Germanic titles, became 1st Marquess of Milford Haven, Dickie Mountbatten had been especially close to the King's elder brother, at least up to his Abdication. It was then that he changed horses and re-aligned his loyalties. If the King saw through him, but nevertheless enjoyed his naval jokes, their shared interests in the service to which they both belonged, in uniforms and in decorations, the Queen was not so amused by Dickie and his wife Edwina's hedonistic lifestyle or their champagne socialism.

Rarely, however, can Mountbatten's ambitions have been quite so transparent – at least that is how it seems today – than during the royal family's visit to Dartmouth. On the Sunday morning, the King and Queen were advised that two of the cadets had gone down with mumps. Rather than put the Princesses at risk by allowing them to attend chapel, it was thought wiser that they should wait at the Captain's House with the Dalrymple-Hamilton family who lived there.

Curiously, of all those who might easily have qualified to entertain the two Princesses, the only cadet who appears to have been allowed anywhere near them was Dickie Mountbatten's eighteen-year-old nephew, Prince Philip of Greece who, when he became a naturalized British subject ten years later, dispensed with his family name, Schleswig-Holstein-Sonderburg-Glücksburg, and assumed his uncle's name, becoming plain Philip Mountbatten.

At Dartmouth, however, it was Prince Philip who was delegated to keep the King's daughters amused at the Captain's House, first by playing with a clockwork train set and then at the tennis courts where, at Philip's suggestion, they could 'have some real fun jumping the nets.'

If Crawfie thought the tall, blond, Nordic-looking cadet with piercing blue eyes, 'showed off a good deal', the Princesses, especially the thirteen-year-old Elizabeth, were most impressed. 'How good he is', was one of her famous remarks, 'how high he can jump.'

Although it appears he did not pay Princess Elizabeth any special attention, preferring instead to tease the plumper and younger Princess Margaret, Philip was present at lunch that day and came back the next for both lunch and tea, at which, to the admiration of both Princesses, he consumed several platefuls of shrimps as well as a banana split. It is a matter of record that Princess Elizabeth fell in love with Prince Philip that day.[9]

Early the following month, after a slight delay in their departure, which led Princess Margaret to ask indignantly, 'Who *is* this Hitler, spoiling everything?' the royal family left London for their annual summer holiday in Scotland. Not three weeks later, on 22 August, however, news that Germany and Russia had entered into a pact, and that in consequence Parliament had been recalled to meet the next day, sent the King back to London by the overnight train.

A little under six months' earlier, having already occupied Prague, and made a German protectorate of Bohemia and Moravia, Hitler had demanded the port of Danzig from Poland. It was the British and Commonwealth Governments' pledge of support for Poland – which, after Mussolini's invasion of Albania in April, was extended to include Greece, Romania, Denmark, the Netherlands and Switzerland – that would lead to war with Germany.

On 1 September, German troops crossed into Poland. Two days later, the British Government issued Hitler an ultimatum to which there was no response. At 11.15am that day, Sunday, 3 September 1939, Prime Minister Neville Chamberlain opened his wireless address to the nation with the famous words:

I am speaking to you from the Cabinet Room at 10 Downing Street. This morning, the British Ambassador in

Berlin handed the German Government a final note stating that unless we heard from them at 11 o'clock that they were prepared at once to withdraw their troops from Poland, a state of war would exist between us. I have to tell you now that no such undertaking has been received, and that consequently this country is at war with Germany.

That evening, George VI also spoke to his people throughout Britain and the Empire. He said, in part, 'In this grave hour, perhaps the most fateful in our history, I send to every household of my peoples, both at home and overseas, this message, spoken with the same depth of feeling for each one of you as if I were able to cross your threshold and speak to you myself. For the second time in the lives of most of us we are at war. Over and over again we have tried to find a peaceful way out of the differences between ourselves and those who are now our enemies. But it has been in vain. We have been forced into a conflict . . . For the sake of all that we ourselves hold dear and of the world's order and peace, it is unthinkable that we should refuse to meet the challenge . . .'

Five days after the King returned to London, the Queen left Balmoral to join him, leaving their daughters at Birkhall in the care of Crawfie and Allah. Princess Margaret asked anxiously, 'Why had Mummie and Papa to go back? Do you think the Germans will come and get them?' Assured that they would not, both Princesses took comfort from their daily telephone conversations with their parents.

Though no definite plans could be made, it was decided that the Princesses should remain safely out of the way at Birkhall for the time being. In fact, they stayed on until Christmas. Soon, the reality of war penetrated even the tranquillity of the Balmoral estate with the announcement on 14 October that the battleship *Royal Oak* had been torpedoed by a German U-boat that had slipped through the defences of the northern naval base at Scapa Flow, with the loss of more than 800 lives. Jumping from her chair, her eyes blazing with anger, Princess Elizabeth exclaimed, 'It can't be! All those nice sailors.'

One way in which both Princesses relieved their fury was in violently bombarding the wireless with cushions and books whenever they heard the anti-British broadcasts of William Joyce, the infamous Irishman known as 'Lord Haw Haw.' 'There was something oddly arresting about that dreadful voice', said Crawfie. 'Some evenings up in Scotland it was almost impossible to get away from it.'

At Birkhall, the Princesses followed much the same sort of schoolroom timetable as they would normally, even though Crawfie began to find that having them both on her hands for lessons all the time soon started to become a strain. Preparing lessons for two children of different ages, 'both extremely bright', was hard work, she said. To the rescue came Mrs Montaudon-Smith, one of their French teachers, who was known to them all as 'Monty.' Dividing the teaching schedule between them meant that Crawfie could take one Princess in more general studies, as she was used to doing, while Monty took the other in French. Because she was keen on singing, something that appealed to the extremely musical younger Princess, Monty also taught them French duets which they religiously rehearsed as a surprise for their parents.

When not at their lessons, the Princesses helped out at the war work sewing parties that Crawfie and Allah organized between them in the schoolroom at Birkhall. Every Thursday afternoon, the wives of local crofters, farmers and estate workers sat together making comforts for the troops, while listening to music from an old-fashioned horn gramophone which was so loud that the Princesses resorted to pushing scarves down the horn in an attempt to muffle the sound. Princess Margaret's favourite record was *Your Tiny Hand is Frozen* sung by Beniamino Gigli which, said Crawfie, was 'astonishingly apt' since they had only one small, if cosy, stove in the centre of the room. At these sewing parties, both Princesses handed round tea and cakes and chatted with the women about their husbands and sons who were all by now in uniform.

By autumn, the weekly meetings were joined by the mothers of children who had been evacuated from Glasgow's slum tenements and who, at the King's wish, had been put up at Craigowan House on the Balmoral estate. These, however, were rough-and-ready city kids, as unused to royal estates and royal princesses as the royal princesses were to having grimy streets as a playground and rough-and-ready city kids as pals. Crawfie may have forgotten that when she said that the 'not noticeably clean' evacuees were 'terrified of the silence, scared to go into the woods, and frightened if they saw a deer.' Balmoral was an alien world and while many of them loved it, many more were unable to make the adjustment.

'The sound of the wind groaning through the trees at night terrified them', Princess Margaret recalled. 'It was, they said, the "sound of witches and devils." In fact, many of the children were so unhappy that they had to be sent home again.'[10]

At the King's insistence, Queen Mary also became an evacuee. On the day war was declared she was at Sandringham enjoying a few days with her Kent grandchildren, the four-year-old Prince 'Eddie' and his not quite three-year-old sister, Alexandra. Instead of returning to London, the King advised his mother to head for Badminton House in Gloucestershire, the home of her niece Mary and her husband Henry Somerset, the 10th Duke of Beaufort, His Majesty's Master of the Horse. Not to return to London, said the Queen Dowager, was not 'at all the thing.' But she agreed to go to Badminton when the King explained that her continued presence in London would only cause needless trouble and anxiety.

During her five-year stay, Queen Mary enthusiastically took part in three much-favoured pastimes. One was the collection of salvage – discarded bottles, tin cans and scrap iron – required for the war effort, which was dumped into her Daimler and driven off to the nearest collection depot. The second was leading her 'Ivy Squad' in tearing ivy from buildings, walls and trees, while the third activity was 'wooding' which, together with her four personal dispatch riders, involved sawing up branches and logs, thinning or clearing thickets or spinneys and tidying up woodland debris in general.

Like the 120 men of the Gloucestershire Regiment stationed at Badminton, the Queen's dispatch riders had not been directed to act as military errand-boys, but as her personal bodyguards. Each one of them, it is said, had embarked on their royal mission with some trepidation, but 'quickly came to regard the Queen with personal affection', recalling 'the wiles [she] would employ to discover the dates of their birthdays so as to give them surprise birthday presents, or the way in which she handed round cigarettes during the short break in a 'wooding' afternoon, chatting to them about her family or theirs as she stood amongst them, herself smoking a cigarette.'[11]

When peace finally came and Queen Mary was able to return to London, her farewells were tinged with genuine sadness. As she presented 'thank you' gifts to members of the Beaufort household, the seventy-seven-year-old Queen was reportedly in tears as she said, 'Oh, I *have* been happy here! Here I've been anybody to everybody, and back in London I shall have to begin being Queen Mary all over again.'

At Birkhall, as the first Christmas of the war approached, the Princesses, who had never been in Scotland so late in the year before, were amazed by the severity of the frosts, 'so much whiter and heavier than the southern ones', said Crawfie, and the early arrival of snow. Frozen sponges and face flannels in their bathroom, carafes of drinking water that had frozen solid on side tables in their bedrooms, early morning frost patterns on windows, were all novelties they were experiencing for the very first time.

Together they joined the local Girl Guides company, which met each week in the village hall, and with the Craigowan evacuees they went off on hikes and outings. There were even occasional film shows when the schoolroom was turned into a cinema and the owner of the village projector would screen some of his Charlie Chaplin, Keystone Cops, and Laurel and Hardy films.

'At the end of these performances', said Crawfie, 'we frequently had another, when [Allah] would try to get Margaret to bed.' Bouncing off sofas, weaving and dodging round chairs, the nine-year-old princess would defy her exasperated nanny until Crawfie would fix her with a particularly cold look, 'take her arm and walk her to the door, saying, "*Go to bed!*" Margaret usually went then, quietly.'

If, even at that age, Princess Margaret was capable of unnerving grown men with her 'witty tongue' and sometimes 'sharp way', she had, as Crawfie put it, 'the softest of hearts.' A 'misunderstanding of her lighthearted fun and frolics', she wrote, 'was often to get her into trouble long after schoolroom days were done. It was to be her misfortune that the ordinary exploits of . . . a healthy and vivacious girl . . . made newspaper paragraphs, instead of being dismissed with a laugh.'

To their delight, the Princesses heard from their mother that Christmas would be spent as usual at Sandringham. For a while, not least because of the royal estate's proximity to one of the stretches of North Sea coast thought most likely to be targeted in the event of an invasion, there had been some debate about leaving the Princesses where they were or bringing them further south. With the decision made and the small, sixpenny gifts of china ornaments and costume jewellery which they had bought in the Aberdeen branch of Woolworths, carefully wrapped and packed away with the rest of their luggage, Lilibet and Margaret left Birkhall on 18 December.

On Christmas Eve, as was the custom, the lights on the tall pine tree in the drawing room at Sandringham House were lit and gifts were exchanged. Among those the Princesses received from their mother were their first diaries, which, although she never kept one herself, Queen Elizabeth insisted her daughters should write up every evening.

On Christmas Day, the King, who had not long returned from a successful six-day, morale-boosting, visit to his troops in France, broadcast his first seasonal message to the nation. Because of his stammer and the fear that he might suddenly dry up mid-sentence, broadcasting – in those days of 'live' only transmissions – was, and always would be, an ordeal that filled him with dread. He nevertheless recognized the importance of speaking directly to his people, especially during that first disquieting Christmas when, although war had been declared more than three months earlier, nothing had yet happened.

In what was probably the most memorable broadcast of his reign, George VI warned his listeners of the dark and uncertain times that lay ahead. 'A new year is at hand,' he said. 'We cannot tell what it will bring. If it brings peace, how thankful we shall be. If it brings us continued struggle we shall remain undaunted.' He ended by offering a message of hope and encouragement; one that he himself had discovered in the words of a poem that had recently been sent to him:

> I said to the man who stood at the Gate of the Year,
> 'Give me a light that I may tread safely into the unknown,'
> And he replied, 'Go out into the darkness,
> And put your hand into the Hand of God.
> That shall be to you better than light,
> And safer than a known way.'*

* The poem from which George VI quoted was written in 1908 by Miss Marie (Minnie) Louise Haskins (1875-1957), a lecturer at the London School of Economics. When the Memorial Chapel to King George VI was constructed in St George's Chapel, Windsor, the words of the poem were engraved on a plate to the right of the chapel's gates.

SIX

The Princesses Elizabeth and Margaret stayed on at Sandringham until the first week of February 1940, when they travelled down to Windsor and returned to the Royal Lodge, its distinctive pink walls now re-painted with the murky shades of camouflage to protect it from air attack. Here, officially described by the censors as living 'somewhere in the country', they stayed until 12 May. It was then that the Queen telephoned Crawfie from Buckingham Palace and asked her to take the Princesses to the greater safety of Windsor Castle, 'at least for the rest of the week.' They were to remain there for the next five years.

Two days earlier – having invaded Denmark and Norway only weeks before, leading the Princesses' great-uncle Charles, the Norwegian King, Haakon VII, to seek refuge in London – Hitler had launched a massive ground and air attack on Holland, Belgium and Luxemburg.

Queen Wilhelmina of the Netherlands, it turned out, had escaped capture by German soldiers parachuted into Holland, by only half an hour. With invasion imminent, she left the Hague with the intention of joining that part of her army that was still resisting the enemy in Zeeland. Prevented by German bombardment from landing at either Breskens or Flushing, however, the indomitable sixty-year-old Queen, who had been rescued from Rotterdam by the British battleship *Hereward*, sailed for England. There she planned to petition the British Government for further assistance.

Telephoning George VI when she arrived at Harwich, Queen Wilhelmina was reluctantly persuaded to accept the inevitable. Such was the situation in Holland that an immediate return was not an option. Later that day, the King wrote in his diary, 'I met her at Liverpool Street Station & brought her [to Buckingham Palace]. I had not met her before. She told me that when she left the Hague she had no intention of leaving Holland, but force of circumstances had made her come here. She was naturally very upset . . .'

Hitler's invasion of the Low Countries – the Netherlands finally capitulated on 15 May, the same day the British Prime Minister, by now Winston Churchill, heard from the French premier, Paul Reynaud that 'the war [in France] was lost' – soon led the former Lord Chancellor, Lord Hailsham, to write to Churchill advocating that the King and Queen and their daughters, or failing that, at least the two Princesses, should be evacuated to Canada. 'I observe that the Nazis both in Norway and in Holland made a desperate effort to capture the royal family', he pointed out. 'No doubt they will do the same in this country if they can; and in the British Empire it would be a more serious matter because the Crown is the principal link between us and the Dominions.'[1]

It was not an idea that met with royal approval. 'The children could not leave without me', said the Queen emphatically, 'I could not leave without the King, and the King will never leave.' In the event of the King and Queen having to leave London, three 'safe houses' had already been selected – Pitchford House in Shropshire, Madresfield, near Malvern and Newby Hall in Yorkshire – but there was never any question of them being evacuated from Britain.

Indeed, at both Buckingham Palace and Windsor Castle, George VI had shooting ranges laid out where he and the Queen, as well as other members of the royal family and their Household, were taught to use revolvers, rifles and tommy-guns.

'I shan't go down like the others', the Queen declared. The King, moreover, had already expressed his determination to offer his services to the leader of a British resistance movement should his country be invaded.

In the meantime, the daily pattern of life for King George and Queen Elizabeth, now under the protection of a handpicked company of officers and men from the Brigade of Guards and the Household Cavalry, meant commuting between London and Windsor by armoured car, the ever-present tin helmets and gas masks, together with a sten gun concealed in a dispatch case, by their side. During the course of the war they also visited towns and cities up and down the country when, often for days on end, the royal train became 'home.' In all, the King and Queen made no fewer than 300 such journeys throughout Britain, and covered 40,000 miles in the process.

Almost without exception, King George and Queen Elizabeth went everywhere together in their attempts to boost morale. Unhurriedly picking their way through scenes of total devastation, they did their best to console, encourage and sympathize. They toured hospitals, ARP centres, Home Guard stations, barracks, munitions factories, and feeding centres. They stood in stunned silence on the edge of immense craters where once people's homes, sometimes entire streets, had stood, and they shared air raid shelters with ordinary men and women.

There was one visit, however, which the King insisted on undertaking alone, so that the Queen might be spared the full horror. That was to Coventry where, on the night of 14 November 1940, from a clear, moonlit sky, 500 German aircraft dropped 543 tons of high-explosive bombs and incendiaries on the city. In the first hour of the attack, the entire town centre was ablaze. One-third of the area was devastated while another third had to be demolished. Two hundred fires raged that night and 600 people lost their lives.

Accompanied only by Alexander Hardinge, his Private Secretary, and Joey Legh, then his equerry, the King drove to Coventry from Windsor on 16 November to witness the devastation for himself. 'The cathedral, hotels, shops, everything was flat & had been gutted by fire', he wrote. 'The people in the streets wondered where they were, nothing could be recognized . . .'

The King's unexpected and unannounced presence in their midst gave the city's inhabitants a tremendous psychological boost. One later recalled, 'We suddenly felt that if the King was there everything was all right and the rest of England was behind us.'

It was the bravery, resilience and gallantry of ordinary people that he and the Queen saw everywhere they went, that inspired the King to create two new civilian honours bearing his name. One was the George Cross, the other the George Medal.

Though it seems to have been an extraordinary oversight, it was not until 1941 that a proper air raid shelter, complete with gas-proof chamber, bathrooms and kitchen, was built for the King and Queen at Buckingham Palace. Up to that point, they had had nothing more substantial than a housemaids' sitting room in the basement, which had been reinforced with timber and steel, furnished with an odd assortment of Regency sofas and gilt chairs, and equipped with a bottle of smelling salts, a hand-pump and buckets of sand for emergencies.

Between September 1940, with the start of the Blitz, and July 1944, Buckingham Palace was bombed nine times, with various parts of the building and its precincts receiving direct hits. These included the private Chapel, one of Nash's original conservatories housing the recently completed swimming pool, the roof and ground floor, the West Front, the forecourt, and the North Lodge. It was at the North Lodge that Police Constable Stephen Robertson, who had swapped duties as a favour to one of his colleagues, and who was attempting to deal with phosphorous incendiary devices, was fatally injured by falling masonry, when another aircraft released a stick of six bombs. One of them fell on Wellington Barracks nearby, another on the lawn of Queen's Gardens opposite the Palace,

two exploded in the forecourt, while another scored a direct
hit on the North Lodge, burying PC Robertson beneath a pile
of rubble.[2] Fifty years later, during a private ceremony, Queen
Elizabeth was to unveil a memorial plaque to Steve Robertson
on the garden wall of Buckingham Palace. During another
raid, one equerry who had fought in the trenches during the
1914–18 War, said 'this great house continuously shook like a
jelly . . . for two or three hours it was like a front-line trench
under bombardment.'

While the King and Queen usually slept at Windsor Castle,
they were invariably found in London during the day. It was
then that most of the attacks on Buckingham Palace took place.
None was more audacious, however, than that which occurred
on 13 September 1940. On that morning, taking full advantage
of low cloud cover, a German bomber flew straight up the Mall
and released two sticks of six bombs each on to the Palace.
Having just arrived from Windsor, the King – who later
suspected that, given its accuracy, a cousin in the Luftwaffe may
have carried out the raid – said 'we heard an aircraft making a
zooming noise above us.' He then saw '2 bombs falling past the
opposite side of the Palace, & then heard two resounding
crashes as the bombs fell in the quadrangle about 30 yards away.
We looked at each other & then we were out in the passage as
fast as we could get there . . . We all wondered why we weren't
dead.'

A little later, as the King and Queen toured the Palace to
inspect the extent of the damage, they arrived at the kitchen to
find their chef, Monsieur René Roussin, surrounded by the
debris of the shattered glass ceiling, but otherwise cheerful and
well, and remarking on the fact that there had been a '*petit
quelque chose dans le coin, un petit bruit.*'* As the Queen later told
Queen Mary, 'The *petite quelque chose* was the bomb on the
Chapel just next door!' Delighted though he was to find
Monsieur Roussin alive, the King was no less pleased to discover

---

* 'A small something in the area, a small noise.'

that, along with his chef, the cooker had also survived and in it his lunch that was still fit to be served.

The bombing of Buckingham Palace did at least mean that, in the Queen's famous words, 'We can now look the East End in the face.' And it was the East End, or more specifically the areas of East and West Ham, that the King and Queen were able to visit as planned on the afternoon of 13 September.

In a letter to her mother-in-law describing what they had seen, Queen Elizabeth wrote, 'The damage there is ghastly. I really felt as if I was walking in a dead city, when we walked down a little empty street. All the houses evacuated and yet through the broken windows one saw all the poor little possessions, photographs, beds, just as they were left. At the end of the street is a school which was hit, and collapsed on the top of 500 people waiting to be evacuated – about 200 are still under the ruins. It does affect me seeing this terrible and senseless destruction. I think that really I mind it much more than being bombed myself. The people are marvellous, and full of fight . . . We *must* win in the end.'[3]

At Windsor the two Princesses, like other evacuees, were largely spared the horrors of war, even if they knew something of its discomforts. When they were first moved from Royal Lodge to Windsor Castle, they went to bed in their own rooms in the Augusta Tower, overlooking the Little (or Home) Park and the Long Walk. Then, as Princess Margaret recalled, enemy aircraft, 'always seemed to come over when we had just got to sleep.'[4] That meant their being roused, hurriedly dressed in siren suits and, with their small suitcases containing their most important possessions, being taken down to one of the dungeons through long, subterranean passages 'smelling disgustingly damp.'

There they would hear the drone of German bombers overhead and, through the Castle's chalk foundations, feel the reverberations of explosions in and around Windsor, as well as further afield, all the while anxiously awaiting the all clear. As at Buckingham Palace, a purpose-built, fully-equipped bunker, or 'concrete box', as Princess Margaret described it, was eventually built beneath the Victoria (now the Queen's) Tower, where they could rest, if not always sleep, at night, in greater safety and with more comfort.

Occupying the only naturally defensive site in that particular part of the Thames Valley, 100 feet (30m) above the river, Windsor Castle was built by William the Conqueror more than 900 years earlier, in about 1080. From that time to the Great Fire of 1992, the Castle, both as fortress and royal palace, evolved under successive monarchs, some of whom achieved more than others. None built or rebuilt on the scale or with the grandeur of George IV, however, who was a truly great Francophile and transformed many of the State and semi-State Apartments into gilded treasure houses the equal of Versailles. Though always beloved of Kings and Queens and their families as a home, the Castle in the role of fortress during the years of the Second World War became a dark, physically gloomy and frequently icy cold place, lit by reduced-voltage electric light bulbs, warmed by log fires which were allowed only in sitting rooms, never bedrooms, and supplied by a reduced boiler system which meant that hot water was no longer an everyday utility. Baths were marked with red or black lines indicating the five-inch restriction on bath water, while notices warned of the need for economy. To Crawfie, the royal as well as non-royal residents of the Castle all 'seemed to live in a sort of underworld.'

Priceless paintings, drawings and tapestries, state portraits, sculpture and chandeliers, antique porcelain and plate, together with a myriad other moveable treasures belonging to the Royal Collection, were taken away for safe keeping. George IV's magnificent gilded furniture was covered in dustsheets, glazed cabinets were turned to face the wall, and heavy blackout curtaining was drawn every night across windows protected by an adhesive mesh overlaid with wire-netting.

Outside in the grounds, members of the 300-strong No. 1 Company Grenadier Guards, otherwise known as the Castle Company, that had been detailed to the protection of the King and his family, dug slit trenches which the Princesses then named after the guardsmen responsible, 'Denny's Delight', for example, and 'Peter's Folly.' These were useful for the Guides and Sea Rangers to duck down into when daytime air raid warnings sounded, but were otherwise something of a 'menace' as Crawfie put it, because 'you did not know when you would trip over one while on a walk through the grounds.'

Of the more defensive trenches that were laced with barbed-wire fences, Princess Margaret said with mild amusement, 'They wouldn't have kept anybody out, but they kept us in.'[5]

So that they too could 'dig for victory', both Princesses cultivated their own plot of land as a vegetable garden, while on a broader scale, all the land in the Home and Great Parks that could be used for food production was put to the plough or used as pasture for sheep and cattle.

Not far from the Royal Lodge, on the wide expanse of Smith's Lawn where Edward VIII as Prince of Wales had had an airstrip laid out for his personal use, the United States Air Force established a base consisting of some twenty-five officers, in tented accommodation, and fourteen aircraft, all of them Dakotas.

The Princesses not only got to know a number of the American airmen from the Smith's Lawn base, but also met a great many GIs who visited the castle. Though fascinated by the King's young daughters, the American soldiers invariably used the same opening line when they were introduced: 'I have a little girl at home just your age.' It wasn't long before the Princesses knew what was coming and fought to suppress their giggles. Only once did Princess Margaret lower her guard and then only to her Governess. 'Crawfie', she whispered, 'the children there must be in America, all our age. *Billions* of them!'[6]

American military personnel often visited Windsor Castle during the war years but on one occasion, without ever realizing it, one group of VIPs managed to take the King and his family completely by surprise. Margaret Rhodes, the youngest of Queen Elizabeth's Elphinstone nieces, recalls that 'during the high summer of either 1942 or '43, when I was taking a secretarial course nearby, the King and Queen invited me to stay at the Castle. One afternoon we were all having tea on the terrace overlooking the garden. The table was fully laid with a long white cloth, silver tea service, and so on, when we suddenly heard American voices coming closer. The King or the Queen said it was General Eisenhower, and they had completely forgotten that he and a group of soldiers were coming to look round the Castle. Rather than be seen, the four of them, the King, the Queen and the two Princesses, dived under the table, leaving me sitting there all alone and feeling rather foolish.'[7]

Windsor, according to Princess Margaret, came into its own during the war. 'There was a tremendous spirit', she recalled, 'everybody was always cheerful.'[8] Not everyone saw it through the eyes of a happy and exuberant teenaged Princess, of course, and not everybody felt the same way about the 'spirit' of the place.

Returning from distinguished service with the Fifth Battalion, Coldstream Guards, in north-western Europe, Michael Adeane, then Assistant Private Secretary to the King, said the atmosphere at Windsor Castle, 'was rather like that of a convent.'[9]

Despite the cloistered world in which they were fast growing up and the predictable rhythm of their days, the Princesses' lives were far from inactive. Cockney evacuees from the East End of London were put up on the royal estate at Windsor, in much the same way that children from the back streets of Glasgow had been evacuated to Balmoral.

The Princesses got to know most of them, particularly those who enrolled in either the Guides or the Sea Rangers. Other evacuees followed their example and when, four years after the war ended, Princess Margaret flew out of London at the start of a European tour and spotted a familiar face among the airport staff, she greeted her with an informal, 'Hello, Jo. How nice to see you.' She had recognized Josephine Burwell-Smith, who had been a member of her Guide company at Windsor and was now an air stewardess.

'It was amusing and no doubt very instructive for the two

Princesses to mingle with the children', said Crawfie of that time, 'for if among the children of Court and other officials there had been a tendency to let them have an advantage, win a game, or be relieved of the more sordid tasks, there was nothing of the kind now. It was each for herself.'

Indeed, when they camped out in the Great Park – which was something Princess Margaret enjoyed far more than her sister – there was firewood to be collected, food to be prepared and greasy dishes to be washed. The Princesses were expected to muck in and get their hands dirty, which they did.

Even in later life, one friend was to say that, Princess Margaret 'loves great big roaring fires'. Indeed, no matter where she might have been spending an autumn or winter weekend, whether with members of her family or with friends, 'she thought nothing of getting down on her knees in front of a fireplace, screwing up newspapers, getting the logs together, and then getting a good fire going. And she makes frequent trips to the log basket. She doesn't expect anyone else to do it for her.'[10]

Similarly, when the Princess was staying at Windsor Castle on one occasion, a footman discovered her down on her knees collecting newspapers and logs from a cupboard in the corridor outside the familiar rooms in the Augusta Tower that were always reserved for her use. Remonstrating that it was his job to take care of making up the fire, the Princess looked up at him and said, 'I was a Girl Guide you know.'[11]

Throughout her life the Girl Guide in her continued to surface in 'domestic' tasks that nobody but Princess Margaret herself was allowed to take care of. Removing her considerable porcelain collection from antique breakfront cabinets and glazed display cupboards in the hall, Drawing- and Garden-rooms of her apartment at Kensington Palace, she alone carried it through to the glass pantry where, donning rubber gloves and an apron, she would stand at the sink for hours carefully washing and drying every last object. Before putting them back, the Princess first cleaned all the shelves before repeating the process with her collection of sea-shells which, in the opinion of specialists at

London's Natural History Museum, was one of the finest collections in private ownership.

Becoming part of life at the Royal Village in Windsor Great Park suited London's East End evacuees. Not only were they friendly and easy to get on with, but they seemed well able to take their changed surroundings in their stride. Thirty or so even attended the Royal School, which was founded by Queen Victoria and housed in a picturesque, red-brick building with pitched roofs, barge-boarding and mullioned windows. Built in 1846, it functions still as the Royal School, albeit a Crown-Aided First School, under the direction of the county's Education Department.

Then, however, it was directed by a colourful headmaster, Mr Hubert Tanner, a one time Gilbert and Sullivan actor whom Princess Margaret and her sister would come to know as well as any of the village children. The Princesses' own education, meanwhile, continued to follow much the same undemanding course as it always had but with one or two significant additions. Under the tutelage of Antoinette de Bellaigue, a Belgian Vicomtesse known as 'Toni', the Princesses were given lessons in French language, French literature and European history. Far more able than Crawfie, or even Mrs Montaudon-Smith, to instruct them in these subjects, the Vicomtesse, who became a great friend of both her students, was as important a tutor to the Princesses as Sir Henry Marten, the Provost of Eton, was to Princess Elizabeth.

Knighted by the King in March 1945, on the steps of the College Chapel in the presence of the Queen and their daughters and in full view of the school, Sir Henry gave Princess Elizabeth one-to-one tutorials in general history, but with the emphasis on constitutional matters of interest to her as Heiress Presumptive to her father's throne.

These lessons took place twice a week, either at Eton or at Windsor Castle, where Sir Henry – who would absent-mindedly address Princess Elizabeth as 'Gentlemen', pronounced 'Gen'lemen', the manner in which he addressed his schoolboys –

would arrive in a dog-cart transporting a heavy Gladstone bag full of books, but without the pet raven he kept in his study.

Though four years younger, Princess Margaret deeply resented the fact that she was not allowed to share these tutorials with her sister, or even permitted to follow her lead in gaining the higher education she would like to have had. It would always be, as she put it, 'a bone of contention.'[12]

The decision not to allow Princess Margaret to take history lessons with Sir Henry was also ironically short-sighted, not least because it overlooked the historical fact that both her father and grandfather had been second sons and both, as a consequence of their own lack of education, had felt at a distinct disadvantage when called to the throne. Princess Margaret was also a second child and at that time second in line to the same throne. Yet it did not seem to have occurred to her parents or to her governess that a gentle, 'lady-like' curriculum of reading, writing, dancing, drawing and riding for the heiress presumptive to the Crown Princess, as it were, was no longer sufficient.

If, however, the Princess minded missing out on Sir Henry's tutorials, she was also unhappy at not being permitted to take singing lessons which, she said, 'I would very much have liked. My father said no, because his sister, my aunt Mary, had asked for singing lessons and they hadn't worked out. She hadn't been taught properly, so that when you stood next to her in church and it came to singing hymns you never knew what was going to come out. Sometimes there were the most awful noises. So my father said "*No!*" to my having singing lessons.'[13]

In an appraisal of Princess Margaret's character, the writer and historian Kenneth Rose said, 'We show no lack of sympathy for those denied a vitalizing education by poverty or colour. But there are shortcomings at both ends of the social scale. The undemanding course of study at the hands of the governess Crawfie left an unsatisfied appetite in the younger of her two pupils.'[14]

It was precisely because of that 'unsatisfied appetite' that Princess Margaret became an autodidact; absorbing the Arts-oriented subjects – history, art, architecture, dance, theatre – that fired her imagination then and for the rest of her life. She also read widely, taking advice on which of the Classics she should read and keeping two or three books – a biography, a history of some description, a volume of memoirs or a new novel – on the go simultaneously. But as one of her friends put it, 'Princess Margaret, like all self-taught people, only looked at what interested her, not at the "nuts and bolts." There was no slaving over Latin verbs, if you see what I mean.'[15]

The entertainer in Princess Margaret was already much in evidence by the time she was ten years old. At lunch each day, to which two or three Guards officers, among them Sir Francis Manners, Mark Bonham-Carter, who became a life-long friend, and Hugh Fitzroy, later Duke of Grafton, were invited, she came into her own. Once she had organized who she wanted to sit on either side of her she proceeded to keep the entire company amused. 'If you sat at Princess Margaret's end of the table', said one young Grenadier, 'the conversation never lapsed for a moment. You did not have to worry at all yourself. She was amazingly self-assured, without being embarrassingly so. In fact, she was already a good companion.'

Even Queen Mary, who had expressed disappointment that her granddaughter was 'so spoilt', was won over. Confiding in her old friend and lady-in-waiting Mabell, Countess of Airlie, she confessed she found the Princess 'so outrageously amusing that one can't help encouraging her.' She was '*espiègle*' – a mischievous little rogue.

One way of tapping musical talents was the Windsor Castle Madrigal Society to which both Princesses belonged. Its members included some of the young officers of the Castle Company, as well as a handful of boys from across the river at Eton, one of whom was the Honourable Angus Ogilvy, grandson of Mabell Airlie and future husband of Princess Alexandra. Another was performing in concerts from which the Queen's Wool Fund, the Red Cross or some other charity would benefit from 'box office' receipts. At one of these concerts, Herbert

White, a young Guardsmen from Norwich, who had been invited to join the small band of musicians, recalled playing a violin solo while Princess Elizabeth danced a French minuet and later a Scottish reel.[16]

Dances became frequent events at Windsor and even at Buckingham Palace. The King, who was a particularly good dancer, was up for everything from a waltz or foxtrot with his wife, his daughters or a member of the household, to leading a conga. In July 1941, following one of the Princesses' special benefit concerts, the King and Queen held a dance for them at Windsor Castle. 'My very first dance', as Princess Margaret, who was then just a month short of her eleventh birthday, would later recall.

Describing the 'ball as everybody calls it now' in a letter to her cousin Margaret Rhodes, Princess Elizabeth wrote: 'Jack Jackson was the band. Everybody was full of praises about it. I can't think how they played from 9.0pm to 2.30am with only two intervals. Margaret stayed to the very end and the result is that she retired to bed two days after from pure exhaustion. I must explain that we had a concert the day before the dance. Margaret & I danced, sang and played so that everything in the programme had either Princess Elizabeth or P. Margaret in it. We did not have programmes so Mr Tanner, the Schoolmaster and our producer compèred it. We made about £80 for wool.'[17]

Hubert Tanner was also the driving force behind the Princesses' most famous wartime theatricals at Windsor. Staged in the magnificent Waterloo Chamber, which George IV conceived to commemorate the defeat of Napoleon and where Queen Victoria's children enacted *tableaux vivant* for their mother's entertainment, pantomimes were produced each Christmas from 1941 to 1944 with a professionalism that took some audiences by surprise.

The Princesses' pantomimes had their origin in quite a different production, however. Performed in December 1940 in St George's Hall, next door to the Waterloo Chamber, *The Christmas Child* was a nativity play in which a number of the evacuees became involved. Some were cast as shepherds while two others, one of whom had his face made up with cocoa, were chosen to appear with Princess Elizabeth, who was dressed in a golden crown and velvet tunic, as the three kings. In what Crawfie described as 'a most beautifully clear voice', Princess Margaret in the role of the Little Child sang *Gentle Jesus, Meek and Mild* so effectively that the King was moved to write afterwards, 'I wept through most of it.'

The success of *The Christmas Child* led Crawfie to suggest, though partly in fun, that they would be quite capable of putting on a pantomime the following year. 'From that moment', she wrote, 'I had no peace. Margaret was after me incessantly. "Crawfie, you *did* say . ." she would begin a dozen times a week.' So keen was the young Princess, in fact, that she made her own drawings for *Aladdin*, planned all the roles, and talked about nothing but pantomime. With the King's approval, the idea was soon taken a step further when the capable and enthusiastic Hubert Tanner – who would also direct and take part in the productions – produced a script for *Cinderella*.

Even some of the twenty and more empty frames on the walls of the Waterloo Chamber that usually contained Sir Thomas Lawrence's portraits of the allied kings, statesmen and commanders who had contributed to Napoleon's defeat in 1815, added to the sense of occasion. Claude Watham, a young, part-time art student and one of the London evacuees who was staying with the Camm family at their house on the edge of Windsor Forest, was asked to produce a series of pictures portraying characters from popular children's stories. This he did while sharing a studio at Windsor Castle with Sir Gerald Kelly, later to become President of the Royal Academy, who was then at work on the State portraits of the King and Queen in their coronation robes that now hang in the Castle's Crimson Drawing Room.

Produced on rolls of wallpaper that were then pasted up by the Castle decorators, Cinderella together with Aladdin, Jack and the Beanstalk, Dick Whittington and his faithful cat, and others, were hung inside frames that normally identified portraits not, as Crawfie erroneously claimed, of 'Charles I . . . Queen Henrietta Maria, and so on . . .' but of King George IV, Pope Pius VII, the Prince of Orange, Cardinal Consalvi, the Emperors of Russia and Austria, and other eminent figures. When the war ended and the rightful owners were returned to their frames, Claude Watham's pantomime posters stayed where they were, only to be seen when portrait-cleaning or redecoration became necessary or in times of emergency, such as the Great Fire at Windsor Castle in November 1992, when the canvases were hastily removed from the path of the inferno that engulfed St George's Hall and the Grand Reception Room, immediate neighbours of the Waterloo Chamber.

In preparation for *Cinderella*, the first of the pantomimes, a stage was erected at one end of the Waterloo Chamber complete with scenery that had been specially built and painted by volunteer carpenters and decorators, while drapes of velvet and brocade were put to good use as backcloths. Costumes were hired, programmes were printed and seats were priced according to their situation: seven shillings and sixpence (37½ pence) for the best seats, five shillings (25 pence) for the second best, and one shilling (5 pence) for the less advantageous positions. Everybody was rehearsed until they knew their lines, songs and special stunts perfectly.

On the morning of each performance, however, Princess Margaret, who appeared in the leading role of Cinderella playing opposite Princess Elizabeth, who was suitably attired in powdered wig, white satin jacket and knee-breeches as 'Prince Florizel', was always to be found in bed 'pea-green' with nerves. But ten minutes before curtain up, with her make-up and costume on, the star of the show was ready for her first entrance. One highlight of each performance was the scene in which Cinderella arrived in her golden coach to attend the royal ball. At that moment, Princess Margaret who was dressed in a silver-white wig and white and silver crinoline trimmed with pink roses, appeared on stage in a Georgian sedan chair that had been specially adapted for the occasion and, according to Crawfie, 'brought the house down.'

One member of the cast also thought that Princess Margaret was 'the best in our little company. The star, I guess you would say. It had nothing to do with being who she was. Princess Elizabeth was rather stiff. She was never bossy with the other children, but she was quick to correct her sister if she did not approve of her behaviour. Princess Margaret liked doing little pranks – moving props, things like that, and she giggled a lot.'[18]

The following year, the royal ensemble staged a production of *The Sleeping Beauty*. When the roles were being cast on that occasion, Princess Margaret firmly stood her ground against taking the lead. 'I felt I had hogged the limelight quite long enough in *The Christmas Child* and in *Cinderella*,' she explained, 'besides which, I didn't think I was pretty enough [for *Sleeping Beauty*], and another girl in the company was.'[19] In 1943, the Princesses' young cousins Eddie and Alexandra of Kent were also found parts in the third pantomime, *Aladdin*, in which Princess Elizabeth appeared in the eponymous role and Princess Margaret featured as the exotic 'Princess Roxana'.

By then, the royal pantomimes had become so well known that weeks before they were staged, the Castle post office received a flood of enquiries about times of performances and availability of seats, while some extremely eager would-be members of the audience even sent blank cheques in the hope of obtaining tickets. The final pantomime in the quartet was *Old Mother Red Riding Boots*, in which some of the Grenadier Guardsmen appeared in full uniform for a finale that called for Union Flags to be unfurled to the sound of a patriotic tune called *Red, White and Blue Christmas*. It was at this point while watching one of the rehearsals that the King found himself re-arranging the scene in order to avoid the confusion of marching Guardsmen, to say nothing of waving flags, from getting in the way of other and smaller members of the cast.

Almost inevitably, not everyone who knew Princess Margaret during these years was amused by her precocity. Indeed, while one member of the Royal Household, albeit many years later, expressed the view that 'The root of Princess Margaret's trouble is that she was spoilt by her father',[20] the daughter of another courtier, who thought she had been allowed to grow up too quickly, said, 'She could be *very* tiresome. She was always late.' Recalling one occasion, she said, 'There was a dinner for one of the ambassadors, and everybody except Princess Margaret, who was then only thirteen, had assembled in the Drawing Room. Everybody waited and there was still no sign of Princess Margaret. Getting very impatient with this, Joey [Legh, Master of the Household] sent a page to fetch her. When she finally sauntered in, making no apology, the King simply chucked her under the chin and said, "I suppose you've been listening to Tommy Handley [a popular comedian] on the wireless", to which she replied airily, "Yes, I have." She really wasn't at all concerned about keeping everybody waiting.'[21]

If the pantomimes helped take the children's minds off other aspects of the war, as Crawfie maintained, it also acted as a brief diversion for the adults involved, not least the King and Queen who, despite the inevitable gulf that existed between their way of life and the infinitely tougher conditions endured by the majority of their subjects, still knew the basic human emotions of anxiety and grief.

In 1941, while serving with the Scots Guards, Queen Elizabeth's nephew John Bowes Lyon, Master of Glamis, was killed on active service, while another of her nephews, Andrew Elphinstone, who later entered the church and eventually became vicar of Worplesdon, near Guildford in Surrey, was captured and held as a prisoner-of-war. Similarly, the King's nephew, George Lascelles, elder son of the Princess Royal, was wounded while serving as a captain in the Grenadier Guards and imprisoned in Colditz. It was the death of the King's youngest brother, however, that stood out as the royal family's most serious war-time tragedy.

In the late summer of 1942, Prince George, Duke of Kent, then acting as a Group Captain in the Royal Air Force, had been detailed to carry out an inspection of RAF bases in Iceland. On 25 August, having taken the night train from London to Inverness in Scotland, he drove with the Commanding Officer No. 4 (Coastal) Operational Training Unit to Invergordon. There, after lunch, he joined the highly experienced crew of eleven officers on board Sunderland flying boat W4026 DQ-M, which had been flown from Oban the previous weekend and was now moored on the Cromarty Firth, whose surface that day, according to one observer, was as smooth as grey slate. Minutes after take-off that afternoon, the Sunderland turned north-east to follow the coastline on the first part of its flight to 'the frozen north', as Prince George put it.

Inland, no more than half an hour later, a farmer and his son who were rounding up their sheep heard the aircraft's approach but because of a dense mist known in Scotland as 'haar', could not see it. The horrific sound of an immense explosion then followed as the Sunderland – which had already cleared the 2,000 foot (610m) summit of Donald's Mount, situated at the eastern end of the Scaraben ridge, on the Duke of Portland's Caithness estate – inexplicably descended in the thick mist and hazardous terrain to an altitude of only 700 feet (200m) and ploughed into a gently sloping hillside.

As the King himself noted when he visited the crash site, '. . . the ground for 200 yds [183m] long & 100 yds [62m] wide had been scored and scorched by its trail & by flame. It hit one side of the slope, turned over in the air & slid down the other side on its back. The impact must have been terrific as the aircraft as an aircraft was unrecognizable when found.' To this day, though a special Court of Inquiry at the time blamed it on pilot error, the cause of the accident has never been satisfactorily explained.

While the King, who had received the news of his brother's death in a telephone call from Sir Archibald Sinclair, the Secretary of State for Air, had to break the news to the Queen and to his brother Harry and sister-in-law Alice, the Duke and Duchess of Gloucester, who were staying with them at Balmoral, it fell to Princess Elizabeth to tell her sister of the loss of another uncle. 'I came down to breakfast,' remembered Princess Margaret, 'to be given the news by my sister. The entire family was devastated . . . we adored him.'[22]

Though the King and his family rallied to support Georgie's thirty-six-year-old widow, Princess Marina, who had given birth to their third child, Michael, only seven weeks earlier, her misery was such that she was all but unreachable. Queen Mary, who had more in common with Prince George than with any of her other sons, found her daughter-in-law, whom she saw the day after the accident, in a pitifully desolate state, one moment sobbing uncontrollably, the next staring blankly into space, utterly motionless.

It was not until the King, with the approval of his Prime Minister, Winston Churchill, took the politically delicate step of inviting Marina's eldest sister, Olga, the exiled and effectively imprisoned Princess Paul of Yugoslavia, to come to England from Kenya, that his brother's young widow was able to begin the slow process of recovery from the blow her husband's sudden death had dealt her.*

The public image of King George VI, Queen Elizabeth and their teenaged daughters as a happy and devoted family was every bit as true in private. To frequent visitors, such as the photographer Lisa Sheridan, it was obvious 'that home was to the Royal Family the source of life itself and that there was a determination on the part of the King and Queen to maintain a simple, united family life, whatever calls there might be to duty.'[23]

---

* In March 1941, Prince Paul, Regent of Yugoslavia, yielded to pressure from Germany and her allies and signed a Tripartite Pact which, in essence, guaranteed Yugoslavia freedom from attack as long as German troops and equipment were allowed free passage through to Greece. Subsequently branded a traitor and quisling, Prince Paul and Princess Olga were exiled to Kenya as political prisoners where, subject to British jurisdiction, they were held under house arrest. Prince and Princess Paul were finally allowed to leave Kenya for South Africa where they lived until the end of the war, when they returned to Europe and established themselves in Paris.

Queen Elizabeth, of whom he 'thought the world', was the most important person in the King's life. From the earliest days of their marriage, she had given him the love that he had never known. With her support and encouragement, there grew a confidence and strength that in other circumstances, this good, yet basically shy and retiring man, might never have realized.

'With [the King]', wrote Cecil Beaton after one of his wartime photographic sessions with the royal family, 'the Queen is miraculously clever – always handing him the stage – but saving the situation as soon as the Monarch has got into difficulties.'[24] Like her mother, Princess Margaret had the same ability to save the King from himself in an awkward moment or when his notoriously short temper flared into one of his 'gnashes'.

In his adored younger daughter with her ebullient and loving personality, George VI appreciated some of his own traits: 'the same quick mind', as Sir John Wheeler-Bennett observed, coupled with 'a vivacious charm, a sparkling sense of wit, an appreciation of the ludicrous, and a brilliant gift of mimicry. She also possessed an amazing ability to play the piano by ear, passing from classical items to songs and music-hall tunes of the First World War, to modern dance music, with equal facility. She it was who could always make her father laugh – even when he was angry with her – and who, perhaps more than any other of her family, could reduce him to giggles. She it was who could entertain him by the hour with songs and tunes and drolleries. Yet both she and Princess Elizabeth could talk to him on serious subjects.'[25]

The King, as another observer was to say, 'used to look at Princess Margaret in sort of amazement that he had produced this object who found everything so easy and was a pretty little thing.'[26] An indication of the love that existed between them was always seen in the way they greeted one another. The King wouldn't just kiss Princess Margaret on both cheeks, as was customary in the royal family, but would do it twice – and then add an extra kiss for good measure.[27]

Though in character and temperament the complete opposite

of her sister, Princess Elizabeth had what Cecil Beaton called an 'easy charm', adding, 'each time one sees her, one is delighted to find how much more serene, magnetic, and at the same time meltingly sympathetic, she is than one had imagined.'[28]

In 1944, the last full year of the war, the King, who had already made visits to the British Expeditionary Force in France in 1939, to the victorious 1st and 8th Armies in North Africa, as well as the island of Malta, in June 1943, crossed the Channel to visit the Normandy beaches ten days after the D-Day landings. Sailing from Portsmouth aboard the cruiser *Arethusa* on the night of 15 June 1944 in a choppy sea and cold and gusty weather conditions, he not only wanted to visit the Allied Forces, but to hold a public investiture, decorating officers and men on the beachhead where Field Marshal Montgomery waited to meet him.

In Italy the following month, George VI undertook a strenuous eleven-day programme, from 23 July to 3 August, in which he travelled 8,000 miles by air and 1,000 miles by road, visiting British and Imperial troops as well as some of the American, French, Polish and Brazilian Forces which comprised General Alexander's composite army.

In his absence, the by now eighteen-year-old Princess Elizabeth was appointed a Counsellor of State for the first time, which meant that under the Regency Acts of 1937 and 1943, she joined her mother, and three other Counsellors of State, her uncle and aunt, the Duke of Gloucester and the Princess Royal, and their cousin Alexandra, Princess Arthur of Connaught, in temporarily acting for the King in Privy Council; the oldest form of legislative assembly still functioning as part of the machinery of government.

Appointed Colonel of the Grenadier Guards in succession to the late Duke of Connaught, not long before her sixteenth birthday, and already undertaking public engagements in her own right, Princess Elizabeth was now a young adult. The four-year difference between the two Princesses was becoming ever more noticeable. No longer dressed alike, the elder Princess was given her own suite of rooms, a move away from the nursery suite she had shared with her sister, and before long her first ladies-in-waiting, Lady Mary Strachey and the Honourable Mrs Vicary Gibbs.

In addition, she was now able to participate in royal shooting parties as more than a spectator and, more practically, was permitted to enlist in the Auxiliary Territorial Service, the ATS, as a Second Subaltern. Now in uniform, albeit unflattering and khaki, she finally achieved the rank of junior commander, commenting, 'I've never worked so hard in my life.' Over and above all these things, she was in love with Philip of Greece and he with her.

A marriage between the distant royal cousins had been mooted for at least two years, with Chips Channon, adopted Briton and inveterate collector of royalty great and small, claiming as early as 1941 that Philip 'is to be our Prince Consort, and that is why he is serving in our Navy.' More reliably, Queen Mary confided to Mabell Airlie shortly before her granddaughter's eighteenth birthday that Elizabeth and Philip had 'been in love for the past eighteen months. In fact longer, I think . . . But the King and Queen feel that she is too young to be engaged yet.'

With all the developments that were taking place in Princess Elizabeth's life and once again disqualified by age from following her sister onto the Scottish moors or into the ATS, which she confessed made her 'very cross', Princess Margaret began to feel left out and just a little resentful. 'I was born too late,' she once said angrily to Crawfie's amusement. 'She was now at a girl's most awkward age', said Miss Crawford, 'neither quite a child nor quite grown up, and she took the interlude much harder than ever her sister had done. Perhaps because Lilibet had always been far more firmly disciplined.'

Wishing she was old enough to do the things her sister was now doing, and frustrated by the restrictions that her youth as well as the schoolroom continued to impose on her gave rise to some of the earliest fictions that Princess Margaret was not only jealous of her sister, but also of her sister's more elevated position. From that point on, as the Princesses started to lead their own lives with sharply diverging interests and different circles of friends, there evolved a welter of often incomprehensible, sometimes irresponsible, but invariably highly colourful stories. Evidently disregarding the fact that Princess Margaret's personality was too strongly defined to allow her to play second fiddle to anyone – and, indeed, overlooking her personal popularity which, on a global scale earned her a following that ran into millions – one of the most persistent of media inventions was that as the 'younger daughter', then the 'younger sister', she was always 'fated to be second best'.

Although it doesn't mean there were never times when she minded the difference in status – and the privileges that were accorded to Princess Elizabeth and not to her – there is no tangible evidence to suggest that Princess Margaret was jealous of her sister either in a personal sense, or as Heiress Presumptive and subsequently as Queen. Unsupported claims to the contrary, however, generally fail to consider one important fact. That having been born into a family which, unlike any other, functioned within a rigidly structured framework of rules and protocols, both Princesses were brought up to understand the meaning and subtleties of rank, status and precedence. Put another way, they were taught to understand what the line of succession was all about, and with room for neither argument nor rancour – though there were those, notably Princess Marina, a true thoroughbred when it came to royal pedigree, who resented being ranked after the non-royal wives of her husband's elder brothers – were made aware of who took precedence over whom and why.

Princess Margaret's own response to the ill-informed claims about her feelings at growing up as the King's younger daughter, and her subsequent position as the Queen's only sister, was to say, 'I have never suffered from "second daughter-itis." But I did mind forever being cast as the "younger sister." ' [29]

After almost six years, VE Day (Victory in Europe Day) finally arrived on 8 May 1945.* At three o'clock that afternoon, Prime

---

* VJ Day (Victory in Japan Day) came with Japan's unconditional surrender three months later.

Minister Winston Churchill spoke to a war-weary but exultant nation in a wireless broadcast that was also relayed through loudspeakers that were set up in public places so that all could hear. There were loudspeakers as well as floodlights outside Buckingham Palace where men, women and children converged in their tens of thousands, calling for the King and Queen. Together with the Princesses, each of King George and Queen Elizabeth's appearances on the Palace balcony received tumultuous applause and the crowds called them back again and again.

That evening, Princess Margaret with Princess Elizabeth, dressed in her ATS uniform, and a group of friends including their uncle David Bowes Lyon, joined the throng outside in the streets. Linking arms and singing such popular songs as *Run, Rabbit, Run* and *Roll out the Barrel*, they danced and strolled, pushed and pulled their way from Whitehall to Piccadilly and, via the Ritz and Hyde Park Corner, back to Buckingham Palace where, still unrecognized, they joined the crowds still yelling for the King and the Queen.

Recalling that day on 8 May 1995, in a specially recorded television programme shown as part of the BBC's commemoration of the fiftieth anniversary of the end of the war, Princess Margaret said, 'What was very exciting was when the floodlights came on, because it was the complete antithesis to the blackout. And you can't imagine how awful the blackout had been; everything was dark and everything was gloomy.

'Suddenly, the lights came on and lit up the poor old battle-scarred Palace. My mother was wearing a white dress with a tiara . . . and it all sparkled, and there was a great roar from the crowd which was very exciting. VE Day was a wonderful sunburst of glory. I don't think I'll ever forget it as long as I live.'[30]

SEVEN

By the time she was sixteen, Princess Margaret was already a self-assured young woman. Gone were the velvet-collared coats and berets, tweed suits and frilly party dresses of childhood. Gone, too, were the hand-me-downs that had originally been made for Princess Elizabeth and which had then been passed on to do a turn for her uncomplaining sibling. In their place were now stylishly tailored coats and dresses, designer hats, silk stockings and shoes with heels for day wear, and long dresses of silk, satin or chiffon for evenings. Soon to have her own lady-in-waiting, Princess Margaret had already been granted her own coat-of-arms,[*][1] which in time would be followed by a specially-created cypher or monogram for her personal use. Taking the form of a classically-styled capital 'M' beneath a coronet composed in heraldic jargon of 'crosses patée and fleur-de-lys', it would, for

---

* Princess Margaret was first granted 'Arms' on 21 April 1944. Their form, which is identical to that of the Sovereign's or Royal Coat of Arms, save for certain heraldic differences, was later amended on 26 March 1960 when, at the Princess's request, two alterations were made. One was a change in the style of harp, or 'stringed argent', in the third (or lower left) quarter of the Royal Shield, which was changed from the plainer Celtic harp to one ornamented with a female figure or bust (reminiscent of carved figureheads on sailing ships), and much favoured by Britain's Hanoverian royalty. The second alteration was the addition of the Royal Victorian Order, otherwise GCVO, of which the Princess was appointed Dame Grand Cross in 1953, that was incorporated to encircle the diamond-shaped Shield.

example, be embossed in red on the Princess's private stationery, etched on glassware, worked into table linen, and so on.

By now, she had even started to perform official public engagements in her own right, although at the start of her career invitations were invariably approved, if not chosen for her, by her parents. As an active member of what Prince Philip is credited with calling the 'Royal Firm', Princess Margaret had made her début in July 1944 when, chaperoned by her mother, she visited the Princess Margaret Royal Free School, named in her honour, in Windsor. That afternoon, feeling 'dreadfully sick' with nerves, she made her first public speech, which she realized then and there was an aspect of her role she would never enjoy.

Not quite two years later, on 26 March 1946, Princess Margaret performed her first solo engagement when, at the invitation of the Save the Children Fund, she opened the Hopscotch Inn, a new children's play centre in Camden, North London. It was an event that was considered sufficiently newsworthy for the BBC to commission a report from Audrey Russell, one of its most respected broadcasters, who had been the Corporation's only fully-accredited female war correspondent.

'One has to remember that she was only fifteen at the time,' she recalled, 'but I was first struck by her marvellous poise. I think she was trying very hard to follow her mother's example, talking to everybody and asking questions all the time, which she did very professionally.'[2]

Earlier that month, the King had accepted a formal invitation from the Governor-General of the Union of South Africa, Gideon Van Zyl, to visit the Union the following spring. This was something South Africa's prime minister, Field Marshal Jan Smuts, a formidable adversary during the Boer War, who had since become a steadfast friend, had discussed with the King on more than one occasion during his wartime visits to London.

If, as is generally the case with visits of this kind, the underlying objectives of George VI and Queen Elizabeth's tour of South

Africa were essentially political – to strengthen Britain's post-war ties with the Dominion and, with an election due the following year, 'to save Smuts and the Crown of South Africa', as one South African historian put it[3] – it also provided the royal family, 'we four', with an opportunity to experience their first and, as it was to transpire, last official overseas tour together. For both Princesses, it would also be the first time they had been abroad.

If Princess Elizabeth, so much in love with Prince Philip, didn't relish the thought of a tour that would mean a separation of ten never-ending weeks, Princess Margaret, who still retains vivid memories of it all, not least the vast open spaces and, unlike austerity Britain, an abundance of good things to eat, was tremendously excited. At home, long before departure, the tour's sometimes tortuous route was traced on maps in the Buckingham Palace schoolroom. Cape Town, Port Elizabeth, East London, Bloemfontein, Basutoland, Natal, Swaziland, the Transvaal, Southern and Northern Rhodesia, and Bechuanaland, were to be traversed by air, road and rail, the latter on board the fourteen-carriage 'White Train' which, since it would not only be the royal family's home for much of the time, but also the King's office and operational headquarters, was designed not so much with luxury in mind as efficiency, reliability and comfort.

On 1 February 1947, the King and his family sailed from Portsmouth on board the Royal Navy's newest battleship, HMS *Vanguard*. Behind them, much to the King's concern, they left one of the most severe periods of cold weather the country had ever experienced. So cold, in fact, that only two days before their departure, Big Ben struck once then ground to a halt. By the time they neared the end of their voyage to Cape Town, during which they themselves encountered seas rough enough to confine them to their cabins with sea-sickness, weather conditions in Britain – where there were serious fuel shortages – suddenly worsened as heavy snowstorms and sub-zero temperatures plunged the country still deeper into the worst winter in living memory.

More than four million workers were made idle by power cuts, thousands of homes were without heat or light for long periods of the day, and towns and villages were isolated by the kind of 10- to 20-foot-high snow drifts that blocked the Great North Road, Britain's north-south artery, for twenty-two miles. Even the Thames at Windsor froze over which, when the thaw eventually came, led to severe flooding.

So concerned was the King by the severity of conditions at home that he seriously considered curtailing the South African tour. Having shared so much with his people throughout the war, he felt very strongly that he should be in England sharing the present crisis. Government advice argued firmly against such a course of action, however. The King's return, it was reasoned, 'would magnify unduly the extent of the difficulties'[4] and might even lead the nation to feel that an already severe situation was in danger of becoming even worse.

Aboard HMS *Vanguard* once the seas had calmed down and the skies cleared, the royal party took advantage of the sunshine and enthusiastically joined in deck games with members of the ship's company. Watched by the King in tropical kit and the Queen in a light dress and towelling turban, one particularly energetic game of 'tag', in which Princess Margaret is seen to receive a hefty shove from behind, was caught on film and shown to cinema audiences at home as part of newsreel coverage of the royal progress. There was also miniature rifle practice in which, firing at fixed targets, the King and Queen both took part, lying flat on their stomachs on pallets laid out on the deck.

Once the tour was under way, a long and strenuous schedule of audiences, opening sessions of parliament, civic welcomes, pageants, presentations, formal lunches and state dinners, wreath-layings, reviews, march-pasts, garden parties and the like, often in soaring temperatures, eventually began to take its toll on the King's nerves. Seven weeks into the tour, while driving in an open-topped car through townships of the East Rand, the heat and dust caused the King to lose his temper with the chauffeur. Blaming him for the condition of the roads and the unavoidably rough ride, the King's persistent and biting tirade meant that, despite their apparently happy smiles, none of the royal visitors was in the most relaxed of moods as they drove into Benoni.

It was there, as delighted if over-enthusiastic crowds of towns-folk pressed towards the slowly moving car that the only ugly incident of the entire tour occurred. Breaking from the crowd, a shouting Zulu sprinted purposefully towards the royal family. With something clutched in one hand, he grabbed the car door with the other. Fearing they were about to be attacked, the Queen began beating the Zulu with her parasol – 'The worst mistake I ever made,' she is said to have remarked later – until he was dragged off and knocked senseless by local police.

Only later did they discover that what the unfortunate man had in his hand, as he raced towards the car crying 'My King! My King!' was nothing more threatening than a ten-shilling note which, with her twenty-first birthday only three weeks away, he wanted to give to Princess Elizabeth as a present. Upset by the incident, the King enquired after the Zulu well-wisher; and later apologized for his own ill-tempered behaviour. 'I'm sorry about today,' he said. 'I was very tired.'

When on form, however, George VI's humour glowed. Returning from a visit to the grave of Cecil Rhodes in the Matopos Hills, for example, the King cried 'Off parade at last' and threw his hat to the ceiling. Caught by his equerry, the King then threw it on to the floor and the Queen kicked it into the dining room.

Although it did not secure victory for Field Marshal Smuts and his United Party in the general election of May 1948, the royal tour was considered a great success. Writing to Smuts on his way back to Britain, the King said the effect of the visit, 'has given me a new outlook on life after those terrible war years . . . which to me were a period of great strain . . . I have been able to relax for a bit, & I feel that I shall now be able to return to my work in London with renewed energy.'[5]

If, as the King hoped, the royal family's tour of South Africa had helped to strengthen popular feeling towards the Crown and alter the 'conception of monarchy in the eyes of some South Africans', as he put it, Britain was about to lose control of its greatest 'possession'. For 163 years, since the days of Robert Clive and the East India Company, India had been subject to British rule; and from Queen Victoria's proclamation as Empress of India on 1 January 1877, the vast sub-continent had been seen as the 'jewel' in the Imperial Crown. Now, partitioned into two separate states under proposals submitted by Dickie Mountbatten, whom the Government of Clement Attlee had appointed to the post of last Viceroy, India faced a new and independent dawn.

With independence greeted by cheers and the sound of a conch shell reverberating round the Constituent Assembly in New Delhi on 15 August 1947, Imperial rule finally came to an end and King George VI ceased to reign as Emperor of India.

Two months before, on 12 June, his daughters were among the very last recipients of the Crown of India, an Order which Queen Victoria had established at the end of her first year as Empress. Though it is one of her proudest orders, it is perhaps ironic that, unlike her sister, Princess Margaret has never been to India. 'Oh,' she is known to have said, 'they wouldn't want to see the daughter of the last Emperor.'[6]

With the formal engagement of Princess Elizabeth to the recently naturalized Philip Mountbatten on 10 July, Princess Margaret became painfully aware that with her sister's marriage, she would soon lose her closest companion. Perhaps recognizing that fact, Philip was careful not to exclude her from the boisterous pastimes and amusements such as ball games and races along Palace corridors, in which he and Princess Elizabeth indulged 'like high-spirited children.' What he wouldn't put up with from Princess Margaret, however, was any show of tardiness. 'Margaret,' said Crawfie, 'was fond of Philip in an entirely sisterly fashion, and he was very good for her. He stood no nonsense. She was then at adolescence's most tiresome stage, apt at times to be comically regal and overgracious, and Philip wasn't having any. She would dilly-dally outside the lift, keeping everyone waiting, until Philip, losing patience, would give her a good push that settled the question of precedence quite simply.'[7]

Married at Westminster Abbey on 20 November, the wedding of Princess Elizabeth and the newly-created Duke of Edinburgh was the culmination of a week of royal celebrations that included what the Princess's Private Secretary, Sir John Colville, described as 'a magnificent evening party' at Buckingham Palace. Attended by most of the crowned heads of Europe and not a few ex-royalties besides – among the guests were King Frederick and Queen Ingrid of Denmark, King Haakon VII of Norway, Queen Frederika of the Hellenes, Crown Princess Juliana of the Netherlands, the Crown Prince and Princess of Sweden, and King Peter and Queen Alexandra of Yugoslavia – it was a glittering party that one lady-in-waiting likened to a 'scene out of a fairy tale.'

During the evening, however, 'An Indian Rajah became uncontrollably drunk and assaulted the Duke of Devonshire', the King's recent South African host, Field Marshal Smuts, told a bemused but, as ever, jewel-bedecked Queen Mary, 'You are the big potato; the other Queens are all small potatoes',[8] while the King himself, enjoying one of his favourite dances, led an uproarious conga line through the State Apartments.

On the day of the wedding itself, which dawned wet, cold and windy, crowds up to eighteen-deep in places thronged the processional route to and from Westminster Abbey to cheer the bride and bridegroom. At the same time, the display of royal pageantry was described by Churchill as, 'A flash of colour on the hard road we have to travel', the like of which had not been seen since the coronation a full ten years before.

Dressed by Norman Hartnell in Botticelli-inspired ivory satin embroidered with York roses, stars, ears of wheat and orange blossom worked in pearl and crystal, Princess Elizabeth drove to her wedding in the Irish State Coach, the King in the uniform of an Admiral of the Fleet by her side. At the Abbey, they were met by two kilted pageboys, the Princes William of Gloucester and Michael of Kent, and the Princess's eight bridesmaids, each dressed in star-spangled ivory tulle. Chief among them was Princess Margaret, then her cousins Alexandra of Kent, Margaret Elphinstone and Diana Bowes Lyon, and Philip's cousin Pamela Mountbatten. 'I hope', wrote Crawfie, 'that people were not too taken up with the bride . . . to notice her younger sister. She moved with extraordinary dignity and grace . . . More than once the King and Queen exchanged a smile and a reassuring glance.'

After the Edinburghs, as Princess Elizabeth and her new husband were known, had moved into the newly-refurbished Clarence House – a late seventeenth century addition to St James's Palace, originally built by Henry VIII for Anne Boleyn in the mid-1530s – Princess Margaret became the only Princess at Buckingham Palace.

Yet, while hers was a formal and in many ways lonely life, massively circumscribed by conventions and disciplines that had all but disappeared from English life elsewhere, the Princess was soon gathering around her a circle of friends much wider and increasingly more diverse than almost any other member of her family. The one exception was her highly cultured aunt Marina, Duchess of Kent, whose well established sense of style, eclectic company of friends and love of the artistic, would soon be reflected in Princess Margaret's own lifestyle.

One of the Duchess of Kent's intimates was the American actor Danny Kaye who, instead of booking into an hotel whenever he was in England, invariably stayed with Marina at Coppins, the former Buckinghamshire farmhouse that her late husband had inherited from his aunt Princess Victoria. Other members of the Duchess's and, for that matter, the Mountbatten's, circle whom Princess Margaret would also befriend, were Douglas Fairbanks and the even more celebrated Noël Coward.

It was Coward, in fact, who paid the Princess an early

compliment about her musical abilities that she has never forgotten. After a private dinner party at the American Embassy in November 1949, he noted, 'Princess Margaret obliged with songs at the piano. Surprisingly good. She has an impeccable ear, her piano playing is simple but has perfect rhythm, and her method of singing is really very funny.'[9]

There were occasions, though, when Princess Margaret's choice of songs was not always seen as appropriate. When a Scottish minister was invited to tea with the King and Queen, the Princess was asked to sing. Sitting down at the piano she plunged straight into the rather saucy *I'm Jist a girl who cain't say No*, from the American musical *Oklahoma!* Deliberately ignoring her mother's discreet attempts to stop her, the King suddenly roared with laughter, while the minister, having recovered from an initial moment of shock, was also said to have enjoyed the performance. Show tunes, as Noël Coward discovered, were invariably a popular feature of the Princess's repertoire, even arousing the interest of her grandmother. Sir John Colville recalled, 'Queen Mary took Lord Cambridge, Lady Helena Gibbs and me to see *Annie Get Your Gun*. H.M. revelled in it . . . After the song "I'm an Indian too, a Sioux", she turned to me and asked, "Is *that* one of the songs Margaret sings?" I said it was, to which she remarked, "What a pity!" I thought I had said the wrong thing and done Princess Margaret ill-service, but a minute or two later her grandmother reverted to the subject and said, "What a pity I have never heard her!" '[10]

In the opinion of one of her friends, Princess Margaret missed a golden opportunity to make more than she did out of her 'particularly good theatrical talents.' Rather in the manner of Marina of Kent's maternal grandmother, the Grand Duchess Marie Pavlovna, doyenne of Russian society in the closing decades of Imperial Romanov rule, she 'could have used her musical talents to have attracted her own 'Court' of actors, singers and dancers around her. Although she didn't do so, she was in an ideal position. Who would have refused an invitation from Princess Margaret?'[11]

In her late teens and very early twenties, the Princess's friends were predictably aristocratic and well-to-do, drawn from the families she had always known. Among them were two of the 'gilded young men', as one of her friends puts it, who along with David, Lord Ogilvy, later 13th Earl of Airlie, were regarded as potential suitors. As Marquess of Blandford, John Spencer-Churchill, known as 'Sunny', was heir to the 10th Duke of Marlborough, whose family seat, Blenheim Palace at Woodstock in Oxfordshire, built by Vanbrugh for the 1st Duke in the early eighteenth century, was not only one of the largest mansions in England, but also one of the richest.

The Duchess of Gloucester's nephew, Walter Montagu Douglas Scott, Earl of Dalkeith, who was known as 'Johnny', (John was the last of his three forenames), was heir to two dukedoms, Buccleuch (created in 1663) and Queensberry (created twenty-one years later in 1684), of which he would become the 9th and the 11th Duke, respectively. He also stood to inherit half-a-million acres and three huge family estates, including Drumlanrig Castle in Dumfriesshire. It was Johnny's father, the 8th Duke of Buccleuch, who as Lord Dalkeith almost thirty years earlier, had been in love with Princess Mary (and she so deeply with him), until an outraged Queen Mary shattered their dreams and married her daughter off to Viscount Lascelles.

Then there was Billy Wallace, grandson of the distinguished architect Sir Edwin Lutyens, and the only surviving son of Captain Euan Wallace, who had been Neville Chamberlain's Minister of Transport. Quick-witted, tall, dark and, like Sunny Blandford, all but chinless, Billy was a shambling Wodehousian figure, with a distinctive way of speaking and an entertaining personality. Renowned for the excellence of his parties, he was also well read and had a good – even shrewd – eye for pictures, collecting a number of paintings by the British impressionists Sickert and Matthew Smith long before they became fashionably collectable. Though plagued by ill health – kidney problems meant he underwent so many operations as a young man that he no longer had a navel – Billy, who was to die of cancer at the age of forty-nine, did what he was physically able to in the pursuit of a career as an executive with Silver City Airlines.

The Honourable Colin Tennant – then heir to Lord Glenconner – who, to his evident amusement, was 'Second Lieutenant Tennant' of the Irish Guards, when he first met Princess Margaret in 1947, became a life-long if somewhat eccentric friend; as did Mark Bonham-Carter, the future Liberal Member of Parliament for Torrington, and Simon Phipps, a cousin of the actress and comedienne Joyce Grenfell. After Cambridge, where he revealed a flair for writing revue sketches, Phipps served with the Coldstream Guards, in which he was promoted to the rank of major and was awarded the Military Cross. Later, the man with whom Princess Margaret loved to debate theology, entered the church, was ordained, became a curate in Huddersfield and was eventually appointed Bishop of Lincoln.

Peter Ward, second son of the Earl and Countess of Dudley, Tom Egerton, Henry, Lord Porchester, grandson of the famous 5th Earl of Carnarvon (discoverer with Howard Carter of the tomb of the young Pharaoh Tutankhamun), and the Earl of Minto's son Dominic Elliot, a one-time boyfriend who, if rumour is to be believed, the Princess might have married had it not been for religious differences, were also members of the inner circle. 'Dommie' Elliot, who always regarded the Princess as his 'best friend', not only commended her particular gift for loyalty in friendship, but also corroborated what others have said about her capacity for understanding. 'You really can talk to her about *anything* on a one-to-one basis,' he said. Similarly, another friend was of the view that because she, herself, was 'very open', the Princess, liked 'people to be up-front with her', adding, 'one of the reasons she is such a good friend is because she wants to feel needed.'[12]

Jamie and Robin McEwen, the eldest of what has been called a 'Renaissance family' of six sons and one daughter, saw a lot of Princess Margaret throughout the late 1940s and '50s at Marchmont, their family house in Berwickshire, which Colin

Campbell described as 'a kind of Camelot.' There she spent some of her happiest and most carefree days at house parties that might or might not have included other friends such as Johnny Dalkeith, David Ogilvy, and Simon Phipps. The Princess followed the local hunt, albeit on foot – she has never ridden to hounds – showed her flair for dancing Scottish reels at the Berwickshire Hunt Balls, joined the family on leisurely picnics, always one of her most enjoyed activities (even if the royal family's own idea of a picnic still meant sitting on a chair at a table) and, even more simply, relaxing at the water's edge whenever Robin went fishing.

Of an evening, the Princess and the McEwens – Jamie and Robin, their younger siblings Rory and Alex (who would later earn fame as a singing and guitar-playing duo on popular television shows), David, John-Sebastian, and Kisty (later Lady Hesketh), would play the sort of parlour games such as charades or sardines that were enjoyed in all the big houses, or gather round the piano for musical soirées, or settle down at the card table for a game of canasta or gin rummy.

Though Princess Margaret would always prefer male company – in years to come that occasionally meant the deliberate exclusion of wives, not all of whom she liked, and vice-versa – her circle of friends included Johnny Dalkeith's sister, Lady Caroline Montagu Douglas Scott, who later married the politician Ian Gilmour and whom the Princess described as a 'VBF' – 'Very Best Friend', Sunny Blandford's sister Rosie, otherwise Lady Rosemary Spencer-Churchill (now Muir), Marigold Bridgeman, Laura and Kate Smith, daughters of Viscount Hambleden, and Lady Caroline Thynne.

Once the attention of media and public alike, at home, across Europe, and in the United States, had started to focus on Princess Margaret in a way – though today's younger generations may not be aware of the fact – that far exceeded anything Diana, Princess of Wales, was to experience thirty years later, the press began to scrutinize the lifestyle and background of all her friends, particularly her male friends, to whom they looked in the hope of discovering a burgeoning romance. Not surprisingly, the American press put great emphasis on any connection with their part of the world, and enjoyed the fact that Sunny Blandford's paternal grandmother was Consuelo Vanderbilt, that Henry Porchester's mother was a Wendell of New York and his step-mother the actress Tilly Losch; and that Billy Wallace's stepfather was the American writer and publisher, Herbert Agar.

Yet, though he may never have realized it, the responsibility for introducing a direct Transatlantic influence into the heart of Princess Margaret's circle of friends lay with the American President Harry Truman, when he appointed Lewis W. Douglas of Arizona, a former adviser to President Roosevelt and one-time Vice-Chancellor of McGill University, to succeed Averell Harriman as United States Ambassador to the Court of St James's.

When they arrived in London, Lewis Douglas and his wife Peggy – known respectively as 'Winkie' and 'Blinkie'; he because he wore a patch after losing an eye in a fishing accident, she because she constantly squinted when she spoke[13] – were accompanied by their twenty-one-year-old daughter, Sharman. Tall, blonde and vivacious, with a slight Southern drawl to her voice, 'Sass' as she was known to her friends, first met Princess Margaret, who was two years younger, at an official Embassy reception. They became the best of friends soon after.

Almost from the moment of their arrival, the Douglas' gregarious daughter gathered around her a circle of young friends who could meet informally and have fun away from the glare of media attention at the ambassadorial residence, Winfield House in Regent's Park. Before long, Sharman's lively gatherings became a regular feature in Princess Margaret's social diary, including one widely reported dinner party which, to the vicarious delight of the tabloid press, went on until four o'clock the next morning and found the Princess dancing the samba, foxtrot and Charleston with the Lords Blandford, Ogilvy and Westmorland.

From get-togethers such as this – at least so far as the popular press was concerned – emerged the so-called 'Margaret Set', conjuring up images of a pack of well-heeled 'ravers' sashaying their way across town, with the King's irrepressibly wild daughter in the lead.

'Most of the people who became my friends – and they generally had other and much closer friends of their own,' said the Princess, 'were Sharman's friends first. So, if anything, it was *her* set, not mine. There never was a "Margaret Set." '[14]

In support, Dominic Elliot said the Princess and her friends, including those she met through Sass Douglas, 'Never went round together as a "gang"; so there never was a "set" in that sense. They didn't flock round Princess Margaret, because everyone, including the Princess, did their own thing and only occasionally came together en masse when there was a big party or something of the kind.'[15]

Into this circle during the early 1950s, somewhat later than everyone else, came Judy Montagu. Large and plain, lacking in vanity, but with a personality that was as immense as her generosity, Judy – who was the daughter of Venetia Stanley, H.H. Asquith's confidante, by her husband Edwin Montagu, and granddaughter of Lord Swaythling, a prominent merchant banker – was a great friend of both Billy Wallace and Colin Tennant, through whom she met and became close friends with Princess Margaret.

Like Billy, Judy was also to die, from a sudden heart-attack, at the age of only forty-nine. Afterwards, the Princess, together with Colin Tennant, the Marchioness of Salisbury, Lady Lambton and others among her twelve godparents, helped to look after Anna, Judy's daughter by her marriage to the Rome-based, American publisher, Milton Gendel.[16]

'During the post-war years,' said Margaret Rhodes, 'there were a lot of parties, and Princess Margaret was the star in the middle; a planet round which everyone revolved. She simply sparkled.'[17]

In fact, no party or high society event from a wedding to a charity ball, was ever considered complete without the Princess being there or at least putting in an appearance. From the time of her eighteenth birthday, when the Chaplain at Crathie Church on the Balmoral estate was moved to say, 'And let us pray . . . for Princess Margaret, that God may bless and prosper her in such purposes as she has in her heart',[18] the world – and the world's press – were in love with her. It was quite as simple as that. Never before had there been a Princess like her. Though she had a sophistication and charisma far in advance of her years, she was young, sensual and stunningly beautiful. With her vivid blue eyes – 'the only thing about me worth looking at', she once said – an archetypal English complexion 'as smooth as a peach,' and lips that were described as both 'generous' and 'sensitive,' she was acknowledged to be one of the greatest beauties of her generation. In addition, she was curvaceous, extremely proud of her eighteen-inch waist (though not so proud of her nose, which she thought was a little too long, or her hands, which she thought a little too short), unpredictable, irrepressible and coquettish.

It was she who brought sex appeal into a royal family that, for all its qualities, was decidedly unsexy. Without even realizing it, she had already embarked on a path which, paradoxically, would do much to change royal attitudes and bring the monarchical ideal into the modern world. To her friends, though they might still have to bow and curtsy and call her 'Ma'am', she was simply, 'the life and soul of the party.'

During the late '40s and throughout the 1950s, years that might best be described as the defining decade of Princess Margaret's life, scarcely a day passed without her photograph making the front page of newspapers and magazines, if for no other reason than whatever she did appealed to the public and was good for sales. At nineteen, she caused a sensation when, though using a three-inch cigarette holder, she first smoked in public at a charity Hallowe'en Ball at the Dorchester Hotel.

In what was to become something of a familiar refrain some years into the future, she set newspaper editors snarling at one another over issues of good taste when a long-range photograph of the nineteen-year-old, swim-suited Princess sun-bathing on a private Italian beach filled the world's press. And she made headlines that read *Princess Margaret High-Kicks It!* when, at a ball attended by 300 guests given by Lewis Douglas at the American Embassy, she, Jennifer Bevan, her first lady-in-waiting, Sharman Douglas and three other girl friends, danced the *Can-Can* dressed in authentic frilly petticoats, black fishnets and feathered bonnets.

Preparing to photograph her at Buckingham Palace at around this time, Cecil Beaton noted, 'Princess Margaret is great news value. She is grown-up – an independent character showing more signs of interest in unconventional life than any member of the royal family since Edward Prince of Wales. She likes dressing up, flirtations, going to night clubs until all hours. Her "press" is rather scandalous. The American papers most anxious for any snippets they can get of her . . .'[19]

It was this, perhaps, that led Tory MP and famous diarist, Chips Channon, to observe, 'Already she is a public character and I wonder what will happen to her? There is already a Marie Antoinette aroma about her.'

'I wonder what he meant by that?' the Princess once asked.[20] Who can say? Whatever he meant and whatever it was that prompted Channon's comment is forever open to conjecture. Did he foresee a tragic future for the Princess, or simply fancy that he heard an echo of the young French Queen's unhappy refrain, 'I am terrified of being bored'?[21]

Boredom at that time was never going to be an issue in Princess Margaret's life. She was too popular, too busy and having too much fun. Following an evening engagement or after dinner at a fashionable restaurant such as the Bagatelle the Princess, escorted by Dommie Elliot, Sunny Blandford, Johnny Dalkeith, Colin Tennant, and perhaps two or three other friends, would dance the night – and the early hours of the next morning – away at London's most exclusive night clubs, Les Ambassadeurs, the Milroy in Park Lane and the 400 in Leicester Square.

With swing the popular dance mood of the time, the Princess, who Lady Mary Clayton says has 'perfect rhythm' as a dancer,[22] 'swung' with the best of them as the Paul Adams Band played tunes such as *My Very Good Friend the Milkman* and *Good Morning, Good Morning*. It was, said one of the Princess's friends 'very Fred Astaire and Ginger Rogers, because that is what the music loaned itself to.'

Even Frank Sinatra, who soon became a friend, paid his own compliment to the Princess in the 'hip' American jargon of the time, when he said, 'Princess Margaret is just as hep wide-awake as any American girl, maybe more so. She is up on all the latest records and movies, and has a lot of wit and charm too . . . She is the best Ambassador England ever had.'[23]

Leaving the nightclubs of Mayfair and the West End in the small hours of the morning meant that dawn was often reflected in the rear view mirror by the time Princess Margaret and an escort or two returned to Buckingham Palace, frequently slipping through the tall black gates of the tradesmen's entrance on Buckingham Palace Road. It was all fuel for the headline writers and gossip columnists who, in those drab post-war years, loved nothing better than to regale their readers with stories of the Princess's colourful escapades.

Princess Margaret's Week of Late Nights, was one banner headline the London *Sunday Pictorial* splashed across its front page after she had attended a number of parties in the space of a week. For Crawfie, who was still part of the Royal Household despite the fact that Princess Margaret no longer had any need for a governess fussing over her, too much partying and far too many late nights was sufficient excuse for candour.

'Margaret,' Crawfie wrote, 'was all over the place . . . She had a wonderful time, but I was very worried about her. I spoke to the Queen quite openly. "I can do nothing with her. She is tired out, and absolutely exhausted with all these late nights." The Queen replied, "We are only young once, Crawfie. We want her to have a good time. With Lilibet gone, it is lonely for her here." '

Then, as if to confirm the view that the King and Queen had

spoilt and indulged their younger daughter to the extent that even they were anxious to avoid upsetting her, Crawfie went on to say that while realizing 'all this gaiety was not entirely desirable', neither the King nor the Queen could 'bring themselves to cross her . . .' Finally, however, 'an arrangement was come to, by which [Princess Margaret] spent one or two nights of every week quietly at home.'

If this meant that Fleet Street's posse of cameramen, as they were called, could also take a night off from 'door-stopping' the Princess at theatres, restaurants, night clubs, private parties and the rest, attention in other directions remained as relentless as ever.

The Princess's role as a leader of fashion was a source of never-ending fascination, as much to readers of up-market fashion journals as to those of the women's weeklies. While shades of lipstick, perfumes, (even cocktails), were named after her, many of her coats and dresses, hats, handbags and shoes, were copied by high street retailers and bought by untold numbers of young women to whom the Princess was a glamorous and inspirational role model.

For Princess Margaret herself, always interested in her appearance, perfectly groomed and impeccably dressed by Norman Hartnell, Christian Dior, Victor Steibel and other celebrated couturiers, the idea that she was ever a leader of fashion – even though the New York Dress Institute listed her among the fourteen best-dressed women in the world – is very firmly dismissed.

Adamant that she was neither muse nor pioneer, the Princess said 'I was never a trend-setter. That was only what the fashion correspondents said. I *followed* fashion. You had to. Otherwise what would I have looked like?'[24]

In another, altogether more official capacity, Princess Margaret was expected to be more than purely decorative; and at a time when the royal family consisted of relatively few working members, hers was to be a vital role in the life and function of the monarchy during the second and more progressive half of the twentieth century.

Even at seventeen – proving Lady Mary Clayton's point that although, 'delightful, vivacious and carefree in private, she would become totally absorbed and professional in her official work'[25] – Princess Margaret made a favourable impression on a number of Foreign Ministers who were entertained by the King at Buckingham Palace. Among them was the Soviet Union's hard-liner Andrei Vyshinski. Sir John Colville recalled, 'Princess Margaret engaged Vyshinski in a twenty minutes' argument which much impressed him. He said to me that if only she had not been a Princess she would assuredly have made a most formidable advocate.'[26]

In September the following year, little more than a fortnight after her eighteenth birthday, Princess Margaret undertook the first important mission of her royal career. To her delight, the King had asked her to represent him in Amsterdam at the inauguration of Crown Princess Juliana as Queen of the Netherlands. The daughter of his wartime guest Queen Wilhelmina, Juliana was to ascend the throne of the House of Orange-Nassau on 4 September when her mother, who had become Queen fifty-eight years earlier at the age of ten, formally abdicated. The new Queen's ceremonial installation, as opposed to coronation, a ritual other European monarchies do not observe, was to take place on 6 September.

Travelling to Amsterdam with her great-aunt Princess Alice, Countess of Athlone, a first cousin of Queen Wilhelmina, her husband 'Alge', Queen Mary's brother, and the Duke of Beaufort, the King's Master of the Horse, Princess Margaret was also accompanied on her four-day visit by another member of the Royal Household, her father's equerry, Group Captain Peter Townsend.

A thirty-four-year-old fighter pilot, tall, slim, with wavy brown hair, finely-drawn features and blue-grey eyes, who had once been likened to 'a shy Gregory Peck', Peter Wooldridge Townsend, a Battle of Britain hero decorated with the DSO, DFC and Bar, had been appointed by the King to his personal staff in March 1944 at the recommendation of Air Chief Marshal Sir Charles Portal, Chief of the Air Staff.

Succeeding Wing Commander Pelly Fry who, at the conclusion of his three month period of service as equerry to the King, had returned to his Company, Townsend became the second (and, as it transpired, last) RAF officer George VI would appoint as part of a new system he introduced to honour officers who had distinguished themselves during the war.

Born in Rangoon, on 22 November 1914, the fifth of Lieutenant-Colonel Edward Copleston Townsend and his wife Gladys's seven children*, Peter had been brought back from Burma, where his father, an Indian Army officer, was currently serving with the Burma Commission, at the age of five months. Educated at Haileybury, formerly known as the East India College, Townsend later chose to enlist in the Royal Air Force because of a burning ambition to fly.

When war came, Townsend was to be found commanding Hurricanes of B Flight, part of the famous No. 43 Fighter Squadron with which, in February 1940, he shot down the first German bomber, a 250-mile-an-hour Heinkel, to be brought down on British soil since the First World War. In July of that year, by which time he had been given command of 85 Squadron, based first at Debden in Essex and then in Croydon, the words of his first citation described how, 'while leading the section of a squadron to protect a convoy, [Townsend] intercepted about 20 or 30 enemy aircraft, destroying one and severely damaging two others. The enemy formation was forced to withdraw. Under his command the squadron has destroyed eight enemy aircraft, while protecting convoys against sporadic attacks.'

* Peter Townsend's brothers and sisters were: Audrey, who won a scholarship to Oxford and married Commander C.J.O. Malcolm, RN; Michael, who became a Rear Admiral in the Royal Navy, distinguished himself as a destroyer commander and was awarded the DSO, DSC and Bar as well as the OBE; Philip, who became a Brigadier in the Gurkha Rifles, was twice wounded in the war and won the Distinguished Service Order when fighting bandits in Malaya; Juliet, who married Deryck Flint, a partner in a London firm of chartered accountants; Stephanie, who married Arthur Gaitskell, brother of Hugh Gaitskell, leader of the Labour Party; and Francis, who also enlisted in the RAF. After the war he went to Oxford and then into the Colonial Service. In 1956 he was District Commissioner of the Masai when, at her request, he was introduced to Princess Margaret during her visit to East Africa.

The following month, according to his second citation, Townsend's 'squadron attacked some 250 enemy aircraft in the Thames Estuary. He himself shot down three enemy aircraft; the squadron as a whole destroyed at least ten and damaged many others. The success achieved has been due to Squadron Leader Townsend's unflagging zeal and leadership.'[27]

Some months later, in what was almost a fatal encounter, the detection at 8,000-feet of a formation of Me. 110 fighter bombers with an escort of Me. 109s, led to 85 Squadron being scrambled to intercept the attack. 'We were having lunch', Townsend recalled, 'and those so-and-so Germans came and interrupted us. It was the most basic bad manners, and so we just had to go up and chase them.'[28]

In the ensuing dog-fight, he hit two of the Me. 109s, while a third passed so close below him that he could clearly see the pilot at the controls. As Townsend fired, the bullets from an Me. 110 that he saw out of the corner of his eye struck his Hurricane, tearing open the centre fuel tank and sending the nose cap of a cannon-shell smashing into his left foot. Soaked in petrol and blood, Townsend baled out, landing in a wood near Hawkhurst in Kent, from where he was recovered, taken first to the local cottage hospital and then to Croydon General Hospital. There, on the day the *London Gazette* announced that he had been awarded a bar to his Distinguished Flying Cross, the big toe of his injured left foot was amputated.

Three weeks later, walking with the aid of a stick and his foot still bandaged, Townsend was again at the controls of a Hurricane, not only flying operations every night, but as the squadron diary revealed, 'to the amazement of onlookers', carrying out 'aerobatics'. On yet another occasion, when November fog shrouded the air base and visibility was nil, Townsend crash-landed. Although he was slightly injured and his aircraft badly damaged, he refused to rest and was flying again the following night.

For twenty consecutive months of day and night operations, during which he flew some 300 missions, Peter Townsend who, according to his biographer Norman Barrymaine, 'hated what he did in the war, but did it because he knew he had to,' faced his obligations with relentless courage. By early 1941, however, when 85 Squadron moved to Hunsdon in Hertfordshire, exhaustion gave way to nervous collapse and Townsend was grounded. It was during his enforced period of rest that he met Rosemary Pawle, the attractive dark-haired daughter of Brigadier and Mrs Hanbury Pawle, who lived in a neighbouring village.

That July, only two months after their first meeting, Townsend and Rosemary were married in the thirteenth century church at Much Hadham, where a Guard-of-Honour formed by men of 85 Squadron flanked the church door as bride and bridegroom left after the ceremony. When their first son Giles was born nine months later, his father was to say, 'I had been living in an environment of death and, with my own hands, destroying life. I now found, before my eyes, a life that I had actually created. It was a welcome compensation, if only a symbolic one, for the lives I had taken.'

By the time the Townsends' second son Hugo George – named in honour of the King, who stood as godfather – was born in February 1945, Peter had been equerry to George VI for almost a year. Although he would ultimately remain in royal service for nearly ten years, it was already far longer than the three-month tenure intended for temporary post-holders under the scheme the King had recently introduced.

It was beyond all doubt a mark of royal esteem, even affection, that Peter Townsend – 'brave, good-looking, full of charm and very efficient,' as he was described by the daughter of one senior member of the Royal Household[29] – became a permanent member of His Majesty's personal staff; not least because his middle-class background and middle-class education, though backbone of Empire and all that, was not socially or academically the stratum from which courtiers were traditionally drawn. But then, both men had hit it off from the moment Townsend went to Buckingham Palace for his very first audience with the King.

'The King did not try, or even need, to put me at my ease', Townsend later wrote. 'The humanity of the man and his striking simplicity came across warmly, unmistakably . . . sometimes he hesitated in his speech, and then I felt drawn towards him, to help him keep up the flow of words. I knew myself the agonies of a stammerer.'

Becoming ever more indispensable, the King put Adelaide Cottage in the Home Park at Windsor at the disposal of Peter Townsend, so that he could be close at hand. Together with her sister, Princess Margaret, who was then little more than fifteen, made the first of many visits following Hugo's christening in St George's Chapel on 3 November 1945. Thereafter, invariably in the company of the Queen or Princess Elizabeth, she would look in at Adelaide Cottage for tea or to while away an hour or two in the garden with Peter and Rosemary and their two young sons. On one occasion, Giles, the elder boy, stood behind a rhododendron bush pulling faces at Princess Margaret, until to his astonishment, she stuck her tongue out at him.

Riding together in the Home or Great Parks with both the Princesses before the elder sister married, and with Princess Margaret afterwards, was more pleasure than duty for Townsend, who was a good horseman and enjoyed risking his neck as much racing a horse as an aircraft, which he also did competing several times in the famous King's Cup Race. Not everyone thought highly of his dropping everything when the telephone rang to go out riding with Princess Margaret, however, particularly when it meant leaving a birthday party that was being given for one of his sons. 'He was not on duty. And he went,' said one of the adult guests. 'He was a double crosser . . .'[30]

By then, however, the Townsend marriage, based on a passing attraction and hastily entered into, as so many wartime marriages were, was floundering. When not on duty, which was soon most of the time, Peter grew bored being at home and briefly filled his free time working in the City as an underwriter for Lloyds. Rosemary, who was no less bored with spending her days at Adelaide Cottage with her children and the servants, complained that, 'Peter spends more time at his work than in his home.'

The result was that while he 'fell in love with the royal family', as one Courtier put it, she, socially ambitious and 'tiresomely flirtatious', began an affair with an attractive baronet and Guards officer who walked away from the relationship as soon as he heard tell that Rosemary was talking about marriage.

'The first intimation that all was far from well with Peter and Rosemary', said one friend, 'was when Peter asked, "How do you think a divorce affects children?" '[31] To this point, close though he was to the royal family, there had been little sign or suggestion of the mutual attraction that would develop between Townsend and Princess Margaret, though by the time the eighteen-year-old Princess and the thirty-four-year-old Group Captain visited Amsterdam in September 1948, there were those at Court who had started to notice a certain chemistry at work as 'They made eyes at one another, even on the most official of occasions.'[32]

It was at the celebrations marking Queen Juliana's accession to the Dutch throne that the first stories of a romance between Princess Margaret and her father's equerry began to appear in the foreign press. After the Dutch Queen herself, the King of England's daughter was the cynosure of all eyes. At the installation ceremony, looking 'too sweet, charming and shy, and lovely to look upon', as her great-aunt Alice described her in her floor length pink dress, ostrich-feather-trimmed hat and fur cape, she, rather than any of the other senior European royalties present, was invited to inspect the Guard of Honour drawn up in front of the royal palace, while Townsend looked on.

During the ceremony itself, it was noticed that she looked round – 'like a child lost among so many grown ups', as Norman Barrymaine put it – for Townsend's reassuring smile, while at the celebratory ball that evening, she was said to have been 'noticeably radiant' when dancing with the Group Captain. In addition, though such a public display of familiarity was not, it must be said, very likely, there were also claims, emanating from who knows where, that the Princess 'leaned against' Peter and 'took his arm' while touring the Rijksmuseum the following day. For the moment, whatever passed between them was innocent enough; nothing more, as Townsend's biographer described it, than an 'easy, quite unselfconscious relationship based on liking, trust, shared tastes and interests, and admiration.'[33]

EIGHT

Despite the success of Princess Margaret's visit to the Netherlands, the public and private celebration of the King and Queen's Silver Wedding anniversary and news that Princess Elizabeth was expecting her first baby at the end of the year, an ever-deepening shadow was cast over the royal family during 1948, caused by concern for the King's health.

Physically and mentally the war years had exhausted him. He had been, said the historian Robert Rhodes James, 'one of the best informed people in the country. Churchill saw to that. He was one of six people who knew about the atomic bomb programme and he had access to virtually all top secrets.'[1] For a man who could never stop worrying, being party to highly classified and often extremely disturbing intelligence put the King under an almost intolerable strain. As a consequence, too many late or sleepless nights, too many cigarettes and too many anxiously gulped decanters of whiskey at dinner, all conspired to undermine his health. Even the tour of South Africa, which it had been hoped might restore the King, imposed its own strain; the tour had been too long and the schedule much too demanding. By the time it was over, he had lost 17 pounds in weight.

From early January 1948, though he kept it to himself, King George VI had been suffering from cramp in both legs which, if he had but realized it, was an early indication of Buerger's disease or arteriosclerosis, hardening of the arteries. Caused by smoking, the condition restricted the flow of blood to his legs and feet.

By the time the royal family left for their annual holiday at Balmoral in August, the King was in discomfort most of the time. When he found that negotiating even the smallest of slopes caused him severe pain, he complained to Peter Townsend, 'What's the matter with my blasted legs? They won't work properly.' By early October, the King's left foot was numb all day and pain at night prevented him from sleeping. Presently, to the alarm of Sir Maurice Cassidy, his general medical adviser, the problem had switched to his right foot. Recognizing the serious nature of the King's condition, Sir Maurice, in consultation with Sir Morton Smart and Sir Thomas Dunhill, respectively Manipulative Surgeon and Serjeant-Surgeon to the King, called in Professor James Learmouth, one of the country's foremost authorities on vascular complaints. When he saw the King on 12 November, his diagnosis was that the fifty-three-year-old Sovereign's condition was one of early arteriosclerosis, giving rise to the threat of gangrene and the fear that his right leg might have to be amputated.

Though major spinal surgery proved unavoidable – Professor Learmouth was to perform a successful right lumbar sympathectomy on 12 March the following year – the dramatic possibility of amputation at least receded once the King finally, if reluctantly, agreed to a strict regime of bed rest and careful treatment designed to improve his circulation. As an indication of just how exhausted her father was at this time, Princess Margaret said, 'When Papa decided he could no longer struggle to keep going, he went to sleep for two days.'

In the meantime, despite the King's own suggestion that a modified itinerary might be considered, rather than disappoint all those who had worked so hard and made such plans, his doctors were emphatic that the tour of Australia and New Zealand which he, the Queen and Princess Margaret were to have undertaken in the spring of 1949, should be cancelled.

'Though His Majesty's general health, including the condition of his heart, gives no reason for concern', said the cautiously worded statement announcing the cancellation of the tour, 'there is no doubt that the strain of the last twelve years [since his accession to the throne] has appreciably affected his resistance to physical fatigue.'

The seriousness of the King's state of health which, for the rest of his short life would always be precariously balanced, had at his insistence, been kept from his elder daughter. Only two days after Professor Learmouth's first visit to Buckingham Palace, Princess Elizabeth gave birth to her first child and eldest son, Charles, shortly after nine o'clock on the evening of Sunday, 14 November.

As the crowds that had gathered outside Buckingham Palace cheered practically anything that moved, including the arrival of Queen Mary, eager for a glimpse of her first great-grandson, Princess Margaret, who had been given the news during an official visit to Sheffield, was to be found dancing round a bonfire lit in celebration in the grounds of Sandbeck, the home of her host Lord Scarborough, joking that from now on she would no doubt be known as 'Charlie's Aunt.'*

Later that month, Jennifer Bevan arrived at Buckingham Palace to take up her duties as Princess Margaret's first lady-in-waiting. The elder daughter of Colonel John and Lady Barbara Bevan, and granddaughter of the 5th Earl of Lucan, who had been ADC to King George V in the 1920s, Jenny had already experienced something closely related to Court life. Having been evacuated to Boston in the United States during the early 1940s, she subsequently spent two years in Ottawa acting as lady-in-waiting to her aunt Margaret, Countess Alexander of Tunis, when Earl Alexander was Governor-General of Canada.

Now, from the end of 1948, until shortly before she married Captain (afterwards Sir) John Lowther, in February 1952, Jenny was companion, friend and right hand to Princess Margaret;

* A reference to the title of the ever-popular Victorian comedy *Charley's Aunt.*

responsible for keeping her engagement diary up to date, dealing with correspondence, answering press enquiries and accompanying – in Court terms, 'attending' – the Princess, on both public and private engagements.

One summer weekend – captioned *Operation Sunshine* in Jenny's photograph album – Princess Margaret accepted the Bevans' invitation to stay at their house in Midhurst, Sussex. Also there as friends of Jenny's parents were the comic actress Joyce Grenfell and her husband Reggie. Celebrated as a mimic and satirist of contemporary manners, especially of middle-class wives, daughters and teachers, (her famous monolgue, *George, Don't Do That* is a classic of its kind), Mrs Grenfell and Princess Margaret entertained their hosts and fellow guests with amusing characterizations, complete with appropriate accents and facial expressions. Years later, the Princess was to say that as mimics, she and Joyce Grenfell were agreed that they 'shared a talent' not for impersonating particular individuals, but 'for doing *types* of people.'[2]

At nineteen, to the evident satisfaction of newspaper editors with an ever vigilant eye on circulation figures, and the unconditional delight of an adoring public happy enough to wait for hours in the hope of catching a glimpse of her, Princess Margaret was undertaking an increasingly full diary of official engagements in her own right. So popular was she and so great a crowd-puller that when, to cite but one albeit typical example, she visited Warrington during a three-day visit to Lancashire, 6,000 school children lined the route she took into town while crowds – which contemporary photographs show stretching away into the distance as far as the eye can see – had to be controlled by extra police drafted in from neighbouring districts.

On occasions that involved long car journeys Princess Margaret and Jennifer Bevan always wiled away the time in the back of the Princess's gleaming black Rolls-Royce singing duets such as *Baby, It's Cold Outside*, which Jenny admitted, 'I was never very good at' – because, said the Princess, 'she would never keep in tune'. Other favourites included songs from

Princess Margaret's vast record collection, such as *C'est Si Bon, Bewitched, Bothered and Bewildered, Autumn Leaves, La Vie en Rose* and *Just One of Those Things*, as well as show tunes from hit musicals such as *South Pacific* and *Kiss Me Kate*.[3]

At the same time as the Princess's official diary, now planned months in advance, became occupied with engagements that were frequently connected with the growing number of presidencies and patronages she was invited to accept,* Princess Margaret was able to make a number of unpublicized, largely private visits to the House of Commons, the Law Courts, the Old Bailey, the Thomas Coram School, Citizens Advice Bureaux and the like, in order that she could see something of the Parliamentary, judicial and educational systems at work or, in her own words, so that she could 'learn about life.'

Attending a session at the East London Juvenile Court at Toynbee Hall, she listened to the cases of a dozen young offenders, girls as well as boys. 'Few in court realized who she was', reported the *Star*, 'as, with chin in gloved hand, she listened intently to the evidence. She sat with two probation officers near the magistrates [who] were asked questions on matters about which the Princess was not clear. Sometimes her sympathies were unmistakably on the side of the small culprits. "How can you expect them to be perfect when they live under such hard conditions?" she said several times. She heard that one child's family lived five and six in one room and that the child shared a bed with three brothers and sisters. "What is receiving?" she asked when one child was charged with this offence. She also wanted to know about conditions in a remand home and what remand actually meant.'[4]

---

* By 1950, Princess Margaret was already President or Patron of a dozen organizations including Dr Barnardo's, The Sunshine Homes for Blind Babies, the Victoria League (Young Contingent), and the Sadler's Wells Foundation, Union of Girls' Schools for Social Service, the Scottish Community Drama Association, and the University of London Musical Society. She was also Colonel-in-Chief of the Highland Light Infantry; the Rand Light Infantry (South Africa); and the Highland Light Infantry of Canada.

Jenny Bevan, who was with the Princess, noted afterwards that, although the session was 'very interesting', it was also 'rather upsetting. The cases were all pathetic and their homes and often the parents left the children small chance of being honest.'

Less absorbing was one of the Princess's first visits to the House of Commons. In her diary for March 1949, Cynthia Gladwyn, whose husband, Sir Gladwyn Jebb, later Lord Gladwyn, was one of the most prominent diplomatists of his day, described how David Eccles, later 1st Viscount Eccles (and a one-time Minister of Education), 'had been in the House of Commons when Hector McNeil was making a speech which was so excessively boring that, for want of something better to do, he suggested to his neighbour that they should ogle the pretty girl who had come to hear the debate from the Speaker's Gallery. They made signs to her, to which she quickly responded. Imagine his consternation on learning . . . that this had been Princess Margaret. He was annoyed with himself for making such a mistake, but also surprised that she responded so readily.'[5]

It was by way of compensation for the cancelled tour of Australia and New Zealand that the King and Queen agreed to a suggestion put forward by Major Tom Harvey, then the Queen's Private Secretary, that their younger daughter might be allowed to visit Italy during the spring of 1949, with the aim of seeing some of the British military cemeteries and battlefields such as those at Bellizzi near Salerno, where Major Harvey himself saw action, Cassino and Monghidoro.

As one idea superseded another, however, a thirty-five-day programme evolved which not only resembled a mid-twentieth century version of the Grand Tour but, in reality, developed into something of a royal progress; beginning with the Princess's arrival in Naples on 27 April and, having arrived there, by way of Capri, Sorrento, Rome, Florence, Venice, Stresa, and Montreux, ending with a four day visit to Paris, from where she returned to London on 1 June. For much of the time in Italy, *La Bella*

Margherita as she was hailed by an exultant press, wasn't able to move without being surrounded by photographers, excited locals and just about anyone else who cared to join the throng. Such scenes prompted an editorial in the *Giornale d'Italia*, to remonstrate that such excessive interest in the Princess's visit was blighting her chances of seeing much more of the country's spectacular scenery and architectural heritage than the valiant, if unremarkable, backs of the *Carabineri*, as they struggled to clear a path for her.

Matters did improve, but not before a chambermaid at one of the hotels in which the royal party stayed had been bribed into letting reporters into the Princess's bedroom. The inevitable news item that appeared soon after described every last detail of the room and its contents, right down to the brand and colour of the Princess's nail varnish.

Although Vicomtesse de Bellaigue and Sir Arthur Penn were significant influences in stimulating and directing Princess Margaret's cultural awareness, her first European tour or, perhaps more correctly, her first visit to Italy, a country with which she fell in love and to which she was to return almost every summer, was in a sense her cultural awakening.

At the Vatican, where to begin with as she recalled, 'I was so nervous that I couldn't stop shaking,'[6] the Princess, dressed according to protocol in black – a floor-length velvet coat with a lace mantilla worn as a veil – was conducted through the State Apartments to her private audience with Pope Pius XII by a reassuring Cardinal Giovanni Montini, the future Pope Paul VI, and an escort of the papal Swiss Guard, dressed in the medieval red, blue and orange uniforms that Michelangelo had originally designed.

During their meeting in the Pope's private library, the elderly Pontiff asked the Princess about her family for whom, he said, he prayed often, particularly for the health of her father. At the end of the audience, as the Princess remembered, Pius XII asked, 'almost shyly', whether he might give her a gift. 'It was a small crucifix', she said which, to the Pope's obvious relief – he had evidently been uncertain about giving a crucifix to a devout Protestant – she 'was pleased to accept.' Later, Cardinal Montini guided the Princess on a tour of the Vatican Museums' collections, showing her some of the world's finest examples of early Christian, Medieval and Renaissance religious art, including works by Giotto, Bellini, Carravaggio, Botticelli and Raphael.

The Princess visited Rome's most famous religious and secular landmarks, among them the Basilicas of St Peter, Santa Maria Maggiore, and San Giovanni in Laterano,the Roman Forum and the Palatine Hill. She absorbed the uniqueness of medieval Venice, and the incomparable art collections and marble clad cathedrals and churches of Renaissance Florence, the city she found the most fascinating of the entire tour. The experience inspired in Princess Margaret a love of Italian art and architecture that was to become one of her deepest and most scholarly interests.

Leaving Venice – from where she had also visited the picturesque islands of Torcello and Burano – Princess Margaret made the 95-mile journey to Stresa on Lake Maggiore by car, from where, via the Simplon Pass, she travelled to Montreux and on to the lakeside villa of her distant cousin, ex-Queen Victoria-Eugenie of Spain, at Lausanne. Switzerland was no more than a two-day stop-over on Princess Margaret's itinerary, during which she attended a reception given by the Swiss Government, took a 20-mile cruise by launch on Lake Geneva, went shopping, and otherwise enjoyed catching up with her 'Cousin Ena'. Widow of King Alfonso XIII of Spain and grandmother of the present King, Juan Carlos, (whom the Spanish dictator General Franco, groomed to succeed him), the 62-year-old ex-Queen, had been born at Balmoral, the thirty-second grandchild of Queen Victoria, and only daughter of Princess Beatrice and Prince Henry of Battenberg.

Speaking of her young guest, Queen Ena remarked that Princess Margaret had 'blossomed out deliciously', and added, 'what a success she will be in Paris.' If the Italian press had given her little respite from their relentless attention, the French media found her just as exciting and were no less uncompromising. They were in hot pursuit every time she left the British Embassy, whether to visit a hairdresser in the Faubourg St Honoré, to lunch at the Elysée Palace with Madame Auriol, wife of the French President, visiting Versailles and Fontainbleau, or attending divine service at the British Embassy church. When she heard a nightclub band playing *Mean to Me*, Princess Margaret remarked, 'That's a tune that is dedicated to some photographers.'

At home, where the British press had reported the tour just as assiduously, the question of romance was always a favourite subject for speculation, never more so than when Princess Margaret reached her early twenties. Like her own sister, who had married at twenty-one and was the mother of two children by the time she was twenty-four, the Princess was fast approaching the age at which most women of their generation were following the traditional, even expected, path to marriage and motherhood.

One by one, the Princess's boyfriends, escorts, even dance partners – virtual bystanders – found themselves under the scrutiny of the tabloid press and, one by one, they married other girls. Hugh Fitzroy, Earl of Euston, who had been a friend of both Princesses, married as early as 1946, and others followed suit. Soon, although her name had been linked with no fewer than thirty-one eligible young men, the three who were looked upon as the most likely contenders were Sunny Blandford, Johnny Dalkeith and Billy Wallace.

By 1951, however, three had become two when Sunny Blandford announced his engagement to his first wife Susan Hornby and, in the presence of Princess Margaret, and the King and the Queen, married her at St Margaret's, Westminster, on 19 October. 'No sane person would want to marry into the royal family and take on all those pressures,' said one of Princess Margaret's friends, 'it's a colossal undertaking.'[7] Though there is certainly no suggestion that Sunny Blandford married from any sense of unrequited love, another friend who has been close to her since childhood, is of the belief that Sunny did propose to the Princess who, despite her fondness for him, and having told her parents that he would make a good husband, gently rejected him.[8]

In what was now a diminished field, with no sign of any newcomers, attention focused ever more keenly on Johnny Dalkeith and Billy Wallace.

During the first week of August 1951, not long before her twenty-first birthday, the Princess, with Jenny Bevan, spent a few days at Petworth in Sussex as the guest of Billy's mother, Mrs Herbert Agar, for Goodwood race week. It was, as the press noted, the third time Princess Margaret had been a member of the same house party.

With other friends and fellow guests, Rosemary Spencer-Churchill, Tom Egerton, Peter Ward and Charles Smith-Ryland, Billy and the Princess attended the races, went out riding and one evening drove to Dickie and Edwina Mountbatten's Palladian house Broadlands, at Romsey in Hampshire, for a party, 'one of the most brilliant of the year', as it was described, which was given for their younger daughter Pamela, or 'Pammie,' as she was called. Also attended by Princess Elizabeth and the Duke of Edinburgh, it was noted that Princess Margaret, 'danced one of her favourite dance tunes, *Diamonds are a Girl's Best Friend* with Mr Wallace.'[9]

In an album of press cuttings that she kept at that time, a note Jenny Bevan wrote next to a piece from the front page of the local *News Chronicle*, read 'The press were very "hot" on to Billy at this time, as everyone thought that HRH was going to become engaged to him. This is one of the many tiresome articles that was published . . .'[10] Beneath a series of four indistinct photographs, the *News Chronicle*'s on the spot reporter filed a story which described how, 'Princess Margaret sat on top of the boot of an open red sports car to watch a polo match . . . in Cowdray Park. The car belonged to 24-year-old Mr Billy Wallace, the son of Mrs Herbert Agar, with whom the Princess has been staying this week at Lavington Park. Mr Wallace (in the driver's seat), Princess Margaret (next to him) and behind Miss Jennifer

Bevan, Lady-in-Waiting, arrived little more than an hour after leaving Goodwood Races – where they had spent their third successive day . . .'

Though nobody could know it at the time, Billy Wallace's one and only real chance of marrying Princess Margaret still lay a few years hence, and when it did materialize, it was over and done with so quickly that neither the press nor the public knew anything about it. For now, however, the *News Chronicle*'s piece was just a miniature version of the sort of headline stories with which the national press ran in those less cynical and somehow more excitable days of the early 1950s.

On the morning of Princess Margaret's twenty-first birthday, for example, the *Daily Express* surpassed itself with front page coverage of Billy Wallace's arrival at what is now a disused railway station, en route to Balmoral. Beneath the main headline, 'MR WALLACE – AND THE CAKE – CAME ON THE 9.46', the *Express* enthused: 'Tiny Ballater station, which calmly receives royalty once a year, went mad yesterday morning over the arrival of the 9.46 from London. In it was the only invited guest outside the royal family and their near relatives to arrive for Princess Margaret's very private twenty-first birthday party in Balmoral Castle tonight. He was Mr Billy Wallace . . .

'The King's gleaming silver Daimler waited for him at the station. Waiting, too, were the station master and the rest of the station staff, holidaymakers, tourists, villagers, cameramen, an electrician, a bus conductress, and a man with a barrow . . . "Is that him?" said the bus conductress breathlessly. It was. Princess Margaret's lady-in-waiting, Miss Jennifer Bevan, was with him. Cameras clicked . . . Four dogs barked. The man with the barrow hurriedly moved it out of the way, and Mr Wallace followed the lady-in-waiting into the King's car.

'As it drove off, a porter staggered from the train with a huge cardboard box. It was Princess Margaret's 30lb cake. Two feet square and a foot high, its twelve sides decorated with the signs of the zodiac in rose pink icing, her personal standard atop, with a man in attendance all the way from the bakers in London.

They were driven eight miles to Balmoral, through the well-guarded gateway and into the grounds where detectives roam as thickly as grouse.'

It was no doubt because press attention was so firmly focused on Billy Wallace, that the *Express* correspondent was unaware of the fact that he was by no means the only non-family member at Balmoral to help celebrate Princess Margaret's 'Coming of Age'. Having driven over from Drumlanrig, where the Princess had spent a few days earlier in the month, Johnny Dalkeith's arrival went almost unnoticed. Nevertheless, he was still very much a part of the royal house party and, more to the point, despite all the speculation about Billy and the Princess, was raising hopes within the royal circle that romance might even be in the air.

One morning soon after his arrival, Sir Alan (Tommy) Lascelles, the King's Private Secretary, remarked expectantly, if not ironically, to Peter Townsend, that, 'Dalkeith [whose own mother had been born a Lascelles] and the Princess were making sheep's eyes at each other last night at dinner.' Even the King and Queen, who were happy to see them together, were hopeful that their younger daughter might accept the proposal that one of the Princess's closest friends believes Johnny made.[11] It would, of course, have wrapped everything up very neatly, with the elder Princess soon to inherit the throne and the younger, with the Buccleuch estates, virtual queen of a realm of her own. As with Sunny Blandford, however, Princess Margaret was fond of Dalkeith, the tall, red-haired twenty-eight-year-old, who really did have so much to offer, but she had no intention of marrying him.

'Margaret and Johnny are great friends,' one of the Earl's cousins is said to have volunteered at the time, 'but they are personally quite incompatible. Margaret adores London, the theatre, nightclubs and dancing. Johnny lives for hunting, shooting and fishing.'[12]

In later years, Colin Tennant, now Lord Glenconner, who was also once tipped as a possible husband for the Princess, seemed convinced that, 'If the King had lived, he would have made Princess Margaret marry Johnny Dalkeith.' No one else appears to agree. 'If the King had lived', said Lady Mary Clayton, 'he would not have made Princess Margaret marry either Sunny Blandford or Johnny Dalkeith,' but she added, 'neither would Peter Townsend have happened.'[13]

Janie Stevens, a close, long-time friend, who was also a lady-in-waiting, offered the opinion that, 'Princess Margaret would not have married Johnny Dalkeith, because it was not what she wanted out of life. She was always much more attracted to creative, theatrical people.'[14]

Just as emphatic was the view of one of the Princess's 'Marchmont' friends, Alex McEwen, who said, 'The King wouldn't have forced Princess Margaret *into* a marriage, but he would have forced her out of making a wrong marriage.'[15]

Not quite eighteen months later, at the start of 1953, the whole Dalkeith question was finally settled when, with Princess Margaret already heavily involved in the love affair that was soon to become a world-wide sensation, Johnny Dalkeith married the fashion model Jane McNeill, daughter of an Argyllshire QC.

Back at Balmoral on Princess Margaret's twenty-first birthday, the moors and public paths surrounding the Castle teemed with tourists, and journalists and photographers from the world's press. The King with the Duke of Edinburgh and other members of their shooting party, including Johnny Dalkeith and Billy Wallace, were out early in the vicinity of Condavon, a local beauty spot, where a picnic lunch had been arranged for Princess Margaret, her family and their guests beneath a canopied tent.

That evening, wearing the romantic white organza evening gown Dior had designed for her, with its delicate gold embroidery and appliquéd sequin and mother-of-pearl flower motif that she jokingly likened to 'bits of potato peel,' the Princess was toasted in champagne at a dinner party for twenty-five guests, during which, in traditional fashion, six of the King's pipers played a medley of Scottish airs. Later on, the same pipers played outside the castle's front door as Princess Margaret and friends danced an eightsome reel on the drive. Then guests and members of the household, all holding torches which they lit in sequence one from another, formed a chain leading to a bonfire on a nearby hill. The fire was then set ablaze by the last torch-bearer. To round off the evening, the younger, more energetic, members of the birthday party set off with Princess Elizabeth and the Duke of Edinburgh to Birkhall, where the Edinburghs now stayed when on holiday at Balmoral, for an impromptu dance.

Reaching the age of twenty-one meant that Princess Margaret now received a Civil List annuity of £6,000 (to be increased on marriage to £15,000) which was specifically intended to cover formal expenses and, when the time came, the costs of running her own Household. She would also benefit from a Trust Fund that the King, on the advice of his brother-in-law, David Bowes Lyon, had set up at Coutts Bank when the Princess was still an infant; and a £20,000 legacy bequeathed to her in 1942 by Mrs Ronald Greville. The owner of Polesden Lacy at Great Bookham in Surrey, where the then Duke and Duchess of York began their honeymoon in 1923, Maggie Greville was a very close friend of the princess's grandmother, Queen Mary, as well as her parents. In addition to the not inconsiderable sum she left to Princess Margaret, she also bequeathed to Queen Elizabeth, with her 'loving thoughts', an exceptionally fine collection of jewels, including 'ropes of milky pearls', some magnificent rubies, and a ring with a 'diamond shaped as a playing card.'[16]

From a press point of view, still hoping for signs of a royal romance, the week of Princess Margaret's birthday had been a bit of a disappointment, yielding nothing more exciting than the sight of her out riding with her father's equerry, Group Captain Peter Townsend. Watching her canter across the moors with the man who, only a year before, had been appointed to the post of Deputy Master of the Household, couldn't on the face of it, have been more routine: an employee simply doing his job by accompanying the boss's daughter on a morning ride.

Even the boss himself, whose own – perhaps more perceptive – mother is said to have noticed something going on between her granddaughter and the Group Captain, would have thought it inconceivable that there was anything more than a decorous, if mildly flirtatious, bond between them. It would certainly never have entered his head that his daughter would become romantically entangled – let alone think of making a life – with a married man, or one who, for all the King's high regard and personal affection for him, was still an employee and socially still out of his league. Not even the sight of the Princess leaning over him in an off-duty moment at Balmoral, seemed enough to alert the King to that possibility.

In a now-famous passage from his autobiography, Townsend recalled: 'One day after a picnic lunch with the guns, I stretched out in the heather to doze. Then, vaguely, I was aware that someone was covering me with a coat. I opened one eye to see Princess Margaret's lovely face, very close, looking into mine. Then I opened the other eye, and saw, behind her, the King leaning on his stick, with a certain look, typical of him: kind, half amused. I whispered, "You know your father is watching us?" At which she laughed, straightened up and went to his side. Then she took his arm and walked away leaving me to my dreams.'[17]

If ever there was a moment at which Townsend, or even Princess Margaret herself, should have pulled back, this was it. For although he was to claim in his autobiography that he first realized he was in love with Princess Margaret in 1952, conveniently placing the revelation after the King's death and at around the time he was granted a divorce from his wife Rosemary, he had, in truth, already confessed his love to the Princess a year earlier, in 1951.*

By then, with his broken marriage and empty home life – for which he himself was at least partly responsible – Townsend had found something in Princess Margaret that he was unable to find elsewhere.

---

* Peter Townsend was granted a decree nisi on 20 December 1952, on the grounds of his wife Rosemary's 'misconduct', otherwise adultery, with export merchant, John de Laszlo (son of the famous portrait painter, Philip de Laszlo), whom she married two months later as the second of her three husbands. After that marriage ended in divorce, she married the Marquess Camden.

'What ultimately made Princess Margaret so attractive and lovable', he wrote, 'was that behind the dazzling façade, the apparent self-assurance, you could find, if you looked for it, a rare softness and sincerity. She could make you bend double with laughing; she could also touch you deeply. I was but one of many to be so moved. There were dozens of others . . . Yet I dare say that there was not one among them more touched by the Princess's *joie de vivre* than I, for in my present marital predicament, it gave me what I most lacked – joy. More, it created a sympathy between us and I began to sense that, in her life too, there was something lacking.'

By this time, and perhaps in a sense it clouded his view of the ever deepening feelings his younger daughter and Peter Townsend shared, the King was a very sick man. In the words of Winston Churchill, 'During these last months the King walked with death, as if death were a companion . . . whom he recognized and did not fear.' It had already proved a demanding year physically as well as psychologically – with concerns over the economy at home, the involvement of British Forces in the Korean war, the crisis in Anglo-Persian relations precipitated by the government in Tehran nationalizing the holdings of the Anglo-Iranian Oil Company; together with a programme of public engagements that included visits to the Midlands and to Cambridge, the opening of the Festival of Britain, and the State Visit of King Frederick IX and Queen Ingrid of Denmark.

Writing to a friend of, 'The incessant worries & crises' that, as he put it, had 'got me down properly', the King, who had already developed a persistent cough, had been running a temperature for some while before his doctors saw him towards the end of May. In a letter to Queen Mary, he wrote, 'At last the doctors have found the cause of the temperature. I have a condition on the left lung known as pneumonitis . . . I was X-rayed & the photographs showed a shadow.' Though he wrote to his mother in optimistic mood, he was still irritated at 'not being able to chuck out the bug.'

Keenly interested as he always was in his own medical history, it is nevertheless believed that, even at its most acute, the King never realized that he had lung cancer, or that the shadow revealed on the X-ray was the start of it. By September, however, his doctors were unanimously agreed that his left lung had to be removed, though they told the King himself that the procedure had been necessitated by a blockage to one of his bronchial tubes. The operation was performed at Buckingham Palace on the morning of Sunday, 23 September, in preparation for which, Princess Margaret was appointed a Counsellor of State for the first and last time during her father's reign.

Over the next two or three months, the King's health showed every sign of improvement. Hopes rose that while Princess Elizabeth, with the Duke of Edinburgh, would represent her father on the tours of Australia and New Zealand that he had originally hoped to undertake, early in the New Year, the King, accompanied by the Queen and Princess Margaret, would make a private health-restoring visit to South Africa. To that end, Peter Townsend had already been tasked with the job of flying out immediately after Christmas to inspect Botha House, the Prime Minister's official residence in Natal, which had been put at the King's disposal.

In the meantime, having returned to London at the end of her twenty-first birthday visit to Balmoral, Princess Margaret continued with her own official programme of autumn and winter engagements. Chief among them that November, was her second four-day visit to Paris in two years, during which she was guest-of-honour at a grand charity ball, held in aid of the British Hertford Hospital, and at which the press took a particular, if predictable, interest in some of the young French aristocrats – among them Prince Marc de Beauvau-Craon, the Duc de Liancourt and Prince Henri de la Tour d'Auvergne – who were members of the Princess's party that night.

With her aunt Marina, who was on a private visit to Paris, the Princess lunched with President Auriol, the Prime Minister, Monsieur Pleven, and their wives; and attended a dinner and firework party given by the former British Ambassador, Duff Cooper, and his wife, Lady Diana, at their home in Chantilly. It was there that Princess Margaret met Greta Garbo, and while the Princess presided over the first of two tables, the legendary film actress held sway over the second. Later that evening, according to a contemporary account, the Coopers' son, John Julius, played the guitar for half an hour, before the pianist, Jacques Fevrier, sat down to entertain his fellow guests. Later still, 'came the surprise that set all Paris talking . . .' when, a little after midnight, Princess Margaret unexpectedly walked to the piano and for an hour played and sang English, Scottish and French songs, 'both serious and comic.' Of all those who heard her, none was louder in their applause than Garbo, who was reported to have made 'the request for the Princess's last song, *La Ronde de l'Amour*, from the film, *La Ronde*.' This, after it had been publicized in the popular French press, led to a rather bizarre rush for 'gramophone records, said to be of the Princess singing this song . . . A number of people were foolish enough to believe it was [her] until an official denial was issued.'[18] After a visit to General Eisenhower at Allied Supreme Headquarters at Fontainbleau, Princess Margaret followed in the footsteps of her great-grandfather, King Edward VII, and with Princess Marina, her sister Olga and brother-in-law, Prince Paul of Yugoslavia, dined at Maxim's on the elegant Rue Royale.

At what had been one of the King's favourite Parisian haunts, with its potted palms and rich plush décor, the Princess's party sat at the 'royal' table, otherwise Edward VII's, in front of the orchestra to which, in spite of the numbers of other newly-arrived diners who had flocked to the restaurant when word spread that she was there, the Princess danced until leaving for Montparnasse and the Monseigneur Club. Greeted by the Tzigane Orchestra playing *La Ronde de l'Amour*, as she walked in, Princess Margaret 'danced waltzes, rumbas and sambas until nearly 3 am.'

Although aged beyond his years, the King, who had celebrated his fifty-sixth birthday on 14 December, was continuing to make good progress after his lung operation three months earlier; and, indeed, following the bronchoscopy that had been performed the day before his birthday, after a further trouble-some cough had developed.

At Sandringham, where sixteen members of the royal family gathered soon afterwards for Christmas, snapshots in Queen Mary's collection that show the King with his sixteen-month-old granddaughter, Anne, on his knee (her brother Charles cuddling up to his grandmother, next to them), reveal him looking thin, though otherwise cheerful and comfortably relaxed. In fact, all the signs were so positive that Sir John Wheeler-Bennett was to write, 'Serene in the affection of his family, the love of the Queen and of his daughters, and his own growing interest in his two grandchildren, [George VI] was more contented in mind and confident in health than he had been at any time since the war.'[19]

Returning briefly to London at the end of January, the King saw his doctors for a routine check-up at Buckingham Palace on the twenty-ninth. The following evening, feeling as confident as they about his progress, King George and Queen Elizabeth, accompanied by the two Princesses, the Duke of Edinburgh and Group Captain Peter Townsend, drove to the Theatre Royal, Drury Lane, where they saw Mary Martin and Wilbur Evans in a performance of the recently opened Rodgers and Hammerstein musical, *South Pacific*.

Next day at Heathrow Airport, the King kissed his elder daughter God Speed as she and the Duke of Edinburgh set out at the start of their tour of East Africa, Australia and New Zealand. Disembarking from the aircraft after he, the Queen and Princess Margaret had said their private farewells, the royal party – which also included the Gloucesters and Mountbattens – made their way to the roof of the VIP Lounge from where, hatless and windblown, a look of intense concentration on his face, the King watched as the aircraft took off and turned in a south-easterly direction. Only when it had completely disap-peared from view did he step back inside the Lounge to drink a glass of champagne and mingle with his prime minister and other members of the official farewell party that in those days always gathered whenever a member of the royal family flew off on an official overseas visit.

Returning to Sandringham the King, together with a handful of friends, spent the next few days shooting on the royal estate. Tuesday, 5 February, a cold but dry and sunny day, was no different. And while the Queen and Princess Margaret drove over to Ludham to visit the painter Edward Seago, the King, in the highest spirits, set off hare-shooting. That evening, after an entertaining dinner with his wife, younger daughter and their guests, the King listened to the radio news which included a report of Princess Elizabeth's arrival in Kenya and then, as Princess Margaret recalled, laughing heartily at a joke he had just heard,[20] retired to his room at 10.30pm. There he read until about midnight, when a watchman noticed him fasten the latch of his window. Moments later, he climbed into bed and fell into the peaceful sleep from which he would not wake. Sometime during the early hours of 6 February 1952, the precise time is not known, King George VI died when a bloodclot stopped his heart.

Devastated by the death of the father she worshipped, Princess Margaret, who would always ask plaintively, 'Why did he have to die so young?'[21] was inconsolable in her grief, weeping bitterly, unable to eat and, until prescribed sedatives, unable to sleep. Like her mother, who not only found herself 'engulfed in great black clouds of unhappiness and misery',[22] at the loss of her beloved husband, but who would also have to come to terms with the myriad changes, great and small, practical as well as psychological, that no longer being Queen would bring, Princess Margaret suddenly felt lost and isolated. 'There was,' she said later, 'an awful sense of being in a black hole [and] feeling tunnel-visioned . . .'[23]

When, some weeks after the King's death, she felt able to reply to messages of condolence, one family friend to whom she wrote on 19 April was Ava, Lady Waverley. On black-edged Windsor Castle notepaper, she said of father, 'He was such a wonderful person, the very heart and centre of our happy family. Everything seemed to come from him and no-one could have had a more devoted and thoughtful father. He was always so very much *alive*, so that at this lovely Easter time he doesn't feel so very far away and one is comforted by all thoughts of happiness for him and his love for us all'[24]

In Kenya on the day of the King's death, it was already early afternoon before the news was finally confirmed and a thunder-struck Duke of Edinburgh found himself having to break the news to his wife that she was now Queen. The following day Elizabeth II, as she chose to be known, arrived back in England, a slight, but dignified figure in black, who had become the youngest Sovereign since Victoria and, like the first Elizabeth, had succeeded to the throne at the age of twenty-five.

That evening, not long after the sixth Sovereign she had known in her lifetime arrived back at Clarence House, Queen Mary drove over from nearby Marlborough House to greet and console her granddaughter. 'Her old Grannie and subject must be the first to kiss her hand,' the late King's eighty-five-year-old mother had insisted.

The following day, as her accession was formally proclaimed throughout Britain, the new Queen travelled to Sandringham to join her mother and sister. There, as darkness fell, they followed the King's coffin by torchlight to the church of St Mary Magdalene where, as estate workers, gamekeepers, foresters and carpenters kept watch in groups of four, those who had known George VI more as the squire of Sandringham than as King of England passed through the church to pay their respects.

Two days later, London witnessed the poignant scene of the King's return, his coffin, like that of his father when it embarked on the same journey from Norfolk sixteen years before, draped with the Royal Standard on which rested the Imperial State Crown. Silently watching as the Bearer Party carried it from the Royal Train at King's Cross Station were the three heavily veiled figures of his widow and their two daughters who, a little later, were joined at Westminster Hall by Queen Mary.

In that ancient hall, the surviving part of William Rufus's original eleventh century Palace of Westminster, where early kings had lived and held great councils of State, and where Edward VII and George V had lain in state before him, the coffin of King George VI, surmounted by the Crown, the Orb and Sceptre, and his personal Insignia of the Most Noble Order of the Garter, would rest high on a purple catafalque for four nights and three days. Tall, unbleached candles burned at the four corners of the dais, and officers from the Life Guards, the Blues and Royals, the Yeoman of the Guard and the King's Gentlemen-at-Arms, stood watch. During the King's lying-in-state, 305,806 men and women, many of whom had waited in freezing temperatures for up to five hours in a queue that at one point was four miles long, filed through the Hall.

Finally, on the morning of 15 February, George VI's last journey began when, as Big Ben chimed fifty-six times, once for every year of the King's life, a gun-carriage drawn by more than 100 naval ratings carried the King's coffin – followed by the new Queen, her mother, Princess Margaret and the Princess Royal riding in the Irish State Coach – on its two-hour journey through the streets of the capital to Paddington Station, hung with drapes of purple and white, from where the Royal Train conveyed it to Windsor.

In the splendid setting of St George's Chapel later that day, almost five hours after the cortège had left Westminster Hall – followed on foot by four royal dukes, including the Duke of Windsor, four kings, twelve princes, three presidents, Commonwealth High Commissioners, heads of foreign delegations and members of the Royal Household – the mortal remains of George VI were lowered into the Royal Vault. As tradition decreed, the Lord Chamberlain, Lord Clarendon, broke his wand of office in two and Elizabeth II, watched by Queen Elizabeth The Queen Mother, as the King's widow would now officially be known, and Princess Margaret, sprinkled earth on the coffin as Dr Geoffrey Fisher, the Archbishop of Canterbury, intoned the words of committal.

Borne into the royal tomb-house, which was originally created for George III beneath what is now the Albert Memorial Chapel, the coffin of King George VI was to rest on a stone platform in the centre of this subterranean chamber for the next seventeen years until 1969. In March of that year, the King George VI Memorial Chapel was dedicated in a private service attended only by the King's immediate family. Designed by the architects George Pace and Paul Paget, and enclosed by gates that are a modern representation of Edward IV's grille, the chapel was the first structural addition to St George's Chapel since the magnificent fan vaulting, carved in stone above the nave, was completed during the reign of Henry VIII in 1528.

Set into the floor of the chapel, the black ledger stone covering the King's final resting place and bearing the simple legend GEORGE VI recalls that which covers the tomb of King Henry VI. On the wall beyond, a portrait medallion bearing a profile relief of the King, is a replica of that by Sir William Reid Dick in the church at Sandringham, while behind the altar, on which stands a simple modern cross specially commissioned by Princess Margaret, daylight filters through stained-glass windows designed by John Piper and made by Patrick Reyntiens.

NINE

With the death of the King and the accession of the new Queen, one of the most sensitive though unavoidable issues that had to be addressed centred on the question of where the Queen Mother (known in royal circles as Queen Elizabeth) and Princess Margaret were to live. Sixteen years earlier, the end of one reign had forced the new King and Queen to move with their two young daughters from their home at 145 Piccadilly to Buckingham Palace. Now, the start of another reign meant that the established tenants were expected at an emotionally vulnerable time to make way for the new. It was a nettle none wanted to grasp.

The widowed Queen and her son-in-law, Philip, Duke of Edinburgh, proved the most obstinate of all. The Queen Mother did not want to leave because Buckingham Palace was not simply a house brim full of memories, but the home she had shared with her husband. The Duke of Edinburgh did not want to move in, because it meant leaving Clarence House, which he and Princess Elizabeth had so recently transformed into a family home, run with the minimum of formality. Buckingham Palace would mean a return to an establishment machine. Almost the executive branch of the Civil Service, it was profoundly conservative, deeply reactionary and operated by hardened old school courtiers like Sir Alan Lascelles, who at the start of her reign, served as Private Secretary to the new Queen; and who, at least in the early years, did not care for the Duke of Edinburgh, regarding him as 'rough' and 'uneducated'.

Taking the line that his four-year-old son would one day need a house of his own, the Duke reasoned that he and his family could remain where they were and use Buckingham Palace for official purposes, as indeed Edward VIII had done, commuting from York House, St James's Palace, which had been his official residence as Prince of Wales. The Duke of Edinburgh's suggestion to stay put was overruled, as he thought it would be, not only by Tommy Lascelles and his cohorts at the end of the Mall, but also by Winston Churchill. All were emphatic that Buckingham Palace was by tradition the Sovereign's official residence. Although the Duke may still have been forced to concede defeat, it might have been argued that that there was a historical precedent for retaining Clarence House as the Sovereign's residence. Before the young Queen Victoria moved into the newly completed Buckingham Palace three weeks after her accession to the throne in 1837 (thereby establishing its status as official residence), her uncle and immediate predecessor William, Duke of Clarence, lived in the Nash-built house that bore his name. After he succeeded to the throne as King William IV in 1830, he and Queen Adelaide remained at Clarence House where a communicating gallery was built connecting it to St James's Palace next door. St James's had itself been designated the Sovereign's official residence by Queen Anne in 1702 after fire destroyed the Palace of Whitehall four years earlier. Even to this day, it is to 'the Court of St James's' that foreign ambassadors are formally accredited.

If, when it came to it, the Duke of Edinburgh remained resentful about moving to Buckingham Palace, which he and the Queen had no choice but to do, despite the continuing presence of his mother-in-law and Princess Margaret, the dowager Queen Elizabeth was scathing about being offered Clarence House in return. After reigning for so many years as châtelaine of palaces and castles, she dismissed it as 'a horrid little house', that may have been suitable for other 'high-ranking royal dependents', but most decidedly *not* for 'an anointed Queen.'[1] Recently renovated and refurbished for her elder daughter, Clarence House was neither 'horrid' nor particularly 'little'. The simple truth was that she really had her eye on Queen Mary's official residence, the still larger and grander Marlborough House which lay a little further down the Mall, just beyond St James's Palace itself.

Originally built by Wren for the 1st Duke of Marlborough, it was subsequently home to a number of royal figures, most famously Edward VII and Queen Alexandra as Prince and Princess of Wales, and Queen Alexandra and her unmarried daughter Victoria after King Edward's death. Now home to the widowed Queen Mary, who had previously lived there with George V when they were Prince and Princess of Wales, she had also known what it was to leave Buckingham Palace and what she called her 'lovely comfortable rooms which have been my happy home.'

In 1952, therefore, any suggestion that Queen Mary might have considered giving up Marlborough House for her son's widow and younger daughter, would undoubtedly have met the same refusal that was conveyed to Charles, Prince of Wales, on behalf of his grandmother, some forty years later. By then, during the early 1990s, when the Prince was in need of a larger London house for his two growing sons and himself, Clarence House would have provided the solution. At that time, Queen Elizabeth was apparently offered but, perhaps not surprisingly, refused to accept apartments at Kensington Palace.[2]

If it is true that by remaining at Buckingham Palace after the King's death, the Queen Mother found herself marginalized and 'under pressure from staff to move out',[3] she finally agreed that she and Princess Margaret should go to Clarence House. Although arrangements took time and the move did not come about until 18 May 1953, fifteen months after the King died, and only a matter of weeks before the Coronation, it still wasn't easy for either Queen Elizabeth or her daughter.

In fact, it was partly due to the reasons why she and her

mother had had to move there, and partly because she no longer had a self-contained suite of rooms to call her own, that Princess Margaret never really liked Clarence House. At Buckingham Palace, when her sister reached sixteen and was given rooms of her own, the Princess had been able to take over the nursery suite, or 'Maggie's Playroom', as Prince Philip renamed it, for her own use. Now, at Clarence House her bedroom together with a 'horrible little bathroom' were on the first floor, while her sitting room was one of two disproportionate rooms that had been created out of a larger drawing room on the ground floor. Divided by a slightly crooked wall, the second room – so narrow it was little more than 'a slither' – was for the Princess's lady-in-waiting. The Garden Room as it is now known, was finally restored to its original design only after Princess Margaret married. Before then, Queen Elizabeth had refused her daughter's requests to have the dividing wall taken away.[4]

Like it or not, Clarence House was to be Princess Margaret's home for the next seven years and here, as at Royal Lodge, Windsor, which remained in Queen Elizabeth's possession, mother and daughter had, in their own way, to come to terms with the loss of the King. For the new Queen, who had the support of her husband and a family life with two small children, the practical demands of the office she had assumed not only kept her busy, but helped her to cope with her own feelings of grief.

The Queen Mother, however, who seemed to be on the point of retiring from public life until Churchill persuaded her otherwise, was for a long time in a world of her own, leaving Princess Margaret, at twenty-one, effectively motherless and sisterless, to cope with her father's death, as well as her own changed circumstances, as best she could. Her immediate response was to look for solace in the conviction of her religious beliefs.

Outside her family and some of her closer friends, the depth of Princess Margaret's devotion, 'focused upon her perception of Jesus Christ as the crucial centre of her faith',[5] as one friend described it, is very little known. 'Religion in our family is inborn,' said Lady Mary Clayton who, as we have already seen, once stood in awe of her grandfather's long and audible conversations with God.[6] Within the Strathmore family, though not exclusively during the time of Princess Margaret's grandparents, religion was a part of everyday life. So much so, that two of her cousins found their vocation within the Church. Andrew Elphinstone, the son of Queen Elizabeth's sister, May, became Vicar of Worplesdon in Surrey, while his sister Elizabeth became an Oblate of the Convent of the Incarnation, an Anglican Order of nuns at Fairacres, near Oxford. Earlier still, the Princess's great-grandfather, the 13th Earl of Strathmore, 'Mortgaged Glamis up to the flagpole, building Episcopal churches across Scotland.'[7]

Described by one of her friends as 'more of a spiritual explorer than any other member of her immediate family',[8] Princess Margaret's religious conviction was such that, although she had to wait until she was sixteen, she felt ready to be confirmed at the age of fourteen. In later years, Derek Jennings, a Roman Catholic priest, and a friend of Janie Stevens, who enjoyed many theological discussions with the Princess, 'was always astonished by her depth of knowledge of the Bible and her commitment to her religious beliefs. But then', said Mrs Stevens, 'clergy frequently were astonished by her ability to hold her own in any discussion.'[9]

No less important to the Princess were the opportunities she had – always in a private and completely unpublicized capacity, and often through Marigold Bridgeman, a close friend with whom she was always been able to share her faith – of meeting individuals with special forms of ministry. One of the first was the Reverend Mother Clare, Superior of the Community of St Andrew, 'who was a much valued speaker to groups of laity in London, and a counsellor to many; who was always ready, over a tray of tea, to respond to Princess Margaret's wish "to talk over a whole range of profound matters such as Heaven and Hell, and the unending mystery of the Trinity." '[10]

Because of her frequently expressed wish to help and encourage those who care for others, the Princess also asked to meet Helen Preston, whose 'remarkable ministry of Christian healing,' she had been told about, and who found the Princess's genuine interest in her work, 'wonderfully supportive and encouraging.' Another example of her lively awareness of the part she was able to play in supporting the ministry of others was seen in her insistence on meeting the Reverend David Bick. A fellow student at theological college of Dr George Carey, who in 1991 was to become Archbishop of Canterbury, David Bick had, at that time, been given the nickname 'Amos.' Years later, when Princess Margaret and Marigold Bridgeman lunched with Dr Carey at Lambeth Palace, he was amused to be reminded of his fellow student.

Intrigued, Princess Margaret told Marigold as they left, 'I must meet Amos.' She did not long afterwards, when a visit was arranged to his Gloucestershire centre, which specialized in 'the teaching and practice of counselling and other skills, psychological as well as theological, which have helped large numbers of clergy and laity engaged in caring for others, to better understand their problems, whether pastoral or spiritual.'[11]

Later still, 'when expressing her concern for the urgent need of imparting the Christian Faith to our increasingly secular society,' the Princess took one or two unsuspecting and distinguished clergy by surprise, by asking them whether they knew anything about a current and growing vehicle of mission known as the Alpha Course.* In this connection, Princess Margaret met Merilyn 'Emmy' Wilson, one of the remarkable individuals at the centre of a growing ministry in prisons, from whom she was impressed to hear of the number of changed lives among those who have received the Christian Faith.

Never deliberately controversial in the views she expressed publicly, the Princess, although a great traditionalist with 'a deep love of the Church of England',[12] who attended Holy

---

* The Alpha Course is an inter-denominational ten-week programme as an introduction to the Christian Faith which, at the start of the new Millennium was running in churches, schools, universities, prisons and so on, in 108 countries around the world.

Communion according to the (1662) Book of Common Prayer, was nevertheless quite prepared to accept the ordination of women without any difficulty.[13]

More than forty years before the issue of women priests became a matter of public debate, bringing the Church into conflict with itself, Princess Margaret looked to her belief to sustain her through the emotional turmoil she experienced at the time of her father's death. With so many questions that needed to be addressed, Elizabeth Elphinstone, who was always devoted to her young royal cousin, suggested she should join 'a group of mainly young people, who were enquiring about their Christian faith in a way that was not possible in a church service, or at a time when that type of gathering was not nearly so usual as it would be now.'[14]

Led by the Reverend Jock Henderson, the Vicar of St Paul's, Knightsbridge, who later became Bishop of Tewkesbury and later still, Bishop of Bath and Wells, the group met regularly at the Rectory. After a talk by him on some Christian theme, teaching or prayer, a question-and-answer discussion would follow.

Surprising though it may seem, if only because it runs contrary to all outward appearances – 'the enamelled self assurance' that one of her friends has already mentioned – Princess Margaret always had a certain lack of self-confidence. And though Jock Henderson's group meetings meant a great deal to her, she was rather diffident about asking questions directly, preferring instead to whisper them to a friend, who would then put them to the group.

It was from that time on that the Princess started to attend the yearly courses of Lent lectures that were held first at St Paul's, Knightsbridge, and later at Westminster Abbey. From time to time, she would also attend the Eucharist, a celebration that was always of great importance to her, on a special Feast Day in the Church, such as Ascension Day or All Saints. As a friend put it, it was 'this experience of Christians coming together to learn more and to exchange matters of Faith outside the more formal church-going practice', that led Princess Margaret to become part of another small prayer group after Jock Henderson had left London for Tewkesbury. Led by Dr Eric Abbott, then Dean of Westminster, who became a close and valued friend, the group's members included Leonard Beaton, whose work as Defence Correspondent of *The Times* provided particular stimulus to the group's exchange of views and whose wit the Princess greatly enjoyed.

While they met most often in a small flat in Cheval Place, Knightsbridge, the Dean would host a breakfast in the Jerusalem Chamber, after Holy Communion in St Faith's Chapel at Westminster Abbey, once or twice a year. The group would also spend at least one weekend each year at Dowdeswell, a Tudor Manor House in Gloucestershire, which belonged at that time to the Bridgeman family. It was a house that Princess Margaret had known for many years and where, in time, she would send her children to stay when she was away. These weekends, in the words of Jock Henderson, would be a combination of 'things serious and not so serious', including singing around the piano and times spent in the Bamboo Bar, a folly created in a wing at the top of the house. The more serious aspect would centre on Eric Abbott's talks on whatever theme had been chosen for the weekend.

In the chapel that existed in the grounds of the house, where a fine representation of Leonardo's *Last Supper* and a cross made from the nails of the bombed Cathedral at Coventry created an inspiring background, Holy Communion would be celebrated by the Dean and prayers offered. So great, in fact, was Princess Margaret's trust in the power of prayer that, 'at times of need', whether in her own life or the lives of those she cared about, the Princess would 'quite simply and directly ask her friends to pray for them', not least for the Queen who, says a friend, was always 'her special concern.'

On one occasion in her life, Princess Margaret's conviction inspired her to write a prayer of her own. With the Princess's permission, it is published here for the very first time:

We thank Thee, Lord,
Who by Thy Spirit
Doth our faith restore
When we with worldly things commune
And prayerless close our door,
We lose our precious gift divine
To worship and adore
Then Thou, Oh Saviour fire our hearts
To love Thee evermore.

Like Princess Margaret, Peter Townsend was deeply religious. Like her, he was also a 'spiritual explorer.' After the King's death, when there was nobody else for her to turn to, grief strengthened their relationship still further and, in Townsend's own words, 'Princess Margaret and I found increasing solace in one another's company.'

'Peter was always there for her', said one who knew them, 'he was incredibly kind, sensitive, gentle and understanding.'[15] Moreover, while there were those who would have preferred to see him removed from royal employment altogether – and who were doubtless quietly satisfied when that eventually happened – Townsend's new appointment as Comptroller of the Queen Mother's Household meant that he was now closer than ever.

It was that closeness – though he would always deny its existence if challenged by other members of the Royal Household – which led to a situation that, given the prevailing moral climate of the times, was as deplorable as it was infallibly human. In April 1953, by which time it has been said Princess Margaret and he had been in love for at least two years, Townsend seized the moment. In the privacy of George IV's sumptuous Crimson Drawing Room at Windsor Castle, where they had 'talked for hours' about themselves and their feelings for one another, it is thought Townsend finally proposed.

Though swept away by the strength of their emotions, it is difficult to understand how either one of them, hardly giddy teenagers, could seriously have imagined that marriage was a realistic proposition. At almost twenty-three, Princess Margaret was an intelligent young woman. Though 'not an intellectual', as Townsend's biographer put it, she was nevertheless 'intellectually above most of the other members of the royal family.'[16]

She was also a practising Christian, well aware of the Church's implacable opposition to divorce. In addition, both within the Court and at Westminster, uncomfortable memories of Edward and Mrs Simpson were astir. Though the implications were not nearly as extreme, the parallels with the events that led to the Abdication were all too obvious. Nobody could afford another scandal, another crisis, not least because as [the late] Lord Charteris, then Assistant Private Secretary to the Queen, was to say, 'We had a new reign to establish.'[17]

At the age of thirty-eight, Peter Townsend, who had been used to positions of responsibility and leadership and who for almost eight years had been close enough to the King to know what was and was not considered appropriate behaviour, ought never to have allowed himself to become involved with the much younger Princess. But if, in the end, he was seen not to be the most worldly of men, he was surely not quite as naïve or disingenuous as the official version he was to publish of his relationship with Princess Margaret, sometimes made him appear.

Whether, or even *if,* time will add anything more to the story of Princess Margaret and Peter Townsend is far from certain. When asked many years later whether he kept the letters the Princess had written to him almost daily, Townsend replied, 'Not a line . . . I was in the middle of the African veld, miles from anywhere, when I took out a pile of letters and . . . tore them up and flung them to the winds . . .'[18] True or not, Princess Margaret certainly kept the letters Townsend wrote to her. Labelled in her own hand, 'My correspondence with Group Captain Peter Townsend', they were boxed up some years ago and entrusted to the Royal Archives at Windsor Castle where, at the Princess's instruction, they are not to be opened until around the hundredth anniversary of her birth.[19]

From the end of the afair, Princess Margaret was unwilling to discuss Peter Townsend or in years to come recall the episode that, more than any other in her life, was responsible for creating 'The Margaret Legend.' Attempts to draw her on the subject simply met with the protest, 'It was a long time ago and I have forgotten it. It was all over and done with.'[20] While writers, journalists and popular historians kept the story alive, her own life moved on; and it was quite possible that, not so very far off fifty years later, she had forgotten it. Or at least, had archived it along with her letters.

Seen from her point of view – and, until his death in 1995, from Townsend's as well – that part of their lives was something that happened in the story-book tradition of 'once upon a time'. When writing to a friend in December 1985 to thank him for the gift of a book in which the relationship was briefly discussed, the Princess said, 'I am always intrigued that Peter Townsend is always an irresistible subject for conjecture in my "Dossier." I'll tell you one day [it is doubtful she ever did] how it was he who wisely advised me not to go through with the marriage. It wasn't anything to do with money – neither of us had any.'[21]

In the spring of 1953, the Princess's acceptance of Townsend's proposal could not have come at a more ill-chosen moment. Even if he had been a suitable contender for the Princess's hand, instead of a divorced commoner in the employment of her mother, now – with the Coronation only a matter of weeks away – was not the time for distractions. Though unavoidable, there had already been a brief pause in the final preparations for that greatest of rituals, when Queen and country bowed their heads in mourning for Queen Mary.

Late on the evening of 24 March, thirteen months after the death of the King, the third of her sons to have predeceased her,* and only two months before her eighty-sixth birthday, the old

---

* Of George V and Queen Mary's five sons the youngest, Prince John, died in January 1919, at the age of thirteen, following an attack of epilepsy. He was buried in the churchyard of Sandringham Church, otherwise St Mary Magdalene. During her widowhood, Queen Mary mourned the loss of Prince George, Duke of Kent in 1942, and King George VI in 1952.

Queen died peacefully in her sleep from a combination of old age and hardening of the arteries. Determined that nothing, not even her own death, should delay the Coronation of her grand-daughter, Queen Mary specifically requested that the ceremonial surrounding her passing should be kept to a minimum. At Westminster Hall, therefore, where she was the first queen consort to be so honoured, Queen Mary's public lying-in-state lasted for just over a day. Then her coffin, which had been borne to Westminster by gun carriage, was transferred by motor hearse to Windsor where, on the morning of 31 March, she was interred beside King George V in St George's Chapel.

Not long afterwards, when Princess Margaret told her sister that she and Townsend wanted to marry, the Queen's immediate response was both kind and sympathetic. Though the time would come when Lord Charteris felt she became 'bored by the whole business',[22] the Queen, according to another source, 'was always nice to Princess Margaret about Peter Townsend.' But, since 'her own life was so uncomplicated and had always been straightforward . . . she couldn't understand why Princess Margaret had to go and fall in love with a married man.'[23]

Over dinner with the Princess and Townsend on the night of her sister's surprise announcement, the Queen, who had asked to see them both together, made it clear that because of her official position as Sovereign, as Supreme Governor of the Church of England, which forbade divorce, and as head of the family, she was unable to give any kind of personal lead. She was also only too well aware that, as with all marriages within the royal family, she would of necessity have to become officially, and in this instance perhaps even controversially, involved.

Under the provisions of the Royal Marriages Act of 1772, which applied directly to all descendants of George II (except princesses who marry into foreign royal houses), the Sovereign's consent had to be given to any proposed royal marriage. If consent was refused, the royal petitioner's only option at the age of twenty-five, was to signify to the Privy Council his or her intention of marrying. Thereafter, unless within twelve months both Houses of Parliament – to whom written notice had to be given – raised any objections, the marriage could legally take place.

Although Princess Margaret was to say that nobody explained the Royal Marriages Act to her[24] (something she would no doubt have learned had she also been allowed extra tuition with Sir Henry Marten), the Queen made only one request. 'Under the circumstances,' she said, no doubt hoping that delay would provide its own solution, 'it isn't unreasonable for me to ask you to wait a year.'[25]

Having told the Queen – and the Queen Mother, who played 'imperial ostrich', as Tommy Lascelles described her usual way of ignoring what she chose not to see – Peter Townsend now spoke to Lascelles himself. He famously exclaimed, 'You must be either mad or bad.' Taken aback by Lascelles' hostile reaction, Townsend wrote, 'Though not entitled, perhaps, to any sympathy from him, it would all the same have helped. He was a friend and I was asking for his help. I was describing to him a state of affairs which, if thoroughly undesirable, reprehensible even, in his eyes (and, eventually, in a good many others'), was, equally, impossible to ignore.'

As the Queen's Private Secretary, Lascelles had every right to be informed. But Townsend was mistaken in thinking that he was a friend either to him or to Princess Margaret. Indeed, in confirming the Princess's own belief that Lascelles did not care for her, Lord Charteris said, 'He was suspicious of her. He thought she was dangerous.'[26] It was undoubtedly because of his mistrust, that Lascelles, as the Princess put it, took it upon himself to make it known at Court that friends of hers and of Peter Townsend in royal service, were neither to see nor talk to them.[27]

Lascelles' duplicity – for, despite his loyalty to the Queen, it would be difficult to interpret his actions in any other way – was first seen when Townsend offered to resign. Lascelles told him to remain in place, fearing that resignation would fuel speculation, but went immediately to the Queen with the advice that

Townsend should be removed from his post as Comptroller of the Queen Mother's Household and found a posting abroad. The Queen did not agree. From her point of view, such a course would have been unnecessarily hard-hearted, as much to her sister, for whom she cared deeply, as to Townsend himself, whom she had always liked. By way of compromise, the Queen agreed to his transfer from her mother's Household to her own, where he again assumed the role of equerry.

In the meantime, while Lascelles never spoke directly to Princess Margaret about her wish to marry Peter Townsend, she was led to believe that a way would be found. 'Had he said we *couldn't* get married,' said the Princess, 'we wouldn't have thought any more about it. But nobody bothered to explain anything to us.'[28] That nobody, either from within Court or Government circles, ever thought to provide any form of constructive counselling to Princess Margaret or Peter Townsend – if only to ensure that they understood their position – was one of the most extraordinary aspects of this entire episode.

Once again, the Princess was left to get on with it. The Queen, though kindly and from the best of intentions, had made her position of non-interference clear. Her sister must know her own mind and be sure of what she wanted. Queen Elizabeth, while never blind to what was happening (she, Princess Margaret and Peter Townsend had shared too many hours together at Clarence House and at Royal Lodge, just the three of them at lunch and at dinner, not to know), remained totally unapproachable. 'She was not a mother to her child,' said Lord Charteris ruefully.[29] Even when the Princess tried to talk to her, Queen Elizabeth became so upset, perhaps at the intrusion of reality, that it had to be left.

There can and should be no doubt that, despite her consummate ability not to see what she chose not to see, the Queen Mother loved both her daughters. It had to be admitted, however, that she was closer to her first-born, whose character was more like her own. With their dogs and their almost obsessional love of horses, horse owning, horse breeding and horse racing, their interests were more closely allied. By inclination, they were much more turf and country. There was also the fact, as one courtier mischievously put it, that the elder daughter also 'held the purse strings.' The relationship between Queen Elizabeth and Princess Margaret was always more stereotypically mother-and-daughter; each guaranteed at times to bait and irritate the other. During the early days of her widowhood, for instance, the Queen Mother acquired a virtual ruin of a sixteenth century castle on the north coast of Caithness, overlooking the Pentland Firth and the Orkney Islands. Carefully restoring it, the Castle of Mey became for the Queen Mother an occasional home. Visiting it for the very first time some thirty or more years later, Princess Margaret remarked, 'I can't think why you have such a horrible place as the Castle of Mey', to which her mother replied, 'Well, darling, you needn't come again.'[30]

But to return to 1953, the stories of Princess Margaret's romance with Peter Townsend were already making headlines abroad, particularly in America where the story threatened to steal the thunder of the Queen's Coronation. As with the events of 1936, however, the British press said nothing. On Coronation Day itself, Tuesday, 2 June, as they drove in the Irish State Coach with an escort of the Household Cavalry to and from Westminster Abbey, Princess Margaret and her mother were greeted loudly by the excited and wildly-cheering crowds that packed London's festooned and elaborately decorated streets.

Once inside the Abbey, as she walked towards her seat in the Royal Gallery, Princess Margaret was momentarily caught in what Norman Hartnell, in a flight of romantic fancy, described as 'a shaft of silvery sunlight [that] suddenly pierced the lofty stained-glass windows and splashed a pool of light.' Dressed by him in pearl and crystal embroidered white satin, her purple velvet train supported by the Honourable Iris Peake (Jennifer Bevan's successor as lady-in-waiting), 'her gaze steadily fixed upon the High Altar, she moved in white beauty . . .'

Then, as trumpets sounded a fanfare and the choir sang

Psalm 122, the Queen, whom Brigadier Stanley Clark, of the Queen's bodyguard, described as 'a lovely picture in diamond diadem and . . . a robe of crimson velvet trimmed with ermine and bordered with gold lace',[31] walked to her Chair of Estate at the start of the long Coronation service. Some three hours later, the newly crowned, anointed and robed Sovereign, followed by her family, returned to the specially-built, temporary annexe complete with retiring rooms which, since the coronation of William IV, has traditionally been added to the west and north-west front of Westminster Abbey.

There, said Peter Townsend, where the air hummed with talk of the ceremony itself or that morning's triumphant news of Sir Edmund Hillary's conquest of Everest, 'a great crowd of crowned heads, of nobles and commons – and newspapermen, British and foreign – were gathered . . .' It was on leaving the royal retiring room that Princess Margaret, looking 'superb, sparkling, ravishing,' found Peter among the throng. 'As we chatted', he wrote, 'she brushed a bit of fluff off my uniform.'

'It didn't mean a thing to us at the time,' he was to tell the journalist Jean Rook many years afterwards. 'It must have been a bit of fur coat I picked up from some dowager in the Abbey. I never thought a thing about it, and neither did Margaret. We just laughed over it. But that little flick of her hand did it all right. After that, the storm broke.'[32]

Not yet twenty years before, during their cruise along the Dalmatian coast, it had taken nothing more than the lightest touch of Wallis Simpson's hand on Edward VIII's bare arm, to tell the world that they were in love. Now, although Princess Margaret despises comparisons with the Windsors, it took no more than the touch of her white-gloved hand on Peter Townsend's tunic to confirm the rumours that had flooded the American and European press. The following day, the New York media majored on the story and other foreign newspapers followed suit. Only at home did the press continue to say nothing. But not for long.

When it became clear that a Sunday newspaper, infamous for

scandal-mongering, was about to break the silence of the British news media – ostensibly to defend Princess Margaret's honour – Tommy Lascelles drove down to Chartwell, Churchill's country house at Westerham in Kent, to let him know of her wish to marry Peter Townsend. The prime minister's immediate response was to say that 'the course of true love must always be allowed to run smooth.' But then, in 1936, he had caused himself considerable political damage by siding with Edward VIII for the very same reason. Seventeen years later, while Townsend was indisputably the 'gallant officer' he spoke of, and Princess Margaret was beyond all doubt the 'beautiful Princess', it was Clemmie Churchill's rebuke, 'Winston, don't be so stupid',[33] that immediately changed her husband's attitude about the desirability of such a marriage.

While Churchill instructed the Attorney-General, Sir Lionel Heald, to look into the constitutional position and, albeit informally, to seek the views of the Commonwealth Prime Ministers, the British Cabinet, infused though it was with its fair share of adulterers, decided it could not give approval to the Princess's proposed marriage. In the meantime, the expected exclusive from *The People*, gleeful in its indignance, declared that it was high time the British public was made aware of the scandalous rumours that were 'racing around the world' about Princess Margaret. 'Newspapers in both Europe and America', it said, 'are openly asserting that the Princess is in love with a divorced man and that she wishes to marry him. Every newspaper which has printed the story names the man as Group Captain Peter Townsend, Equerry to the Queen . . .

'The story', it said with a knowing wink, 'is of course utterly untrue. It is quite unthinkable that a Royal Princess, third in line to the throne, should even contemplate a marriage with a man who has been through the divorce courts. Group Captain Townsend was the innocent party . . . But', *The People* said with surpassing cant, 'his innocence cannot alter the fact that a marriage between Princess Margaret and himself would fly in the face of Royal and Christian tradition. . . .'

With the genie well and truly out of the bottle, Tommy Lascelles and Commander Richard Colville, the Queen's Press Secretary, reiterated their advice that, in view of the endless speculation that would now follow *The People*'s disclosure, Townsend would have to go. It was a view the prime minister also firmly supported. In telling the Queen that the Cabinet and, it transpired, the Commonwealth Premiers, were unanimously against Princess Margaret's marriage, Churchill went on to say that, even once she had reached the age of twenty-five and could petition the Privy Council, Parliament would not allow her as third in line to the throne to enter into a marriage which the Church could not recognize.* If she persisted, however, the Princess's only way forward would be to renounce her right of succession, not only for herself but also for her heirs and descendants, and to surrender her Civil List annuity. In those circumstances, said Churchill, Parliament would be unable to object further.

Of more immediate concern was the removal of Peter Townsend from the Royal Household. While he and Princess Margaret were agreed they should part for the time being, though still looking towards marriage as their ultimate objective, Lord de L'Isle, as Air Minister, received instructions from Downing Street to find Townsend an overseas posting with the minimum delay. Three posts were offered: as air attaché in Johannesburg, Singapore or Brussels. Having only recently been awarded custody of his two sons, who were at school in Kent, he chose Brussels.

On 30 June, Princess Margaret and her mother boarded a BOAC Comet aircraft at Heathrow, bound for Rhodesia. Ahead lay a sixteen-day, 1,500-mile tour of regions the royal family had not visited in 1947. That morning, said Townsend, 'the Princess was very calm for we felt certain of each other and, though it was

---

* As third in line to the throne, Princess Margaret ranked immediately after Prince Charles, who at that time was not yet five years old, and his sister, Anne, who was not yet three. Immediately after Princess Margaret in the line of succession came her uncle Henry, the fifty-three-year-old Duke of Gloucester, and his two sons William and Richard, then aged eleven and eight respectively. They, in turn, were followed by their Kent cousins, Edward, Duke of Kent, aged seventeen, his sixteen-year-old sister Alexandra, and their ten-year-old brother Michael.

hard to part, we were reassured by the promise, emanating from I know not where, but official, that my departure would be held over until her return on 17 July.'

At the Queen's request, made as a gesture of friendship the day before, Townsend also flew out of London on 30 June, but as Equerry-in-Waiting to Her Majesty at the start of her three-day Coronation visit to Belfast. While there to his astonishment, the Brussels appointment was announced from the press office at Buckingham Palace. As unnecessary as it was churlish, the announcement was made without consultation with Townsend himself, who had yet to tell his sons Giles and Hugo. Worse still, and even more medieval, was Churchill's insistence that, far from leaving for Brussels after Princess Margaret's return to London, Townsend was to leave within seven days of his posting on 8 July – two days before the royal party arrived back from Rhodesia.

At that news, Townsend's younger son, Hugo, was particularly upset, fearing he would never see his father again. Townsend himself was later to say that the boy 'never quite recovered from that brutal separation.' But such was the ruthlessness of a system towards those it deemed to have transgressed.

In America, newspaper headlines shouted the news PRINCESS MEG'S BEAU BANISHED and QUEEN 'EXILES' RAF ACE LINKED TO PRINCESS MEG, while in Britain, before Townsend began his 'banishment' and while the Princess was still away, the *Daily Mirror* ran a poll of its readers. Though less than half of one per cent of the newspaper's readership took part, more than 70,000 responded; 67,907 of whom thought Princess Margaret should be allowed to marry Townsend.[34]

Censured by the newly formed Press Council for running the poll, the *Mirror* sat back and enjoyed the spectacle as a number of other newspapers, among them the London *Evening Standard*, *Daily Express*, *Sunday Times* and *Sunday Graphic*, entered the fray. More trenchant than most was the independent socialist weekly *Tribune* whose editor, Michael Foot, wrote, '*Tribune* believes that

Princess Margaret should be allowed to make up her own mind whom she wants to marry. Most other people, we imagine, would agree with that simple proposition. But the British Cabinet does *not* agree . . .

'The objection is based on the fact that Peter Townsend has been involved in a divorce case. That, in the view of the Church, is a reason for preventing him from marrying the Princess . . . This intolerable interference with a girl's private life . . . is not made any more savoury by our knowledge that three members of the present Cabinet [Sir Anthony Eden, Sir Walter Monckton and Mr Peter Thorneycroft] have themselves been involved in divorce cases.

'The laws of England say that a man, whether he has divorced his wife or been divorced himself, is fully entitled to marry again. In some respects, those divorce laws are still too harsh. But no self-appointed busybody has the right to make them still harsher. If those laws are good they are good enough for the Royal Family.'

Making the sort of tart observation that would not be out of place today, Noël Coward noted in his diary, 'During the last week a journalistic orgy has been taking place over poor Princess Margaret and Peter Townsend. He has been posted to Brussels and she is in South Africa with the Queen Mother. She is returning tomorrow, poor child, to face the *Daily Mirror* poll which is to decide, in the readers' opinion, whether she is to marry a divorced man or not! It is all so incredibly vulgar and, to me, it is inconceivable that nothing could be done to stop these tasteless, illiterate minds from smearing our Royal Family with their sanctimonious rubbish.'[35]

With her arrival back in London, feeling 'utterly lost and lonely'[36] at Townsend's banishment, Princess Margaret put a brave face on her feelings and got on with both her public as well as her private life, in spite of another wave of media attention. This time, it was caused by the Queen's wish to amend the Regency Act, which had last been revised in 1937. Now, in what was perceived to be a snub to Princess Margaret over Peter

Townsend, the Queen wanted her husband and not her sister to act as Regent for the young Prince Charles, in the event that he succeeded to the throne before his eighteenth birthday.

Once again, despite the fact that Princess Margaret insists the decision was justified, the timing could not have been more inappropriate or for that matter, more insensitive. Despite the press arguments for maintaining the status quo, that is to say, keeping the Regency strictly within the line of succession – in which Prince Philip did not feature – the new Regency Bill passed through Parliament early in November and received Royal Assent on the 19th, four days before the Queen and the new Regent-designate embarked on their six-month Coronation tour of the Commonwealth, which would keep them away until the following spring.

On the night before their departure, the Queen Mother gave what Noël Coward, one of the thirty guests, called an 'enchanting' private party for her daughter and son-in-law at Clarence House. While Coward inevitably sang, the incomparable Peter Ustinov provided the evening's entertainment. The Queen and Prince Philip left the party amid fond farewells shortly after 3am; and later that day, looking to a dewy-eyed Noël Coward, watching them on television, like, 'A truly romantic couple, star quality *in excelsis*', they flew out of Heathrow. 'We felt truly sad that they were leaving us for such a long time',[37] he wrote.

TEN

By the time the Queen and the Duke of Edinburgh returned from their epic 44,000-mile Commonwealth tour, it was already May 1954. The year Princess Margaret had been asked to wait was over. And though Peter Townsend might still be in Brussels – where he spent his exile perfecting his French, took up show jumping and riding in gentlemen's races, and gave thought to a world tour – their feelings for one another remained the same.

If they hoped the question of their being allowed to marry would now be resolved, both were to be sadly disappointed. When Princess Margaret reminded her sister that she and Townsend had waited the year requested of them and asked what was to happen next, the Queen, doubtless acting on ministerial advice, asked that she wait a further year. It was a hard and unexpected blow. But another year would take the Princess to within reach of her twenty-fifth birthday and a time when she or, more precisely, she and Peter Townsend would have to decide on the next step for themselves.

At the start of 1955, with interest in her as intense as ever, Princess Margaret set off on a month-long tour of the Caribbean. With her went Iris Peake as lady-in-waiting and Elizabeth Cavendish. A childhood friend whose mother Mary, Duchess of Devonshire, was Mistress of the Robes to the Queen, Lady Elizabeth now joined Princess Margaret as extra lady-in-waiting – one reason why the popular press attempted to bribe her mother's butler with substantial sums of money for private photographs of the Princess.[1] These were the years when every section of the news media was obsessed with – and couldn't get enough of – Princess Margaret. Her only rival was the film actress Elizabeth Taylor, whom the Princess got to know through their mutual friend, Sheran Cazalet. The daughter of Queen Elizabeth's racehorse trainer, Peter Cazalet, Sheran had befriended the teenaged actress during the making of the film *National Velvet* in 1946.

Throughout the whole of February, as the Royal Yacht *Britannia* wound its way from island to island, from Tobago to the Bahamas, the euphoric Caribbean welcome of carnivals and steel bands, calypsos and flag-waving children, turned an official tour, one Princess Margaret would never forget, into a personal triumphal progress. 'She was a star and she sparkled,' said Elizabeth Cavendish.[2] One name and one subject that wasn't mentioned, however, was Peter Townsend. That part of her life, even among close friends, the Princess kept very much to herself.

The press, on the other hand, had no such inhibitions and, in what was the start of a gradual build-up to the Princess's twenty-fifth birthday that summer, examined and re-examined every aspect of the issue. Would they marry? Wouldn't they marry? Would she renounce her birthright? What kind of stepmother would she be to Townsend's two sons? In April, when he arrived in Cape Town, Dr Geoffrey Fisher, then Archbishop of Canterbury, curiously if unwisely remarked to one persistent local journalist that rumours of an impending engagement between Princess Margaret and Group Captain Townsend had been orchestrated by the London press. 'The whole thing', he said, 'was purely a stunt. And a most offensive one that that.' To some tabloid journalists the Archbishop's ill-chosen words were irresistible. With a little reinterpretation, it was claimed he had said the Princess's romance was a stunt. He then didn't help matters by issuing a denial that he had said anything of the kind.

By the time August arrived and the royal family left London for Balmoral, media interest had reached new heights. As 300 newspaper reporters and photographers descended on the Balmoral estate, the *Daily Mirror* demanded COME ON MARGARET! PLEASE MAKE UP YOUR MIND! That was what she was trying to do, but she also wanted to talk it through with her immediate family. That, however, was still not an option. While the ongoing saga of her sister's emotional life did nothing to damage their personal relationship, the Queen was as determined now as she had been at the very start that Princess Margaret had to make up her own mind, without anyone influencing her decision. The Queen Mother, though at the very least recognizing the cause of her younger daughter's moody behaviour, remained unable to cope with the situation and was, therefore, incapable of discussing it. Perhaps unsurprisingly, Princess Margaret's twenty-fifth birthday came and went with no announcement and no comment from within the Castle. The following month, Peter Townsend, whom Elizabeth Cavendish felt 'had no realization of what life [for the Princess] would be like had she married him',[3] arrived in London to attend the European Air Attachés Conference and the Farnborough Air Show. With Princess Margaret still in Scotland, the closest they got to one another on that occasion was talking on the telephone. They would not actually see each other again until 12 October.

That day, just hours after the Princess had stepped off the overnight train from Perth and had been driven home to Clarence House, Townsend returned to England, besieged by press and photographers from the moment he flew into Lydd Airport in Kent to the instant he closed the door at 19 Lowndes Square in London's fashionable Knightsbridge, where Lord and Lady Abergavenny, friends of the royal family, had put their flat at his disposal. A little later, the Princess's cousin, Jean Wills, joined Townsend for lunch, before taking him on a much-publicized West End shopping trip for suits, breeches – and fancy cakes.[4] At 6.20 that evening, Townsend climbed into his car and drove the short distance to Clarence House and his first *official* meeting with Princess Margaret for two years. As the ever-present press corps gathered outside reported, they were together for precisely one hour and forty minutes; not long for the passionate reunion some may have wanted to imagine. As he left, blinded by the glare of a myriad flashbulbs, Townsend told newsmen, 'I am sorry, but I can't say anything ...' At Lowndes Square, where the scene of jostling reporters and photographers was repeated, he said the same thing. But when one of them remarked, 'You don't know what a state the newspapers are in about this,' he replied lightly, 'You don't know what a state I'm in.'[5]

The following day, Friday, 14 October, Princess Margaret and Peter Townsend left London separately to spend the weekend at Jean and John Wills's Georgian house, Allanbay Park, at Binfield in Berkshire. At the same time, on the advice of the Marquess of Salisbury, Leader of the House of Lords, a formal statement was issued from Buckingham Palace. It read, 'In view of the varied reports which have been published, the Press Secretary to the Queen is authorized to say that no announcement concerning Princess Margaret's personal future is at present contemplated. The Princess has asked the Press Secretary to express the hope that the press and public will extend to Her Royal Highness their customary courtesy and co-operation in respecting her privacy.'

If it made Buckingham Palace feel as though it had done something towards preserving the monarchy's dignity, it was, in the circumstances, a hollow gesture; a vain and really rather naive appeal that was not going to stop the world's press in its pursuit of news. It certainly wasn't going to call off the pack of reporters and photographers that had descended on Allanbay Park or prevent Berkshire's chief constable from throwing an extensive police cordon round the estate. Nor, realistically, was it going to curb public interest in the life of its 'favourite princess'. Where was it not *the* topic of conversation? Even on a regular BBC radio show, when one comic actor was asked by another to read the day's news, the response was, 'They had tea together again';

while *Punch*, whose editor Malcolm Muggeridge was no admirer of royalty, ran a cartoon of a child counting peas on her dinner plate, captioned 'Tinker, Tailor, Soldier, Group Captain ...'.

In response to the Palace statement, the *Manchester Guardian* opined, 'Whatever our distaste for sensationalism and emotionalism, we have ... to recognize that in the affairs of the Queen's sister we touch matters of State – and Church – that are of public concern.' In both respects, the *Guardian* rightly went on, the question of divorce and the re-marriage of divorcees was no less an issue. Referring in part to Sir Anthony Eden, Churchill's successor as Prime Minister, who had himself been divorced and who subsequently married Churchill's niece, Clarissa, it said: 'If we can have a Prime Minister, Cabinet Ministers, judges, who are "innocent parties" we can, without feeling unduly disturbed in our moral fibre, give the same latitude to the Queen's sister.'

Even the *Daily Express*, an unlikely champion so far as Princess Margaret herself was concerned, came to her defence. In 1936, the Canadian-born Max Beaverbrook, owner of the *Express*, had been a great supporter of King Edward VIII. After the Abdication, his newspaper, under the editorship of John Gordon, became a relentless critic of the new King's younger daughter, always portraying her, despite the amount of official work she undertook, as a night-clubbing, cigarette-smoking, good-time girl. 'I was always told', the Princess said, 'that it was because Lord Beaverbrook couldn't openly attack my father or my mother or my sister, that he attacked me instead.'[6]

At the height of the Townsend affair, however, the *Express* was outraged that the Princess's marriage to a divorcee should demand her status in return. 'It would [be] deplorable that [the Queen's] sister should be required to write herself out of the succession,' ran its leader. 'A marriage "on condition" would suggest a marriage not entirely acceptable. The implication would be that the marriage though within the letter of the law had something wrong with it. The mass of the British people would utterly regret this. Princess Margaret will, of course, be anxious to ease the problems of her sister, the Queen. She may therefore be attracted to renunciation of her Royal succession. This act of self-denial would do her credit. Just the same it would be mistaken …'

On 18 October, the Tuesday of a week in which the Princess and Townsend either met alone or dined privately with friends such as Jean and John Wills, Micky and Laura Brand, and Jenny and John Lowther, Prime Minister Sir Anthony Eden had his usual weekly audience with the Queen. What he is said to have told her then confirmed Churchill's view of two years earlier, that the Government would not sanction Princess Margaret's marriage and that the only way in which she could proceed, if that was what she intended to do, would be to renounce her right of succession and her entitlement to an annuity under the Civil List.

On the morning of 21 October, in the cold and rain of a 'harsh autumn day', Princess Margaret was reminded of her standing as a member of the royal family and indeed her precedence in the line of succession when, surrounded by her family, members of the Royal Household, the Prime Minister and Cabinet, the Opposition and representatives of Church and Commonwealth, she attended a poignant public ceremony. On the steps of Carlton Gardens, overlooking the Mall and St James's Park, the Queen unveiled William McMillan's fine bronze statue of her father, King George VI, in his Garter robes. In the carefully chosen words of her speech, which her younger sibling listened to intently, Her Majesty said, 'Much was asked of my father in personal sacrifice and endeavour. He shirked no task, however difficult, and to the end he never faltered in his duty to his peoples. Throughout all the strains of his public life,' the Queen went on, 'he remained a man of warm and friendly sympathies – a man who by the simple qualities of loyalty, resolution and service won for himself such a place in the affection of all of us that when he died millions mourned for him as a true and trusted friend.'

Having dined that evening with the Brands at their house in Chelsea, Princess Margaret and Peter Townsend spent part of the next day together at Clarence House. The countdown to the moment they would come to a decision had already begun. 'We were both exhausted, mentally, emotionally physically,' Townsend would later say. 'We felt mute and numbed at the centre of this maelstrom.'

On Sunday, 23 October, Princess Margaret drove to Windsor Castle where she joined the Queen, her mother and the Duke of Edinburgh. What was said between them has never been disclosed, but that they at very long last talked about the Princess's situation *together*, no matter how awkwardly, sympathetically or even angrily, was indicated by one exchange between the Queen Mother and her son-in-law. On a matter that would not have entered her younger daughter's head, Queen Elizabeth reflected that the Princess 'hadn't even thought where they were going to live'. Prince Philip replied sarcastically that it was 'still possible, even nowadays, to buy a house', at which the Queen Mother, 'left the room angrily slamming the door'.[7]

As Sarah Bradford, one of the Queen's more eminent biographers, was to suggest, 'Perhaps the surroundings reminded Margaret of her childhood and of her father and what he would have thought of her proposed marriage, and brought home what she would be giving up for love.'[8] Later that day, though 'in great distress', the Princess rang Townsend. 'She did not say what had passed between herself and her sister and brother-in-law,' he wrote, 'but doubtless, the stern truth was dawning on her.'

To this day, criticism of Princess Margaret at that time has all too often been that, had she not 'wanted it all, position, money *and* Townsend',[9] she would have had no hesitation in renouncing her birthright. A simpler, more practical, explanation is that the twenty-five-year-old Princess was ill-equipped for a life beyond the prescribed, structured and safe environment she had always known. Even in years to come when the door was open to a freer, more liberated world, the 'bird in the gilded cage',[10] as one or two of the Princess's friends described her, may have tried her wings, but in the end, really had no idea how to fly.

The alternative to the royal way of life, as Townsend finally conceded, was far too great a risk, for himself as much as for Princess Margaret, with limited means at his disposal, very little money, no prospects of which to speak, and two sons to raise and educate. 'It is my belief', wrote Townsend's biographer, 'that [he] now began to have doubts about the wisdom of their contemplated marriage. Would their love be strong enough to endure the years of strain that would be imposed upon them by the restrictions under which the marriage would take place? Would not the Princess in time feel that their marriage offended her religious conscience? Also there was the problem of Holy Communion, to which the Princess must attach much importance?[11] This, unlike some of the more imponderable questions raised, was a matter of concern. For the Church had threatened that Princess Margaret would be barred from taking the sacrament if she and Townsend married. More than twenty years later, when the marriage that she did make ended in divorce, the then Archbishop of Canterbury, Dr Donald Coggan, and other clerics with whom she spoke, told her the Church had been quite wrong in making so grave a threat.

By the time Princess Margaret returned to London from Windsor on Monday, 24 October, both she and Peter Townsend were, in her own words, feeling 'thoroughly drained, thoroughly demoralized'.[12] That day, before dining with Jenny and John Lowther at their home in Kensington, the Princess and Townsend decided to draft a statement together that would tell the world of the decision they had reached. When it was done, Townsend said, 'we looked at each other; there was a wonderful tenderness in her eyes which reflected, I suppose, the look in mine. We had reached the end of the road.'

The following Thursday, Princess Margaret drove to Lambeth Palace. As she entered the Archbishop of Canterbury's study, Dr Fisher reached for a reference book on a nearby shelf. 'You can put away your books, Archbishop,' the Princess said. 'I am not going to marry Peter Townsend. I wanted you to know first.' After they had talked, the Archbishop, 'rejoicing' as the Princess put it, said, 'What a wonderful Person the Holy Spirit is.'[13] That evening, dressed in a strapless evening gown of pink and white satin, her diamond 'halo' tiara and her royal orders, Princess Margaret joined the Queen and the Duke of Edinburgh at the Royal Opera House, Covent Garden, for a gala in honour of the President of Portugal, General Lopes, who was then on a State Visit to London. The production chosen was Smetana's *The Bartered Bride*.

Princess Margaret and Peter Townsend spent one final weekend together at Uckfield in Sussex, at the country house of their friends Lord and Lady Rupert Nevill. As hundreds of cars brought sightseers who virtually camped out in the lane leading to the house in the hope of seeing the couple, the medieval church at Frant, where it was thought the Princess would attend morning service, was decorated with fresh flowers, brasses were polished and parishioners waited – but in vain. Neither Princess Margaret nor Townsend left Uckfield where, relieved of the pressures of having to make a decision, both were more relaxed than even they might have hoped.

Back in London once more, the couple said their farewells at Clarence House early on the evening of Monday, 31 October. Having drunk a toast to their past and to both their futures, Townsend returned briefly to Lowndes Square to collect some things before driving back to Uckfield where he spent the next few days with the Nevills before leaving for Brussels. As he drove out of London that evening, and Princess Margaret dined at home on her own, the statement they had written, but which by agreement would be made in the Princess's name alone, was finally released. The BBC interrupted its scheduled radio and television programmes to make the announcement, which was simultaneously transmitted around the world. Signed 'Margaret', the statement read:

> I would like it to be known that I
> have decided not to marry Group
> Captain Peter Townsend. I have
> been aware that, subject to my
> renouncing my rights of succession,
> it might have been possible for
> me to contract a civil marriage.
> But mindful of the Church's
> teachings that Christian marriage
> is indissoluble, and conscious of my
> duty to the Commonwealth, I have
> resolved to put these considerations
> before others. I have reached this
> decision entirely alone, and in doing
> so I have been strengthened by the
> unfailing support and devotion of
> Group Captain Townsend. I am
> deeply grateful for the concern of all
> those who have constantly prayed for
> my happiness.

Written and perfected by Townsend and herself, Princess Margaret resisted appeals to delete two items from the text. First, the once divorced Prime Minister had wanted the reference to the indissolubility of Christian marriage to be removed, which the Princess declined. Second, the Queen and the Queen Mother, who would have preferred no statement to have been made at all, asked via Queen Elizabeth's private secretary, Oliver Dawnay, that the reference to Peter Townsend's 'devotion' be deleted. Again, the Princess declined, making it clear that the statement was to be issued exactly as she and Townsend had constructed it.

'Poor Princess Margaret has made a sorrowful, touching statement that she will *not* marry Peter Townsend,' Noël Coward noted in his diary three days later, adding, 'it would have been an unsuitable marriage anyway ... She cannot know, poor girl, being young and in love, that love dies soon and that a future with two strapping stepsons and a man eighteen years older than herself would not really be very rosy.' His hope, he went on to say, was that Princess Margaret would not go on to 'become a frustrated maiden Princess …'[14]

In making that remark, Coward may well have been thinking of the sad lot of Princess Margaret's great-aunt Victoria, the second of Edward VII and Queen Alexandra's three daughters, whose enforced role in life was to act as companion and nursemaid to her emotionally manipulative mother. Known as 'Toria', the Princess was not without suitors. The widowed Prime Minister, Lord Rosebery, for example, was one, as was Admiral Fisher, who wrote admiringly of Princess Victoria's 'opulent figure' and 'rosy, plump face'.[15] Although to many Princess Margaret's own story would have a similar sense of disappointment about it – 'There was never a personal success story in her life,'[16] said one who knew her well – she at least avoided falling into the same trap as Princess Victoria.

Yet any talk or even suggestion, if only in passing and from any quarter, that Princess Margaret might end up a 'maiden Princess' would not even have been mentioned had the full story of the 'Townsend saga', and certainly the real reason behind the Princess's decision, been known at the time. In 1978, Peter Townsend gave a partial version of events in his autobiography *Time and Chance*. Princess Margaret, however, always and resolutely refused to discuss it, even with the present biographer with whom she chose to co-operate in person. Other than to stick to the story that nobody told her anything and that Tommy (Sir Alan) Lascelles had 'ruined' her life, which transpired to be quite untrue, she would merely say, in a tone that clearly meant *drop it*, 'It was a long time ago and I have forgotten it. It was all over and done with.'

On just one occasion, however, there was a small chink in her armour when she said, 'How do you know after two years apart whether you do want to marry somebody?' That admission of doubt is something that was reflected in a crucially significant letter that tells a very different story to the one we had always been given to believe. Writing to Sir Anthony Eden shortly before her all-important twenty-fifth birthday, she said in a four-page letter handwritten on Balmoral Castle letterhead, dated 'August 15th' (1955):

My dear Prime Minister

I am writing to tell you, as far as I can, of my personal plans during the next few months.

I am doing so because I am particularly anxious that whatever may happen may not cause any embarrassment either to you personally, or to the Government.

During the rest of August and all September I shall be here at Balmoral and I have no doubt that during this time – especially on my birthday on August 21st – the press will encourage every sort of speculation about the possibility of my marrying Group Captain Peter Townsend.

I am not going to see him during this time, but in October I shall be returning to London, and he will then be taking his annual leave. I do certainly hope to see him while he is there, although I well know this will provoke the press to still further enquiries & guesses.

But, it is only by seeing him in this way that I feel I can properly decide whether I can marry him or not.

At the end of October or early November I very much hope to be in a position to tell you and the other Commonwealth Prime Ministers what I intend to do.

The Queen of course knows I am writing to you about this, but of course no-one else does, and as everything is so uncertain I know you will regard it entirely as a confidence.

Yours very sincerely

Margaret

This letter, housed at the National Archives in Kew, which was included in a government file headed '1955 Royal Family' and which was originally to have remained classified until 2057, was released from embargo in 2009, five years after other related documents in the same file were declassified under 'an accelerated opening scheme of government papers'.

Importantly, other documents also throw a different light on and rewrite that episode in modern royal history. Far from not being told anything as the Princess claimed, government papers – like her letter to the Prime Minister – prove that she was well aware of what was happening. Indeed, the government itself had shifted from its earlier stance and for three months, August to October 1955, had been engaged in extensive discussions, the outcome of which would have permitted the Princess and Townsend to marry had they still wished to do so.

On 1 October, Anthony Eden flew up to Balmoral and that evening noted, 'Saw Q after dinner – many topics, but Margaret's problems the chief'.[17] After lunch the following day, Eden had a further talk with the Queen and the Duke of Edinburgh and afterwards with Princess Margaret herself. Noting that he explained the 'limitations of [the] Royal Marriages Act' to her, he went on to suggest that if she wished to marry Townsend, 'the best method' was 'for her to write to the Q[ueen] of her own initiative saying so and renouncing her right [of succession to the throne].'[18] Parliament would then be enabled to legislate in compliance with her wishes. 'Princess M accepted this,' he added, 'and Michael [Sir Michael Adeane, the Queen's Private Secretary] and Norman [Sir Norman Brook, the Cabinet Secretary] will now discuss form of letter, though Princess M still seems uncertain or says she is.'[19]

The letter drafted on behalf of Princess Margaret on 17 October read, 'I have come to the conclusion that in all the circumstances the best course for me to follow is to marry Group Captain Peter Townsend and to give up my rights [of] succession both for myself and my descendants.'[20] On the same day, Brook wrote to Eden with the draft of a statement by the Queen in respect of the 'proposed marriage of HRH Princess Margaret with Group Captain Peter Townsend', which said that it was after 'long and anxious consideration' that the Princess had decided to marry Townsend and that, respecting her wish to 'exclude her' from the succession to the throne, 'Her Majesty would not wish to stand in the way of her sister's happiness'.

Yet another draft statement, drawn up on 28 October, made it clear what Princess Margaret's future status would be were she to have married Townsend. Ministers, it said, recognized that it was the Princess's wish 'despite her renunciation to her right of succession' to 'continue to live in the UK and to carry out her public duties as a member of the Royal Family'. The statement went on that 'neither her marriage or renunciation of succession rights affected her style as HRH Princess Margaret, or the provision made for her to receive an allowance under the Civil List'. Indeed, the Princess's annuity, as was customary at that time, would be increased from £6,000 to £15,000.

Moreover, in a step aimed at simplifying the vexing issue of the Royal Marriages Act, which he regarded as 'unpopular, inappropriate to modern conditions, badly drafted and probably completely ineffective', Lord Kilmuir, the Lord Chancellor, who at first was in favour of scrapping the Act entirely, came to the view that it should be reformed, restricting its reach to the marriages of the children and grandchildren of the Sovereign and the heir to the throne.*

By that time, however, all the discussions, draft statements and proposals were academic. For, as Princess Margaret had told Eden in her letter that August, '... it is only by seeing [Townsend] ... that I feel I can properly decide whether I can marry him or not.' Her decision, after they had spent time together, was that she could not marry him. Indeed, in light of what we now know, the most obvious conclusion to be drawn is that her love for him, and in all probability his love for her, was no longer as strong as it had once been and marriage was no longer an issue. As a consequence, it would seem the intention of the famous statement, issued by the Princess on 31 October, which was to be accepted as fact for over half a century, was to save face. After all the hype and international press coverage, the 'Will she? Won't she?' waiting game, it could scarcely be publicly admitted that they had simply fallen out of love.

Still, the events of late 1955 did not bring the 'Townsend saga' to a complete end. Without their having the slightest inkling of what had gone on behind palace and ministerial doors, the media again decided there was something in the air when, in March 1958, at the end of the eighty-week solo journey around the world he had given thought to during his time in Brussels, Townsend arrived in England, ostensibly to see his sons Giles and Hugo. It soon became apparent to the ever-vigilant press corps that he was no less keen to visit Princess Margaret. Indeed, their first pre-arranged meeting was for 4pm on 28 March. That afternoon, Townsend had scarcely jumped out of his car behind the gates of Clarence House before the front page of the early edition of the London *Evening Standard* proclaimed THEY'RE TOGETHER AGAIN. From then on, the press kept watch on Townsend's every move in eight-hour shifts day and night It was as if the intervening two and a half years simply hadn't happened.

---

* In 2013 the Royal Marriages Act was finally replaced by the introduction of the Succession to the Crown Act, under which only the first six in line to the throne would require the Sovereign's consent to marry.

Timing of the visit had, it seems, been determined as much by an imminent two-day official visit Princess Margaret was to make to Germany as the Easter school holidays of Townsend's sons. All the same, it came on the second day of the Queen and Prince Philip's State Visit to Queen Juliana of the Netherlands and all but overshadowed that event. While the royal party on duty in The Hague affected an air of insouciance, the Queen's 'people', like the monarch herself, were said to be piqued, not only because Princess Margaret and Peter Townsend were again, perversely, the headline news item, but because they had been given no advance warning.

Perhaps having been given some kind of warning herself, or maybe just a quiet word of caution, Princess Margaret decided on a last-minute cancellation of her next get-together with Townsend. It would, she is alleged to have said, be wiser not to meet again until the Queen had returned to London. The following day, carrying one of the four dozen red roses Peter Townsend had sent her, the Princess flew out to Germany to visit the Highland Light Infantry.

Of their continuing friendship – and there is little doubt that Princess Margaret would always think of Townsend with affection – this latest episode illustrated how difficult it was for them even to think of meeting. Indeed, the Princess said, 'We had an understanding that if Peter was here he should come in. But it soon became obvious that that would never work.'[21]

There was, however, to be a brief sequel – a final curtain call – to the story of Princess Margaret and Group Captain Peter Townsend. In the summer of 1992, by which time divorce, even within the royal family, had become commonplace, the Princess and Townsend met for the very last time in their lives when she invited him to lunch at Kensington Palace, after which they walked together in the garden. To Princess Margaret, her distinguished-looking guest, though now seventy-seven, 'was exactly the same, except he had grey hair'.[22] 'It was sweet to see them together,' said Lady Penn who, together with her husband, Sir Eric, had also been invited to give the by now sixty-one-year-old Princess some Dutch courage, 'but also a little pathetic.'[23]

By the time Peter Townsend made his last appearance at Clarence House in the very early spring of 1958, Princess Margaret, who, in the words of one friend, had coped with the situation 'in a very adult way and with astonishing resilience',[24] had almost found herself married to Billy Wallace instead. Five years after the press had all but had them marching down the aisle together at the time of the Princess's twenty-first birthday, she finally accepted him when he made his next proposal. It was, she felt, better 'to marry somebody one at least liked'[25] than to end up on the shelf. After all the business over Townsend, however, the Princess told Billy that she would marry him only if they received the Queen's blessing. Convinced that that was an unequivocal 'yes', and in need of some restorative sunshine after a further bout of ill health, Billy took himself off to the Bahamas where he had a brief romance with a local girl. When he returned, either from naivety or just plain stupidity, Billy confessed to his holiday fling and was astonished when his would-be royal fiancée threw him out. Forgiven in time, Wallace eventually married Lord Inchyra's elder daughter, Elizabeth Hoyer Millar, whose younger sister, Annabel, would become Princess Margaret's lady-in-waiting.

Antony Armstrong-Jones, to whom Princess Margaret was introduced early in 1958, was a talented, inventive, unpredictable, charming but contradictory character with a mercurial temperament. Five months older than the Princess and not very much taller, slightly-built with fair hair, simian jaw and very large hands, he would one day be described by his old friend, the equally talented designer Carl Toms, as 'a modern eccentric with an eccentric's absolute determination to have his own way, which can goad people to the brink of assassination only held back by a charm that could halt a ravening beast in its track ...'[26]

By the time Elizabeth Cavendish invited Tony Armstrong-Jones to a private dinner party at her mother's house in Cheyne Walk, Chelsea, on 20 February 1958 – the night he first met Princess Margaret – he had already established himself on the social, fashion and theatre scene as one of the most versatile photographers of his generation. Born at 25 Eaton Terrace, in respectably aristocratic Belgravia, on 7 March 1930, Tony was the son of Ronald Armstrong-Jones, a Welsh-born, Eton- and Oxford-educated barrister of some note who was made a QC (Queen's Counsel) in 1954.

It was from his mother's side of the family, however, that Tony Armstrong-Jones inherited his artistic and theatrical abilities. Anne Messel, who would become the first of Ronald Armstrong-Jones's three wives in 1925, had beauty, style and a most unusual lineage. A descendant of Sheridan, Charlemagne and Thomas Linley – who wrote the music for *The Duenna*, and whose much-admired daughter, Elizabeth, eloped to France with the young dramatist Richard Brinsley Sheridan – Anne was the daughter of Leonard Messel, who had been a lieutenant-colonel in the British army. On his father's side, the family were German Jews who had been highly successful stockbrokers in London. Leonard's father, Ludwig Messel, bought the manor house of Nymans at Handcross in Sussex which, until it was destroyed by fire in 1947, was the family home. It was near there that Tony Armstrong-Jones would one day renovate a cottage that would act as the final catalyst in the terminal decline of his first marriage.

Tony's great-uncle, Alfred Messel (his grandfather Ludwig's brother), was a distinguished architect. A pioneer of designing with glass and steel, he was responsible for the Berlin National Gallery and was honoured when two Berlin streets, the Messelplatz and Messelstrasse, were named after him. Adding further lustre to the family name, Leonard Messel, Tony's grandfather, married (in 1898) Maud Frances, the daughter of Edward Linley Sambourne, who succeeded Sir John Tenniel, the famous illustrator of Lewis Carroll's *Alice in Wonderland*, as chief cartoonist of *Punch*. Tony's mother Anne was the only daughter of the marriage. The only son was the distinguished stage designer and decorator Oliver Messel, whose innovative and elegant designs dazzled post-war London.

Anne and Ronald Armstrong-Jones's nine-year marriage

produced two children, Tony and his older sister Susan, who later married the 6th Viscount de Vesci. Following their divorce in 1934, Ronald remarried twice. Anne also remarried. Her second husband was Michael Parsons, 6th Earl of Rosse. Known because of his good looks as the 'Adonis of the Peerage', he owned Birr, an estate of over 26,000 acres complete with seventeenth-century castle, in County Offaly, in Ireland, and Womersley Park in South Yorkshire.

It was at his father's eighteenth-century house Plâs Dinas, at Bontnewydd, near Caernarvon in North Wales, now a country-house hotel, however, that Tony spent much of his childhood. And it was there that, as a teenager, he fell seriously ill with poliomyelitis. Though it left one of his legs shorter than the other, and though he had to use a wheelchair – the experience of which led to his later work on behalf of the disabled, including the design of a new wheelchair – he did at least survive.

Never academically outstanding, he nonetheless received a traditional education. However, as his parents soon learned from one end-of-term report during his time at Eton, 'Maybe he is interested in some subject, but it isn't a subject we teach here.' In fact, Tony's preferred place of 'study' while there was the engineering workshop, where he spent his time making radiograms, crystal sets and torches. It is said that in an attempt to rouse his son to some other form of interest, possibly even study, Ronald Armstrong-Jones gave Tony a magnificent brass microscope that had belonged to his grandfather, Sir Robert Armstrong-Jones, a leading authority on mental illness. Tony is said to have 'looked at it, admired it, and promptly swapped it with another boy in exchange for a camera'.[27]

His burgeoning interest in photography had, in fact, begun some time before when he had been given his first camera and had impatiently demanded 'a great deal of technical advice', including the art of printing and developing, from William Butler, the local chemist at Birr. Some years later, after Tony had found fame and fortune, Butler said, 'I never thought he would make a photographer, he was too impetuous.'

213

If the level of Tony's academic achievement won him no laurels at Eton, it is remarkable that he ever got to Cambridge. But somehow he did and went up to Jesus College to read Natural Sciences. Once there, however, he switched to architecture, which in turn took second place to rowing and photography. Indeed, during his Cambridge days, Armstrong-Jones's one achievement and sole claim to any distinction was that he coxed the winning boat in the 1950 Oxford and Cambridge Boat Race.

Having failed at Cambridge, Tony decided on photography for a living. With an introduction from his actress stepmother, Carol Coombe (Ronald Armstrong-Jones's second wife), and a fee paid by his father, Tony so impressed the distinguished photographer Henry Nahum, better known as Baron, that he unusually agreed to take him on as an apprentice for three years. Tony learned a lot but left after only six months. Setting up on his own soon afterwards, he established himself in a disused ironmonger's shop at 20 Pimlico Road, which he rented for £4 a week and converted into the epitome of style and elegance. Part studio, part living space – the ground and basement levels were linked by a wooden and copper spiral staircase that he designed – this was where he would work and play, often hosting parties for his friends, a mixed bag of the conventional and unconventional, bohemian and camp, heterosexuals, homosexuals and bisexuals. If not entertaining at home, he might eat out in some small cheerful restaurant that served continental food – then considered very *avant garde* – or with his latest girlfriend, at that particular time the Chinese dancer Jacqui Chan, who had appeared on the West End stage in *Kismet*, *The Teahouse of the August Moon* and *The World of Suzie Wong*, take in a film or a play. 'The young Tony', said Elizabeth Cavendish, 'was extremely hardworking, with a great zest for life. He was great company and a brilliant mimic; always whizzing somewhere on his motorbike.'[28]

Portrait and fashion photography proved lucrative work, as did society weddings. In 1956 he had been on hand when the Hon. Colin Tennant, later Lord Glenconner, married Lady Anne Coke, daughter of the 5th Earl of Leicester. Although

Princess Margaret was a guest at the wedding, she didn't remember the photographer. 'Did Tony take the photographs?' she would ask.[29] Like the *Tatler*, the *Sketch* and *Vogue*, *Queen* magazine, owned by his friend Jocelyn Stevens, also took his work. Theatre and ballet photography was, however, the thing Tony loved best and through Oliver Messel he was introduced to a host of theatre people, to whom his 'refreshingly alive and spontaneous' approach greatly appealed.

When Laurence Olivier played Archie Rice in *The Entertainer*, at the Royal Court Theatre, for example, Tony used immense blow-up photographs front-of-house, commenting afterwards that he saw it as his job 'to get people off the buses' and into the theatre. Later in life he was to say, 'I didn't set out to take photographs ... I only did it because I was failing at drawing. People talk ... about how I created movement in photographs for the first time ... but that is rubbish. I just tried to break away from the routine theatre photographs. I worked for Peter Brook [theatre and film director] and Peter Hall [founder of the Royal Shakespeare Company and later Director of the National Theatre], and I took much more informal and free pictures during rehearsals because it saved me time. It's nonsense that I changed anything.'[30]

True or not, Tony Armstrong-Jones's reputation grew to such an extent that it wasn't long before he was photographing royalty. In 1956 he took the twenty-first-birthday photographs of the Duke of Kent and the following year was invited to photograph the Duke's sister, Princess Alexandra, for her own coming-of-age. A commission to photograph the Queen and Prince Philip with Prince Charles and Princess Anne at Buckingham Palace followed soon after.

'I don't think A.A. Jones's pictures are at all interesting,' bitched Cecil Beaton, who had all but monopolized official royal portraiture for more than a quarter of a century, 'but his publicity value is terrific. It pays to be new in the field.'[31] Tony had quite deservedly become Beaton's arch rival and the older man was piqued. As Tony's royal commissions increased, so did Cecil's jealousy; though he was not always uncharitable. 'Tony Armstrong-Jones had suddenly enormous success and indeed deserved it for his photographs were vital and he himself was a young man of great liveliness and a certain charm,' he conceded on one occasion, adding, 'The fact that he moved in the second-rate world of magazines and newspapers sullied him a great deal, but when I lunched with him in his little basement studio, I thought personally he survived with his freshness pretty well inact.'[32]

Nobody, not even Elizabeth Cavendish, the close friend and lady-in-waiting who had introduced them, knew until shortly before their engagement was announced that Princess Margaret and Tony Armstrong-Jones were seeing one another. There had been no obvious chemistry between them on the night of Lady Elizabeth's dinner party, nor had the Princess expressed a wish to meet Tony again. As she herself was to say, 'It took my friends all their time to persuade me he wasn't queer.' That they did meet again was due entirely to Tony's work as a photographer. Dominic Elliot asked if the Princess would sit for some new photographs. When she agreed, Elliot said he knew just the man to take them. It started from there.

As they became ever more attracted to one another and as they discovered the interests they shared – the Princess would one day write to a friend, 'I can never understand why Tony is always supposed to have introduced me to the theatre, ballet, the arts, etc, when that is what we already had in common and a reason for our marrying'[33] – so she and Tony became increasingly determined to keep their romance strictly to themselves.

Lady Penn recalled, 'We lived in Chelsea at that time and I invited Tony to dinner. He immediately accepted, but when I said that Princess Margaret was also coming, he said, "Oh, can I look in my diary?" Then he came back and said how silly of him, he couldn't make it after all. We didn't know they even knew each other ... but they were obviously trying to keep it under wraps – and succeeded extremely well.'[34]

By August 1959, when Tony's twenty-ninth-birthday photographs of Princess Margaret were published, Alexander McEwen remembered being at Balmoral when she spoke of a photographer 'friend'. 'Up to then,' he said, the Princess 'hadn't been particularly interested in photography. I realized afterwards that she was alluding to something and someone special, and I should have asked, "Who is this man?"'[35] It was, perhaps, an indication of the Princess's certainty that she had found the man she would marry that allowed her, maybe without even realizing it, to allude to Tony. 'Of course, one way of making sure a secret is kept a secret is not to tell anyone,' said one of the Princess's friends. Part of the couple's strategy in making sure their relationship remained a secret was to take care that if they were likely to be seen in public, it was always with other people. In the main, however, though they saw one another at Tony's studio-cum-flat in Pimlico, they would meet somewhere almost no-one else knew about.

Number 59 Rotherhithe Street, in the heart of London's East End, overlooked the Thames in dockland. Built in the seventeenth century, it had been lived in by a succession of ships' captains, merchants and barge repairers. Since the early 1950s, it had been both home and office to Bill Glenton, who ran a shipping news agency from the house. As Tony's relationship with Princess Margaret grew stronger, so Glenton was approached by a friend, who asked him to find Tony a pied-à-terre. Bill offered – and having seen it, Tony accepted – a rent-free, ground-floor room with a square bay window looking straight on to the river, at number 59 itself.[36] Painting the walls white, he scrubbed the beams, built pine cupboards to conceal the pipe work and furnished it with a deal table, rush matting, some easy chairs, a corner china cabinet and an upright piano. And that, save for a floor-to-ceiling portrait of an unknown eighteenth-century admiral that hung on a wall and a hammock slung across one corner, was the famous 'Little White Room' that the press would one day come to learn about.

Describing its location, author Mark Girouard wrote that it was 'down in the Pool [of London] where the river is at its most wonderful, romantic and extraordinary ... there is no embankment, no traffic, no noise except the occasional unearthly bellowing of a ship's hooter; the houses look straight out across the moored barges, the tugs and the occasional great ship, to a tangled skyline of cranes ...'[37]

To Princess Margaret, the room wove its very own kind of magic. 'It had the most marvellous view,' she said. 'One walked into the room and there was the river straight in front. At high tide swans looked in. And because it was on a bend ... you looked towards the Tower and Tower Bridge with the dome of St Paul's behind them to the left, and the docks to the right.'[38]

Once they were married, the Princess and Tony invited friends to the house, either for parties that went on into the small hours or for smaller, more intimate, dinner parties that were made more memorable for having the sights and sounds of the Thames just outside the window. By the mid-1960s, however, 59 Rotherhithe Street – like the passion Princess Margaret and Tony once shared – had gone for ever. In what Bill Glenton referred to as an act of 'corporate vandalism', all the houses in Rotherhithe Street were demolished by the local council to make way for 'a riverside walk virtually no-one wanted'.

It had all been part of a romantic idyll.

ELEVEN

Despite the increasing intimacy of their relationship during 1959, Tony would always, in the presence of others, call Princess Margaret 'Ma'am.' If speaking of her, he would refer to 'Princess Margaret', never, even when the time came, to 'my fiancée' or 'my wife.' It was all perfectly correct, but for somebody as free-spirited as Tony, all rather incongruous. In private, he would call her 'Darling' or 'Margaret' or, if writing, 'Darling M'. To one another, or so it used to be said, they were 'Pet' and 'Tone'. There would also come a time when, with good-natured irreverence, the Beatle John Lennon would call them 'Priceless Margarine and Bony Armstrove.'

Right from the start there was always that suggestion of formality, an unspoken understanding that, no matter who *you* were, royalty's tribal instincts meant *they* would always be a people apart. Tony knew it. Princess Margaret was never entirely able to forget it. As one who has known her all her life, has said, 'There is part of Princess Margaret that is very aware of her royal status.'[1] Gore Vidal, a friend for more than forty years, who was also aware of that side of her character, went further. 'She is far too bright for her station in life,' he once wrote, 'which she takes altogether too solemnly.'[2]

It was that 'solemnity' which could suddenly get in the way and spoil things. A withering, off-hand remark or injudicious word, a swift change of mood, a conversation-stopping correction or contradiction, a thoughtless, though to be fair, often unintentional, disregard for the trouble and efforts of others, seemed to ensure that she would always be the caretaker of her own legend. Woodrow Wyatt, the former Labour MP, life peer and newspaper columnist, once wrote of the Princess, 'Suddenly you may feel her psychologically draw herself up with the unspoken "I am the sister of the Queen", which is instantly crushing.'[3]

There was also the famous cold stare, when her vibrant blue eyes turn to ice, freezing the unsuspecting trespasser who had crossed the undefined – and, for that matter, indefinable – line between the acceptable and the unacceptable; of which only the Princess herself was the arbiter. 'Just when you think you are getting on famously with her', one casualty remarked, 'she hops back on to her twig.'[4] 'It can happen if she feels vulnerable', said one friend, 'or if she is in new or unfamiliar situations. And it can happen if she feels out of her depth.'[5] Another friend is of the opinion that, 'It is slightly her fault if people become familiar. She can be very friendly and that is when people think they know her better than they do. But then, they are all capable of doing the "stare" thing. The Queen and Queen Elizabeth do it, too.'[6]

The Princess's reputation as a house guest was no more encouraging, though as one royal footman put it, 'She can't be that bad, otherwise she wouldn't keep getting asked back.'[7] As with so much else, the press helped to keep that aspect of the 'legend' alive, even though old and very tired stories were shamelessly passed off as new. Who, by now, hasn't heard the one about the police search of a friend's house in which the Princess was going to stay, when even the bath panel was removed. Far from being a routine occurrence, it was a one-off that happened a long time ago. There was also the popular tale of the hostess who allegedly had her bedroom rewired so that Princess Margaret could use her Carmen rollers. Whether that particular story is true or not, one of her friends said, 'Princess Margaret does tend to take over other people's houses. She hates dim lights and candlelight, preferring well-lit rooms. And she once remarked, "A dark dining room upsets my tummy. I can't see what I'm eating." '8

Other friends who invited the Princess to stay understood and accepted the way she was. 'If she's difficult', one was to say, 'it's because she has her own way of living. She has ways in which she likes things done.'9 Another said, 'Having Princess Margaret to stay is not like having anyone else for the weekend. You make an extra effort to make sure that it is a success. But, she can stay in a castle or a cottage and envince the same pleasure if she is having a good time. She can be – and she enjoys – congenial, entertaining company.'10

At the British Embassy in Paris, where she was an official guest one weekend in April 1959, however, Princess Margaret's difficult behaviour exasperated Cynthia Gladwyn, then Britain's ambassadress. On their way back to London from a visit to Rome, the Princess and her mother stayed for two or three days at the embassy. Lady Gladwyn noted in her diary that the Queen Mother's 'sparkling and delightful manner . . . puts everything on an easy footing.' But she said, 'Princess Margaret seems to fall between two stools. She wishes to convey that she is very much the Princess, but at the same time she is not prepared to stick to the rules if they bore or annoy her . . .

'When, after the cocktail party, we went to dress [for dinner], Princess Margaret asked me whether it would be "short or long." I knew that this trivial detail had often been a stumbling block; that if it was decreed that we would all wear short dresses, she would embarrass everybody by making an entry in the most sweeping of ball dresses and vice versa. So, as the occasion was not a particularly formal one, I had given out that the Queen Mother was certain to wear a long dress . . . but that Princess Margaret might well wear a short dress, so that either would be correct. In fact she did wear a short dress which, as one Frenchman commented, "began too late and ended too soon".'

Later that weekend, a number 'of young people' had been invited to the châteaux at Courance and Vaux-le-Vicomte to entertain the Princess. All, said Cynthia Gladwyn, were 'eager to meet this celebrated girl who had become a very popular figure in French eyes from her much-publicized romance with Townsend and her spirited behaviour.' At the last minute, however, the Princess said she had a cold, with which she 'began clearing her throat, cooked up a few coughs, and said that her voice was going.' It meant, of course, that she would not be joining the rest of the party, to the disappointment of all those who had made the arrangements and the younger guests who were looking forward to meeting her.

In the meantime, Lady Gladwyn had been informed that an appointment had been made for Princess Margaret with the famous hairdresser, Alexandre, who was to come to the embassy after lunch that day. 'Clearly', she wrote, 'Princess Margaret's cold was a fake', and said so to Viscountess Hambleden, the Queen Mother's lady-in-waiting, who 'was not in the least surprised.'

On returning to the embassy that day, the Queen Mother and her hostess went to see how the Princess was. 'Her elaborate coiffure', Cynthia Gladwyn remarked, 'showed that something rich and strange had been done to her. Nevertheless the farce of the cold was still kept up, and the difficult girl had not yet decided whether she would come down to dinner or not.' Presently, having enquired through Lady Hambleden which 'important' guests were invited, the Princess appeared. The cold, noted the weary Ambassadress, 'would have been quite impressive if she had remembered to keep it up. But now and then she lapsed and became perfectly normal, to the amusement of those who knew what was behind it all, and the puzzlement of some of those who had been going to meet her during the day, such as the Marquis and Marquise de Ganay.'

The following Monday, before accompanying Queen Elizabeth to the Floralies Exhibition – a Parisian version of the Chelsea Flower Show – which the Queen Mother was to inaugurate, Lady Gladwyn took leave of Princess Margaret who was returning to London that morning after an early dress fitting with Christian Dior. She found the Princess 'in a beautiful sweeping négligé', and went on, 'I asked her how she was feeling, and she said much better. As I curtseyed', Lady Gladwyn said, 'I could not resist remarking, "I'm so glad, Ma'am, that having your hair shampooed did not make your cold worse." '[11]

In October of that year when, at the Queen's invitation, Tony Armstrong-Jones was staying at Balmoral, Princess Margaret received a letter from Peter Townsend. In it he told her that he was about to remarry. At nineteen, Marie-Luce Jamagne, a pretty Belgian girl with more than a passing resemblance to the Princess, was half his age. Stunned by the unimagined nature of Townsend's news, Princess Margaret saw his engagement as the betrayal of an 'understanding' they had reached.

That same afternoon, while they were out walking together, Princess Margaret told Tony of Townsend's letter. But, in anticipation of what already seemed inevitable at some point in their relationship, she asked him not to propose to her. 'He eventually did', the Princess recalled, 'but in a roundabout way. It was very cleverly worded.'[12]

In December, the Princess and Tony were privately engaged, and though the Queen Mother told him with undisguised delight, 'I'm *so* pleased you are going to marry Margaret', he had yet to ask the Queen for her formal consent to the marriage. This he did at Sandringham, one month later, though not without deploying an element of subterfuge in the continuing quest to keep the romance secret. Princess Margaret explained that the elaborately devised smokescreen centred on the need to provide a figure of Buddha, which sat in the garden and was known to the royal family as 'John Chinaman,' with a replacement pergola. As arranged, Tony arrived at Sandringham House one day in January 1960, bringing with him a perfect scale model of the proposed design, ostensibly for the Queen's approval. Once behind closed doors, however, the spurious issue of the pergola and the carefully constructed model were put to one side.[13] Tony formally asked the Queen as Sovereign, as head of the family and, indeed, almost as a surrogate parent, for her permission to marry Princess Margaret.

If either she or the Queen Mother had any private doubts about his suitability, they were kept strictly to themselves. The Townsend episode had been too hard and too painful an experience to deprive the Princess of the almost delirious happiness she had found in Tony. Though it was agreed that the public announcement should wait a few more weeks until after the Queen, who was by now eight months' pregnant, had given birth to her third child, Princess Margaret could not resist taking a handful of her closest friends into her confidence.

In a letter to one of them she said, 'Something so happy has happened to me and I felt I must write and tell you about it before it comes out. It's that I am engaged to be married to the most heavenly person called Tony Armstrong-Jones. This is a dead secret . . . but one which I know you will guard safely. We are so happy it is unbelievable.'[14]

Not everyone shared the Princess's delight. Disturbed by a sense of foreboding, Tony's father, who had just married his third wife, the thirty-one-year-old Jenifer Unite, and was on honeymoon in Bermuda, implored his artistic and much too unconventional son not to go through with the marriage. Jocelyn Stevens, to whom Tony had cabled the news at Lyford Cay, his estate in the Bahamas, also saw a disaster in the making, and responded by return, 'Never was there a more ill-fated assignment.'

If Tony resented the negative reaction of those close to him, it was simply that they could see what he, intoxicated by his own happiness and madly in love with this world-famous, sensual and beautiful woman, could not. In temperament they were much too alike: two peas out of the same pod. And while the Princess thought Tony's way of life daringly attractive, the one she knew had hardly changed since Victorian times.

Tony's was not, and never could be, the world of precisely timed schedules and formal official programmes; of chamberlains, comptrollers and other household officers with grand-sounding titles; of marching bands and military parades. Nor would he be at home in the white-tie, black-tie world of orders and decorations; of hunting, shooting and horse racing; the changing for lunch, for tea, for dinner, and the predictable, clockwork migration from London to Windsor to Sandringham to Balmoral, depending on the seasons. In short, he would not be at one with the prescribed nineteenth century values of Court life.

If those close to Tony were predicting catastrophe, Elizabeth Cavendish thought to ask the Princess if she understood, indeed, would be comfortable in, Tony's world. For all its attraction, she said, it was somewhat 'Bohemian'. Lady Elizabeth recalled, 'The Princess asked, "What does that mean?" I said, "Well, he'll be all over the place, doing whatever he is doing. You won't always know what, you won't always know where he is or where to contact him. He won't always be home for dinner. Can you cope with that?" '[15] Love persuaded her that she could.

When it was formally announced on the evening of Friday, 26 February, exactly one week after the Queen had given birth to her second son, Andrew, at Buckingham Palace, Princess Margaret's engagement took the world completely by surprise.* While there was a palpable sense of incredulity among Tony's journalist and photographer colleagues in Fleet Street, not least because they had known nothing of his relationship with the Princess, there was genuine and widespread delight among the public. Closer to home, however, the mood was again less ecstatic. After Noël Coward had lunched with Marina, Duchess of Kent and Princess Alexandra, he noted, 'They are *not* pleased over Princess Margaret's engagement. There was a distinct *froideur* when I mentioned it.'

---

* The text of the formal announcement from Clarence House read: 'It is with the greatest pleasure that Queen Elizabeth The Queen Mother announces the betrothal of her beloved daughter The Princess Margaret to Mr Antony Charles Robert Armstrong-Jones, son of Mr R.O.L. Armstrong-Jones QC, and the Countess of Rosse, to which union The Queen has gladly given her consent.'

Even though she had spent much of her life in exile before marrying Prince George, Duke of Kent, no member of the royal family was more conscious of her royal heritage than Princess Marina. And although not one of her own children would make a royal marriage, she was far from welcoming in her attitude towards Tony Armstrong-Jones. Not that she was alone. As Sarah Bradford related in her biography of the Queen, 'One old courtier told Harold Nicolson that he lamented the whole thing. "The boy Jones has led a very diversified and sometimes a wild life and the danger of a scandal and slander is never far off." '16

If certain high society families looked down on Princess Margaret's engagement, foreign royalty – including the Dutch and the Scandinavians, so often held up by the ill-informed as exemplars of more democratic and informal systems of monarchy – were no less disdainful. Of those invited to the wedding, which had been set to take place at Westminster Abbey on the morning of Friday, 6 May, only Princess Margaret's godmother, Queen Ingrid of Denmark, and a handful of ex-royalties such as the Hereditary Prince of Hohenlohe-Langenburg, the Princes Maximilian and Ludwig of Baden and Prince Karl of Hesse, accepted.

Nevertheless, royal wedding day itself, with a clear blue sky and bright sunshine, could not have been happier. Nor could the crowds, some 500,000 strong, have been more enthusiastic. All London, it seemed, was *en fête*. Along the Mall, white silk banners emblazoned with red Tudor roses overlaid with the entwined initials M and A stirred in the occasional breeze, while a sixty-foot arch made up of 30,000 pink and red roses spanned the Mall outside Clarence House. Along the way Government buildings were festooned with hydrangeas, stocks and roses, and colourful flower baskets were hung from every lamp post.

Opposite Westminster Abbey, a grandstand with seats at £25 apiece was constructed, while both inside and outside the great church discreet stations were built and camouflaged for television cameras, some using innovative, state-of-the-art zoom lenses for the very first time. This was, in fact, the first royal wedding to be televised and the pageant commanded a world-wide audience of 300 million. Television also meant, as Princess Margaret herself put it, 'that those of my friends who couldn't come could still see it. I loved that idea.'[17]

Among the 2,000 guests at the Abbey, members of the Prayer Group to which the Princess belonged – and which was led by the Dean of Westminster, who would conduct her wedding service – rubbed shoulders with statesmen such as Churchill, Attlee, and Eden, now the Earl of Avon. There were famous faces such as the future Poet Laureate Sir John Betjeman, the long-standing companion of Lady Elizabeth Cavendish, who before the service began was to be seen happily 'gazing up at details of architecture.'[18] Then there was Noël Coward, the actress Margaret Leighton, Dr Mervyn Stockwood, Bishop of Southwark, 'clad in purple like a Prince of the Church',[19] and some of the Princess's closest friends, among them the Dalkeiths and the Blandfords, Dominic Elliot, the Bonham-Carters, the Lowthers and Brands, and the Dukes of Marlborough, Buccleuch, Richmond and Northumberland.

There were other recognizable figures among the minor royal and nearly royal, such as Lady Patricia Ramsay who as Princess 'Pat' had been the Abbey's first twentieth century royal bride in 1919; and Dickie Mountbatten, whose wife, Edwina, had died suddenly of a heart attack while in Borneo only six days before the announcement of Princess Margaret's engagement. Despite the fact that the dress code for male guests at this non-military wedding was morning-dress, he conspicuously wore the full rig of an Admiral of the Fleet, complete with Garter ribbon, stars, and medals.

Not long before the bride, the royal family arrived in a glittering procession of State carriages accompanied by a full Sovereign's Escort of the Life Guards and the Blues and Royals.

The Queen, in full-skirted turquoise silk and lace, restrained her emotions behind an expression stern enough to cause comment. The Queen Mother in soft gold lamé looked, said one guest, 'like a great golden pussy cat, full of sad little smiles,'[20] the disapproving Duchess of Kent was cool and elegant in lemon, and Princess Alexandra, in blue slipper satin, was 'rather bursting out of her seams.'[21]

The bridegroom, immaculate in tailcoat, though described as 'having aged very much in the last few weeks, and a bad colour',[22] was conducted to his seat along with his best man, Dr Roger Gilliatt, Professor of Clinical Neurology at London University.

Shortly afterwards, the eight young bridesmaids gathered at the West Door. Led by Princess Anne, they included Marilyn Wills and Annabel Rhodes, daughters of Princess Margaret's favourite Elphinstone cousins, Jean Wills and Margaret Rhodes, Tony's niece, Catherine Vesey, and Sarah Lowther, daughter of the former Jenny Bevan. All wore long dresses of white organza with puff sleeves and Peter Pan collars. Trimmed with lace and threaded with blue ribbon, they were replicas of the bride's first evening dress, which her father had so admired. Completing the picture, they wore halo-like head-dresses of white swansdown and diamanté, which Carl Toms had designed, and they carried posies of lilies-of-the-valley, Princess Margaret's favourite flower.

The bride herself left Clarence House to the applause of Household staff gathered in the long tapestry and portrait-lined gallery formally known as the Hall. At the front door, beneath the porte cochère, waited the Glass Coach in which, accompanied by an escort of the Household Cavalry, the Princess drove to the Abbey, arriving a few minutes early. This was due entirely to the fact that, with one eye on the clock, Prince Philip, who was to give the Princess away, had kept reminding her that they would be late if she didn't hurry.

All were agreed that Princess Margaret was the very epitome of the 'fairy-tale' princess. Having originated with Tony's own eye for design, Norman Hartnell had been instructed that, in contrast to the heavily embroidered dresses he usually made for the royal ladies, Princess Margaret's wedding dress was to be completely and utterly simple. It was and the effect was stunning.

Worn over stiffened tulle underskirts and made from thirty yards of white silk organza piped with a narrow rouleau of the same material, Hartnell designed the dress with a high V-neckline, fitted bodice and wrist-length sleeves. The diaphanous, almost crinoline, skirt was cut into twelve panels which in turn formed a semi-circular train. Making its effect, said one admiring fashion writer, 'with an art that conceals art', the bridal gown was perfectly complemented by a full-length veil, created in Paris to Hartnell's design by Claude St Cyr. Also made of silk organza so fine that it was as light and transparent as tulle, and edged with the same rouleau as the dress itself, it cascaded from a spectacular diamond tiara that flashed and sparkled with every move of the Princess's head.*

As a fanfare of trumpets heralded her arrival at Westminster Abbey, and the Princess and the Duke of Edinburgh made their way along the blue-carpeted nave towards the high altar, Prince Philip joked, 'I don't know who's more nervous, you or me', and then asked, 'Am I holding on to you, or are you holding on to me?' 'I'm holding on to you', the Princess whispered in reply.[23]

In the main, Tony Armstrong-Jones had left the choice of prayers and music for the service to Princess Margaret, who had several discussions with her old friend Eric Abbott. Music by Bach, Handel, Purcell and Schubert was chosen, together with a reading from the Beatitudes instead of a more formal address.

---

* Superbly worked in a scroll and flower design that can be unclipped and worn either as a necklace or individual hair ornaments, the tiara had been bought some months earlier at the recommendation of Patrick Plunket, the young and artistic bachelor peer who had succeeded Peter Townsend as Deputy Master of the Household. Formally known as the Poltimore tiara - 'Patrick's tiara,' as Princess Margaret called it by way of tribute to Lord Plunket's advice to buy - had been sent for auction by the 6th Baron Poltimore and acquired for something in the region of £5,000.

Married by Dr Geoffrey Fisher, the same Archbishop of Canterbury with whom she had spoken five years earlier at the time of Townsend, Princess Margaret and her new husband left London later that afternoon for a six-week Caribbean cruise on board the Royal Yacht *Britannia*. Like the £25,000 cost of the wedding itself which, predictably, met opposition from certain Labour MPs – and led the Queen Mother to make it known that if need be she would cover the cost out of her own pocket – protests were heard in the House against the use of *Britannia*, her twenty officers and 237 ratings, as a honeymoon cruise ship.

So tightly packed were the streets in the City, however, that as well-wishers slowed the progress of the open-topped royal Rolls-Royce on its way to the Pool of London, there was growing concern that *Britannia* might miss the tide.

It didn't, and as the Princess's personal standard was broken at the main masthead and the arms of Tower Bridge were raised to let the Royal Yacht glide through, the band of the Royal Marines on deck played popular, and highly appropriate, show tunes such as *Oh, What a Beautiful Day*.

Rounding the bend in the river to Rotherhithe and dockland, Princess Margaret and Tony, who had been responding to the cheers of the crowds along the embankments, piers and wharfs, waved enthusiastically to Bill Glenton, now back from the Abbey, who watched them pass by from the open window of the little White Room.

Further down stream at Greenhithe, more than 1,000 cars brought 4,000 sightseers to the river while at the specially decorated promenade at Gravesend, one of the largest crowds the town had ever seen waited to greet *Britannia* and her royal passengers, amid the sounds of saluting ships' hooters and tugboat sirens. At Southend, near where the Royal Yacht paused to let the band of the Marines disembark on to an Admiralty barge, 10,000 spectators lined the pier head, and thirty fishing boats and yachts sailed out to salute the Princess;

at whose appearance the cacophony of sound grew louder still.

Retracing the route it had taken little more than five years earlier, when Princess Margaret first visited the Caribbean, *Britannia* also anchored off some of the smaller islands in the Windward chain. One of them, Mustique, was no more than 1,250 inhospitable acres of thorn-cloaked scrubland, inhabited by giant mosquitoes, a few wild cows and a tiny community of fishermen and cotton growers. Bought by Colin Tennant, whose wife Anne originally thought the whole idea was sheer madness, the Mustique of newspaper headlines, grandiose villas, lords and pop stars, romance and 'Jump-Ups' – all of which, said one visitor, seemed to belong to some kind of upmarket soap opera – had yet to be created.

In May 1960, the Tennants were camping out on their still-primitive island when the *Britannia* came to call, and Princess Margaret invited her old friends on board for dinner with Tony and herself. For Colin and Anne, who had no running water, acceptance of the Princess's invitation was accompanied by a request to be allowed to use the Yacht's facilities. Thus the prospect of a decent dinner was made yet more appealing by the luxury of taking a bath – their first in a fortnight. It was during that honeymoon visit that Colin Tennant asked the Princess – it was not intended to be a shared gift, and Tony never visited the island again – whether she would like a wedding present 'from Asprey's wrapped up in a box,' or a plot of land on Mustique. She chose the land, and a spot was eventually selected on a private peninsula overlooking Gelliceaux Bay, with breathtaking views beyond.

When they returned to London in mid-June, both looking tanned and relaxed, the Princess, radiating happiness and contentment, 'positively glowed.' Even Jocelyn Stevens, who thought Tony should have had an affair with the Princess, but never married her, recognized the brilliance and vitality of their relationship. While it worked, he said, the energy between them 'was like an electric current.' Adoringly attentive in public, they were passionate and intensely physical in private. It was the perfect partnership. They had 'considered every consequence', said the Princess, and agreed on everything.

One subject they clearly were not as agreed on as she believed, was that of children. A family of her own had not been one of Princess Margaret's ambitions. Nor, or so she thought, had it been one of Tony's. In fact, when they'd originally spoken about having children, both had said they didn't want any.[25] Some months after they married, however, it seemed that Tony had changed his mind, and early in the new year, though the news wasn't made public for three months, Princess Margaret discovered she was pregnant. Their first baby was due that November.

It was to be a year of firsts. A joke advertisement which some wag had published in a Sunday newspaper while the Princess and Tony were on their honeymoon, now had an uncanny truth about it: 'Cambridge Blue, 29, well-connected, forced to give up lucrative professional career, seeks release from social round. Own car. Suggestions welcomed.'[26] Not quite a year after that satirical item had appeared, Tony – who had chosen to give up his career before he married Princess Margaret, telling friends, as part of the plan, that he was 'bored' with photography – had started to become restless and frustrated.

With no role or position of his own, there was little for him to do but accompany the Princess on her official engagements; a non-royal consort, always walking the obligatory one step behind. Said Jocelyn Stevens, 'It was like a pilot sacrificing his career for his marriage . . . but watching every plane with the thought, "I should be up there." '[27] The issue of a role for Tony was partly resolved in early 1961 when, as an unpaid advisor, he joined the Council for Industrial Design, later the Design Council. If it pleased Tony to be the first royal husband to have an independent role, it didn't please certain newspaper editors who denounced the appointment as a 'sinecure.' They were no less scathing when with architect Cedric Price and consultant engineer Frank Newby, he designed the new aviary at London

Zoo. 'Tony's Birdcage', it was sneeringly called. One journalist mockingly said that Tony would surely be regarded as one of Britain's leading birdcage designers, 'not an overcrowded profession.' In the end, to his deep satisfaction, Tony had the last laugh. In 1998, almost forty years later, the aviary was awarded Grade II listing.

Design of another, more domestic, kind had focused Tony's thoughts, and those of Princess Margaret, during the summer of 1961. Home since they returned from honeymoon had been Apartment number 10 Kensington Palace. Although by no means large, 'for the first time in my life I have no room of my own except a bedroom', Tony told Kenneth Rose,[28] it was a compact and attractive house on the north side of the palace complex, which had formerly been occupied by Queen Victoria's grandson 'Drino', otherwise Alexander, Marquess of Carisbrooke. When he died early in 1960, the Queen, who did not think it a good idea that her sister and brother-in-law should begin their married life at home with mother, reserved Apartment 10 for their use, if only as a temporary measure. A few months later, she suggested Apartment 1A might be more suitable. Considerably larger, and once containing a communicating passage known as the Stone Gallery, off which were rooms for courtiers, the house was part of Wren's original South-West Pavilion.

When, in 1954, she was offered the entire forty-room house as her official London residence, however, Marina, Duchess of Kent, who had neither the need nor the wherewithal to run so large a property, asked that it be divided in two. This meant the formation of Apartments 1 and 1A and the subsequent neglect of the twenty-one rooms of various sizes and desirability, from basement to attic, that Marina did not want. Now offered to Princess Margaret, the house – or Apartment 1A – had been allowed to fall into decay by the Ministry of Public Buildings and Works.

Last lived in by Queen Victoria's sculptress daughter Princess Louise, Duchess of Argyll, from 1873 until her death in 1939, (she last had it decorated in 1891), the house had previously been the residence of George III's most popular son, Augustus, Duke of Sussex. It was he who had built up a vast library of books – the famous Sussex Library – which, by the time of his death in April 1843, filled ten rooms in the house and contained more than 50,000 volumes. It was the cost of restoring this historic Wren house that found Willie Hamilton, Labour MP and vociferous critic of the monarchy, questioning Lord John Hope, the Minister of Works, about the amount being spent on it. Various sums from £50,000 to £85,000 had been bandied about. In the end, the lower figure turned out to be nearer the mark which, as Dr Stross, another Labour MP, pointed out, would have had to be spent on preserving the property, whether it was occupied or not.

While the grumbling went on at Westminster and was echoed through the media, Tony took Kenneth Rose to see the house. He found it in a 'terribly tumbledown state ... wantonly neglected and allowed to fall into sad decay. Inside it is no more than a ruin ... with gaping holes in the floorboards.

'Tony rightly points out', he noted in his diary, 'that ... the Minister is trying to extricate himself from the responsibility of allowing this Wren palace to rot by implying that the entire cost of restoration is to make it habitable for the Joneses ... I agree with Tony that the public has no idea of the state of 1A ... and make the suggestion that [journalists and photographers should be allowed in]. It would make a good ... news story with pictures.'[29]

If it seems like a storm in a teacup now, it didn't appear so then and from that point on the press were to become increasingly critical of the 'Joneses'. By the time the builders moved out in 1962 and they moved in, Apartment 1A had undergone a complete transformation. From rotten shell the interior now suggested an eighteenth century country house, with all the elegance of the grand *Style Anglais*, into which Princess Margaret and Tony had, as one design writer put it, introduced 'such spirit and detail and colour that the "Dutch solidity" [of Wren's building work for William of Orange and Mary II] has been splendidly transformed into twentieth-century English verve.'

Another transformation that had by now taken place was that of plain Mr Antony Armstrong-Jones into a Peer of the Realm. At the time of his marriage, the Queen had decided to make Tony an Earl, so that any children of the marriage, her nephews and/or nieces, would not be born without a title. It was a sign of changing times and attitudes that not quite twenty years later, her two eldest grandchildren, Peter and Zara Phillips, would be born, and to date remain, plain Mr and Miss. In the early 1960s, however, things like titles mattered much more and while Tony had shelved the idea of a peerage to begin with, the imminent birth of his first child had revived the issue. Yet, he was to become earl of where? Unlike the nonsense surrounding the title Earl of Wessex that was later bestowed on marriage to the Queen's youngest son Edward in 1999, Tony had to be an earl of somewhere real and tangible. Several options suggested themselves, among them, that he assume the title Earl of Caernarvon, where his family had long lived. But since there was already an earldom of Carnarvon, that was discounted. Arvon was then tentatively chosen, as that was the name of the borough in which his father's ancestral home lay. That, too, had to be discounted when the former Prime Minister, Anthony Eden, was created Earl of Avon. At length, Tony chose to become 1st Earl of Snowdon and Viscount Linley of Nymans, which subsidiary title would automatically be given to the baby Princess Margaret was expecting, if a boy.

Tony's elevation was formally announced on 3 October 1961 and, though she had chosen not to use her married name, 'Mrs Antony Armstrong-Jones', as part of her title, 'I didn't want people to think I was a snob, taking a double-barrelled name',[30] she said, she did become Countess of Snowdon.

At Clarence House precisely one month later, at 10.45 on the morning of 3 November, it was as 'Her Royal Highness The Princess Margaret, Countess of Snowdon' that, by caesarian section, she gave birth to or, in the words of the formal statement, 'was safely delivered of,' a 6lb 4-ounce son. Baptized in the Music Room at Buckingham Palace six weeks later, David Albert Charles, Viscount Linley of Nymans,* became the focus of his 'thrilled and delighted' father's attention as he photographed him constantly, with or without his mother, and proudly selected the shots that were to be released to the world.

So besotted was Tony, in fact, that what he did not want to do a couple of months later, was to leave his infant son and fly off with the Princess on a three-week winter holiday to Antigua. Yet this was what had been planned before the birth and, as the Princess – who had herself been raised more by nannies and a governess than by her own mother – pointed out, baby David would not be aware of who was giving him his four-hourly bottle. Whether it was she as his mother, the very experienced and newly-engaged nanny, Miss Verona Sumner, or the capable nursery maid, was of very little consequence. They, she said, knew far better than she did how a baby had to be looked after.

Ever the pragmatist, Princess Margaret and the now Lord Snowdon, flew out of London amid a storm of newspaper criticism at their apparent heartlessness at leaving the new baby. If nothing else, Tony Snowdon must by now have started to become acclimatized to the idea that the press could and most decidedly would make mischief and stir up public opinion at the least opportunity. Later that month, he found himself at the centre of yet another controversy.

If being an advisor to the Design Council had provided him with some sense of purpose, it was not nearly enough to satisfy the range and scope of Tony's artistic and creative abilities. Helping to renovate Apartment 1A – designing the modern stainless steel kitchen, veneering the mahogany doors between the drawing- and dining-rooms, helping Carl Toms create an imaginative Gothic bathroom, or planning his own dressing- and

---

* At his christening, David Linley's five godparents were his aunt The Queen, Lady Elizabeth Cavendish, Lord (Patrick) Plunket, Lord Rupert Nevill and the Reverend Simon Phipps, later Bishop of Lincoln.

study-workrooms – had been fine for as long as it lasted. But Tony's restlessness soon re-surfaced.

The newly-launched *Sunday Times* colour supplement provided a positive solution if not to all Tony's ills – it would soon create as many problems in his home life as it solved – at least to the more pressing issues of his independence, sense of self-worth, purpose and direction. If the question of what he was going to do after they married was another issue on which he and Princess Margaret were not agreed, perhaps because it hadn't been considered, Tony was certain of at least one thing. He had married the Princess because he loved her, not because it was his ambition to spend the rest of his life as some kind of royal appendage. Indeed, if Prince Philip who was generally perceived by the public to be little more than the Queen's husband and side-kick, had already had cause to complain, 'I'm nothing but a bloody amoeba', Tony, as the representative of the modern world, had no intention of going down the same path.

In January 1962, news of Tony's appointment as salaried artistic adviser and photographer to the *Sunday Times* magazine outraged the paper's rivals. When asked why Lord Snowdon and not some other unemployed photojournalist had been given the job, Roy Thomson, the *Sunday Times*' owner, replied, 'Because I don't know of a better unemployed photojournalist.' David Astor, editor of the rival Sunday quality, the *Observer*, responded by saying that 'Mr Thomson carefully avoids the main issue, which is whether linking his expansionist aims to the Queen's family is likely to be good for the monarchy.'

The Queen, however, like Princess Margaret, fully approved of Tony's appointment and, indeed, the Princess had been partly, though discreetly, instrumental in helping her husband secure the position. That is to say, she asked Jocelyn Stevens to make it known to Denis Hamilton, then editor of the *Sunday Times*, that her husband would not be averse to a position if something were available. Tony, on the other hand, put the appointment down to his long-standing friendship with Mark

Boxer, also known as the cartoonist 'Marc', and later a book publisher, who was then working on the *Sunday Times*' new magazine.

However it came about, Tony was back in business and doing what he did best. For the *Sunday Times*, *Vogue*, and *Vanity Fair*, as for all the magazines and journals for whom he worked before his marriage, he accepted assignments and commissions that now, and well into the future, would encompass the familiar realms of theatre, art, dance, literature, and fashion. It would also take him into stark issues of social concern, about which he would also make award-winning television documentaries: old age, mental health, poverty, children, the disabled and the handicapped.

Far less disturbing images of film and theatre personalities, as well as writers, painters and dancers – people such as Sophia Loren, Maggie Smith and Robert Stephens, John Gielgud, and Peter Ustinov; Francis Bacon and David Hockney; Vladimir Nabokov, John Betjeman, and Edna O'Brien; Ashton, Helpmann, Nureyev, Fonteyn and Baryshnikov – seemed to encapsulate the world that had always been his and was now, at least to a somewhat larger extent than it had been before, Princess Margaret's, too.

Of all the royal family, the Snowdons, as they were now known, were the only ones who really moved with the times. As the 'Swinging Sixties' got into gear and really started to 'swing', they found themselves at the heart of the new pop culture. Giving and receiving invitations to fabulous parties, they met, sang and danced to the music of the best bands and singers in the entertainment business at a time when The Beatles were top of the list. 'I adored them', said the Princess, 'because they were poets as well as musicians.'[31] There were other just as famous actors and performers whom the Princess knew and enjoyed, among them Frank Sinatra, Elizabeth Taylor, and Roddy McDowall. There was also the famous American jazz composer and musician Duke Ellington. 'What shall I say to him?' the Princess had asked her friend Colin Campbell, when she was about to meet him for the first time. 'Ask him what it's like to be a duke', Campbell jokingly replied.[32]

During the sixties, the Princess and Tony both kept abreast of fashion, like everyone else with varying degrees of success. Princess Margaret soon adopted mini skirts, caftans, lacy stockings and imaginatively modern costume jewellery. She experimented with hair styles from chic, glossy cuts to elaborate coiffeurs involving hair pieces. Leaving the dukes and princes to their usual impeccably cut, but conservative, lounge suits, Tony wore striped frock coats, scarves, tight trousers, roll necks, leather jackets and boots, and also experimented with hair styles and colour. Meeting them on one occasion at a formal reception at St James's Palace, Cynthia Gladwyn noted that while Princess Margaret looked 'very pretty in a turquoise blue dress, with a beautiful turquoise and diamond tiara and necklace to match', Tony 'had a sun-lamp burnt brown complexion and hair … tinted a curious new colour. Sachy Sitwell afterwards described it as peach, but I would say more apricot.'[33]

Inevitably there were those among the actors, writers, dancers, singers and film makers with whom the Princess and Tony socialized who were not as sold on them as others. One evening when their friends Kenneth and Kathleen Tynan invited them to dinner with Peter Cook and his wife and the playwright Harold Pinter and his then wife, the actress Vivien Merchant, the latter seized the occasion to take an entirely gratuitous swipe at the Princess. Kathleen Tynan recalled, 'The evening started inauspiciously with Ken's failed attempt to introduce the Snowdons and Vivien Merchant. "I put out my hand", Princess Margaret recalls, "which was refused. So I sort of drew it up as if it were meant for another direction." At dinner the actress sat next to Tony Snowdon, who had just photographed her as Lady Macbeth at Stratford. "Of course", we heard her say, "the only reason we *artistes* let you take our pictures is because you are married to her." Whereat she stabbed a finger towards the Princess. Everyone began to drink steadily.'[34]

These were the years when, to all intents and purposes,

Princess Margaret and Lord Snowdon were London society's golden couple. They were, said Lord Ardwick, editor of the socialist *Daily Herald*, 'a new kind of royalty. They had far more contacts among writers and artists and so forth, not among stuffy courtiers. They looked freer and they became the new family model of fast travelling, hard-working, affluent young people.'[35]

By 1964 however, though few were as yet aware of it, and there was certainly nothing to tarnish their popular public image, cracks had begun to appear in the couple's relationship. Though intensely in love with Tony, Princess Margaret had started to become possessive. 'She always wanted Tony to be everywhere with her',[36] said one friend. Another who was discussing some matter with Tony at Kensington Palace when the Princess appeared, noted afterwards, 'Princess Margaret comes in – warm in her welcome. But she tiresomely interrupts everything Tony says . . .'[37]

On another occasion, the Snowdons flew to Greece to holiday with Stavros and Eugènie Niarchos, Sunny Blandford's then sister-in-law, on Spetsopolua, their private island. 'Tony was talking to some people', said one member of the party, 'but the Princess wanted his attention and kept calling, "Tony . . . Tony . . . Tony. . ." She was at fault. But he ignored her and carried on with his conversation. So he was also at fault.'[38] Those who knew Princess Margaret and Tony at this time are agreed that while she enjoyed many aspects of his way of life, the same could not be said for him. 'They were both very strong characters,' said one source, 'too alike, too selfish. Tony wanted his own life, not hers. They both hoped they might be able to change each other.'

One of the realities, perhaps the single most important reality the Snowdons had to face five or six years after their romance had first begun, was the collapse of an illusion, of an idyll. Their relationship was no longer a thrilling secret. Pimlico and Rotherhithe no longer existed. There were no swans outside the window, and reality now told the Princess that she did mind if Tony wasn't home for dinner.

'There are two sides to Tony,' said one who has known

Princess Margaret for a very long time. 'He could be very unkind to her. For instance, we'd make films and he would deliberately leave her out of it. I don't know why he was like that because he was very fond of her.'[39]

Unwittingly, Tony's earliest biographers, Robert Glenton and Stella King, provided a glimpse of that darker side of his character. Writing of one of his childhood visits to Womersley Park, his mother and stepfather's house in South Yorkshire, where he indulged an apparent penchant for building tree houses, Tony evidently wanted to show off his latest effort.

'Wandering through the grounds', they wrote, 'he came across a little group of village children. One of them, a farmworker's daughter, olive-skinned and laughing, fascinated him. Tony . . . coaxed them all to see his tree house. They scrambled up and he glowed under their admiration. Then carefully he helped them to descend. He stood on the branch for a moment, looking down at the scrambling children. He was prey to confused emotions – their happy flattery and his sudden affection for the little girl. He could think of only one way to express himself. He turned, crawled into his wooden hut, and emerged with a can of water . . . Thoughtfully and pensively he looked down once again at his first love, and then with a grin poured the water over her head.'[40]

No less questionable were certain aspects of Princess Margaret's character. The wife of one courtier, for example, is quoted as having said, 'She had everything and then she destroyed herself. Her nature was to make everything go wrong. Nice one day – nasty the next. She was the only one who would come up to you at a party and really talk to you . . . the next day she'd cut you . . . Then she'd be so tiresome in house parties – keeping people up too late and buggering up evenings.'[41]

The Princess and Tony were not merely complex characters, they were both extremely complicated. 'Hurt children', said one friend, 'always smack first.' Perhaps it was the bewildered four-year-old still inside Tony who couldn't understand why the parents he loved were divorcing, that made him behave as he did. Such, indeed, was his relationship with Anne Rosse and Ronald Armstrong-Jones in later life that one who knew him well was to say, 'He was always non-speaks with one parent or the other.'

Though unlike Tony, Princess Margaret was not from a broken home, she was nevertheless part of a strangely dysfunctional and uncommunicative family. What her innermost feelings were, some of which she may even have chosen to deny to herself, nobody will ever know. And although masked by her contradictory character – one moment kind, spontaneous, generous, always willing to help and fun to be with; the next self absorbed, snappy, dismissive and downright awkward – one thing becomes very clear. As a plain statement of fact, untainted by sentimentality, she was always a little girl looking for love. Others have recognized it as well. 'When one realizes that', said one old friend 'you understand everything and you can forgive.'[42] Townsend had also seen it when he sensed, 'that, in her life too, there was something lacking.'

When they returned from holidaying with the Niarchoses in Greece in the early autumn of 1963, Princess Margaret was again pregnant. So, for that matter, were the Queen, who was expecting her fourth child the following March, Katharine Worsley, the young Duchess of Kent, married to Princess Marina's elder son, whose second child was due in April, and Princess Alexandra, whose first baby was expected in February, seven or eight weeks before her first wedding anniversary. Not since the death in childbirth of the twenty-one-year-old Princess Charlotte of Wales, in 1817, when the crown found itself in desperate need of legitimate heirs, had so many royal babies been expected in so short a time.

At Kensington Palace on Saturday, 1 May 1964, again by Caesarian section, Princess Margaret gave birth to a daughter. Ten weeks later, on 13 July, Lady Sarah Frances Elizabeth Armstrong-Jones, was christened in the private chapel at

Buckingham Palace in the presence of her five godparents: Marigold Bridgeman, Janie Stevens, Anthony Barton, Prue Penn and Lord Westmorland. That day, there was no suggestion of the tension between the baby's parents that not so long before had earned Tony a warning about his behaviour from the Princess's doctor.[43] Nor, indeed, was there any sign of it when they flew out to Sardinia the following month as guests of Prince Karim, Aga Khan, otherwise known simply as 'K', who was in the process of launching an exclusive £80-million holiday resort on the Costa Smeralda, which Princess Margaret and Lord Snowdon's presence would endorse. After staying at the Hotel Pitrizza, from where they swam, water-skied and sailed aboard K's yacht, the *Amaloun*, the Snowdons flew to Venice, near where, at the Palladian Villa Malcontenta, they were joined by Janie and Jocelyn Stevens. On the Costa Smeralda, the Princess thought it would be a good idea if she and Tony did nothing more than have fun and relax. Venice, however, would be interesting and cultural.

'I called Princess Margaret the "Master Planner"', said Jocelyn Stevens. 'She loved planning what we were going to do, and [at home] she keeps the most marvellous albums which she faithfully writes up. At the end of each day she would write out her notes, asking us what we had seen. She knew perfectly well, of course, but she wanted to make sure we had noticed as much as she had. It was like being debriefed. We'd all sit in the corner, pretending to be tired or bored, but she took it all very seriously. She loved it. It was the most *marvellous* holiday, and she and Tony got on so well.'[44]

Some weeks later in the garden of Testbourne, the Stevens's country house in Hampshire, the Princess and Tony, with Jocelyn and Janie, Peter Sellers and his young actress wife Britt Ekland, whom he had married earlier in the year, made a rather bizarre home movie which was intended to be a thirty-ninth birthday present for the Queen the following April. In one scene with Sellers, Tony played the part of a camp gangster, while the actor himself, whom Princess Margaret had first met at

Windsor Castle in December 1951 when he and Tony Hancock provided entertainment at a staff party, ran through a repertoire of comic characters. Then, before the small cast lined up for the film's finale singing *We're Riding Along on the Crest of a Wave*, Sellers stood in front of a four-panelled Chinese lacquer screen to announce in suitably goonish voice, 'Following my dramatic success at the Workmen's Institute, Penge, I am presenting this afternoon, in al fresco for the very first time, a few very, very, successful and highly dramatic quick changes. The first will be done in the amazingly short time of eleven seconds flat . . . my impersonation, before your very eyes . . . of Her Royal Highness Princess Margaret.'

Disappearing behind the screen, one or two items of clothing were thrown in the air before the real Princess Margaret, clearly revelling in the theatricality of it all, stepped out, took a bow, curtsied to the camera and, with a final wave, went back behind the screen.

It was by all accounts a film the Queen often showed to guests.

TWELVE

By the end of the sixties, battle lines had been firmly drawn and the Snowdons' marriage was already in an increasingly fast-spinning and destructive downward spiral. To the outside world, their united front concealed ever widening divisions. Some could be temporarily patched up for the sake of appearances, but others would never be bridged. Once the marriage had started to go wrong, it seemed that nothing could save it.

Janie and Jocelyn Stevens were among the first of the couple's friends to notice the change, beginning in 1965 when they joined the Princess and Tony in Italy, for the last part of their summer holiday. The Snowdons' relationship, Jocelyn had once said, had, 'A showbusiness quality' about it. 'When it worked it was sensational, but when it didn't, there was an atmosphere you couldn't kick your way through.' In Rome, disagreement over accommodation had caused one of those atmospheres. Sulky and defiantly silent, Tony had climbed out of the window of the studio their friends Judy Montagu and Milton Gendel had loaned them, and up on to the roof to find escape squatting on a flat-topped chimney. When her anxious pleas to come down were ignored, the Princess rang Jocelyn Stevens who, when he arrived, climbed up to find out what was going on.[1]

With an independent career – and a marriage which he said, made him 'work harder' – Snowdon wanted to be master of his own destiny. Once the novelty of public engagements had worn off, perhaps something else they hadn't seriously considered, Tony no longer wanted to bob along in the Princess's wake as she opened hospitals and housing estates, visited factories, attended charity lunches, dinners, first nights and film premières, and generally by her presence, helped to promote and raise funds for the eighty and more organizations of which she was either president or patron. The restrictions royal life imposed upon him were becoming increasingly difficult for Tony to cope with.

By early November, however, they had clearly called a truce in their burgeoning war of attrition when, to the customary howling of Willie Hamilton, MP, they flew to the United States for a three-week, five-city tour. Tony had been to America before when he'd photographed the fashion model Pagan Grigg standing in the middle of a mountain of precariously balanced scrap cars in one of Manhattan's riverside compounds, and no less perilously had posed her in front of on-coming traffic in Times Square. But this was Princess Margaret's first visit. When the Beatles flew into New York's JFK Airport in February 1964, the roofs of terminal buildings had been packed with screaming fans.

Just over eighteen months later, when Princess Margaret and Lord Snowdon arrived at JFK en route to San Francisco, the rooftop welcome they received from thousands of cheering onlookers was not so very different. 'Everyone is conscious of the royal couple's visit,' quipped Bob Hope. 'I waved at a traffic cop and he curtsied back.'

In the days before America became accessible to all, the Snowdons' tour was seen as something of a media event and followed with a fervour that might nowadays be reserved for some kind of rock superstar. A visit to the set of Hitchcock's *Torn Curtain* at Hollywood's Universal Studios, a tramcar ride in San Francisco which found the royal party besieged by photographers and news camera teams, visits to a working session of the United Nations and to exhibitions of British exports in the stores of Fifth Avenue, and a reception at the White House given in their honour by Lyndon and Lady Bird Johnson, were for most people, glimpses of an America that lived in their imagination. There can be no doubt it had been a positive interlude in the Snowdons' relationship, though not one that would have much effect in the long term. In fact, once infidelity had entered the equation, it was only a matter of time before Tony, playing at home and away, drew the Princess into the game.

Aware that she hated his absences, Snowdon took the initiative before leaving for India on an assignment at the start of 1966, and invited their friend, Anthony Barton, Sarah's godfather, to keep the Princess company. A Bordeaux wine producer whose family firm Barton et Guestier had been in existence since the beginning of the nineteenth century, Anthony and his Danish-born wife Eva, were good friends of the Snowdons, and had shared holidays and socialized together as a foursome. Even so, it seems unlikely that Princess Margaret ever imagined that she and Anthony, whose brother Christopher had been one of Snowdon's rowing heroes at Cambridge, would become romantically involved. But it happened and, as Jocelyn Stevens was to say, 'I've no doubt that Barton was originally encouraged by Tony. If you yourself are playing around, then your conscience is eased if your partner does the same.'[2]

If Princess Margaret surprised herself at the affair, the extraordinary thing is that the 'engineer' seems to have surprised himself by resenting the Princess following his lead in the tit-for-tat infidelity stakes.

Yet, if Tony's amorous adventures were discreet no-name alliances, save for his best known liaison with Lady Jacqueline Rufus-Isaacs whom he met in 1969, Princess Margaret's were no less so, with one or two notable exceptions. Anthony Barton was one, Robin Douglas-Home the other. Not surprisingly, Princess Margaret would much rather the world believe that her month-long romance in February 1967 with Douglas-Home, an unscrupulous, aristocratic piano-player, was the platonic, music-based, friendship she long claimed it to be. However, letters she wrote to him, that he later sold – and which subsequently changed hands on more than one occasion – told a very different story.

But then an emotional fling with Anthony Barton, and a passionate assignation with Robin Douglas-Home, who had charmed, befriended, then, by selling the story, also betrayed Jacqueline Kennedy, did not amount to affairs of lasting significance. They were, instead, more symptomatic of her circumstances. In her late thirties, she was a woman who had lost none of her glamour and none of her physical allure. Nor had she lost the need to be wanted or, indeed, to be loved. If anything, the relationships in which she became involved were little more than impassioned dalliances, which at best lasted no more than a few weeks. Yet, while they were certainly known to have happened, it remained to be asked who her putative lovers were. Warren Beatty, as rumour had it? Patrick Lichfield, whom she once called her 'kissing cousin'? The Italian merchant banker Mario d'Urso, who had been introduced by Imelda Marcos? The film maker, Derek Hart? That nobody knows one way or another is not only testimony to her absolute discretion, but a sure indication that it was her business, not ours.

The one affair that close friends of the Princess are almost certain did not happen, however, was the one Peter Sellers convinced himself did. Described as 'court jester' to the Snowdons, whose close friendship he enjoyed for a number of years, and whom he had showered with expensive gifts, Sellers had all but pressurized the celebrity clairvoyant, Maurice Woodruff, into predicting a marriage between the still-married Princess and himself. Such, indeed, were his delusions that in addition to his belief that they would be married was the certainty – no knowledge of how these things worked here – that he would be king.

This, though, was the man who, according to his biographer Roger Lewis, 'lived by make-believe rules.' An extreme fantasist, he not only insisted to his friends that Sophia Loren was deeply in love with him, but became so obsessed with the actress

Visiting the set of *Torn Curtain* at Universal Studios in north Hollywood in November 1965, during their first American tour, Princess Margaret meets the legendary Alfred Hitchcock.

During their three-week American tour, Princess Margaret and Tony were the guests of President Lyndon Johnson and his wife Lady Bird at a dinner given in their honour at the White House on 17 November 1965.

Princess Margaret photographed with David and Sarah in the garden of Kensington Palace.

As president of the Guides Association, Princess Margaret arrives at the Guides H/Q in Buckingham Palace Road for an AGM.

Princess Margaret photographed during the summer of 1969.

Roddy Llewellyn to whom Princess Margaret was introduced in 1973.

A fiftieth birthday portrait of Princess Margaret taken by Norman Parkinson during the summer of 1980.

Princess Margaret with The Queen and their cousin Jean Wills at the Badminton Horse Trials.

The Princess, president of the NSPCC with Oscar De La Renta at a fashion show in aid of the charity, 1992.

Viscount Linley and Serena Stanhope after their wedding at St Margaret's, Westminster, 8 October 1993.

Lady Sarah and her bridegroom Daniel Chatto leave St Stephens, Walbrook, 14 July 1994.

Princess Margaret with the Queen and Queen Elizabeth, the Queen Mother on the balcony of Buckingham Palace on the Queen Mother's 100th birthday, 4 August 2000.

Princess Margaret photographed undertaking an official engagement in 1997.

The Princess leaving King Edward VII's Hospital for Officers in London, 21 January 2001. The Princess had spent ten days there following a suspected second stroke.

At the close of her funeral service on 15 February 2002, a Bearer Party of the Royal Highland Fusiliers carries Princess Margaret's coffin from St George's Chapel, Windsor Castle.

Nanette Newman that he bought her an E-type Jaguar and rang her husband, Bryan Forbes, both of whom were also friends of the Princess, to negotiate an exchange of wives. Said Forbes, 'He asked me if I'd mind if he married Nanette. I said, "It's not my decision – let's ask Nanette." '³

The only person who, it must be assumed, was prepared to believe the story of Sellers' alleged intimacy with Princess Margaret was the actor's son, Michael. In January 1999, he was to tell one tabloid newspaper that his late father had said the Princess, 'invited him to Kensington Palace. They had dinner and then the servants tactfully withdrew. That is when it happened. He wasn't confessing . . . he was bragging.'⁴ Confessing or bragging, it doesn't much matter. If the story as told purported to be evidence of an affair, it was singularly unconvincing; not least because what Sellers senior would have known and Sellers junior, from what he said, did not, was that Princess Margaret's 'servants' – or in other words her butler – always withdrew from the dining room unbidden once the food had been served and the wine offered. It was the way things were done at Apartment 1A.

The one relationship Princess Margaret had always wanted to work was with her husband. 'It's unlikely the Princess and Tony ever had a proper talk when things were going wrong,' said one source close to them both. 'Tony would probably have run from the room if she had wanted a serious heart-to-heart.'⁵ All the same, they did most certainly seek the help of a noted Harley Street psychologist, in an attempt to sort things out between them.⁶

The closest the Snowdons ever came to putting their troubles behind them, was very probably early in 1967. By chance, the opportunity all but coincided with the first major story of discord when, on 27 February, the *Daily Express* blazed the head-line, TONY DENIES RIFT WITH MARGARET. Arriving in New York from Japan, where he had been working with Brian Moynahan on an in-depth feature for the *Sunday Times*, Snowdon said he was amazed to find the press talking about a 'break up'. At a press conference, he said, 'Nothing has happened to our marriage. When I am away – and I'm away quite a lot on assignments for my paper – I write home and I telephone like other husbands in love with their wives. I telephoned today.' Tony was right about being away a lot on assignments. But, as Princess Margaret herself was to say, 'He never rang or wrote when he was abroad, which made it awkward when friends asked for news of him.'[7]

Ending her month-long liaison with Robin Douglas-Home, the Princess left London on 10 March bound for New York. There, as arranged, she and Tony met at the airport and, chatting as though they hadn't a care in the world, travelled on together to the Bahamas for the holiday they had already planned to take with the Stevens' at Lyford Cay. On their arrival, having smiled through an official welcome, there was a sudden spontaneous spark of fun and daring that the Princess used to know so well. As they left the airport in an official limousine with an escort of police outriders, Tony asked the driver to stop the car. Both then hopped out and, borrowing the motorbike of one of their bemused outriders, climbed on and roared off into the distance. At that moment, it was back to the way it used to be.

Photographed walking together along a jetty with arms entwined or with Janie and Jocelyn strolling on the beach, the Princess and Tony couldn't have been happier. Yet, this was a reunion, not a reconciliation, and while Princess Margaret would have loved it to have worked it sadly wasn't going to. Not six months later, when the royal family's summer programme of official engagements wound down for the holidays and the Snowdons were again guests of the Aga Khan on the Costa Smeralda, the situation had already reverted to one of mutual antagonism. One evening, as an act of awkwardness and defiance, Tony decided to lie underneath the car in which 'K' was about to take them out to dinner.

In London on one occasion when Tony refused to get into the Rolls before a formal engagement, the Princess's good-looking, thirty-something chauffeur, angry at seeing her reduced to tears, turned to the Princess and said, 'Shall I go and thump him one? I will if it'll make you feel better.'[8] Such was the situation between Princess Margaret and Tony, in fact, and so distressing their exchanges, that one lady-in-waiting was always sick with anxiety before she had to go anywhere with the two of them; while the Princess's Private Secretary was often on the point of resigning. 'He'd come home of an evening', said a near relation, 'and frequently say that was it. He'd had enough of them screaming and swearing at one another.'[9]

Though it may be true to say that neither party to this marriage was more, or less, culpable than the other for its erosion, Tony was, said one who saw a good deal of them, 'cleverer at being nasty.' One source close to them both, said, 'Let's say that I had been asked to make up a foursome at dinner. There would be Princess Margaret and Tony, and possibly Peter Sellers or Derek Hart, and myself. During the evening, Tony would do things like stand out of the Princess's line of view and pull silly faces or stick his tongue out. It was all very silly, but he was constantly winding her up. Princess Margaret also loved singing after dinner. But Tony, who was tone deaf, would send her up, again making faces, throwing his eyes to the ceiling or saying, "Oh *not* singing." That hurt her. I don't think she has done it since.'[10]

While the mutual hostility continued with, among other things, Tony leaving shocking notes where the Princess would easily come across them, on her writing table, slipped into a book she was reading, in her glove drawer and elsewhere,[11] the final dénouement so far as she was concerned had been precipitated by the question of a country retreat.

With an enthusiasm she thought Tony shared, Princess Margaret was looking forward to building a house near the lake at Sunninghill in Berkshire, where they used to water-ski. The idea being that it would have been a place of their own, not a crown property that strictly speaking belonged to

251

neither of them, but somewhere they could build from scratch. Tony's preferred option, however, was the renovation of Old House, a cottage that had belonged to his grandmother, on the Nymans estate at Handcross in Sussex; in front of which he had plans to create a lake with an island, crossed by bridges that he would (and ultimately did) design and build himself. Although it was in a pretty dilapidated condition, the Princess had visited Old House and, according to one of her relations, despite the lack of facilities, had tried to be domesticated. 'Even though nobody had ever really shown her how, she tried to cook. Tony more or less threw it in the bin. But at least she tried.'

When they reached an impasse over what to do and where to build – Sunninghill versus Handcross – they asked an associate, their 'business manager', as the Princess referred to him, to act as arbiter, looking into the advantages and disadvantages of both locations. If only in retrospect, the arbiter's choice of Sunninghill, no more than a few miles from Windsor, can have come as no surprise to Tony who, in his determination to have a place of his own, went ahead with renovating Old House. 'Crushed' by this, the Princess blamed Tony for 'ruining everything.'

By the early 1970s, Princess Margaret and Tony Snowdon were all but living separate lives. The Princess admitted that she had finally started to question her own belief in the marriage she had hoped to keep alive while Tony, according to one of the ladies-in-waiting, 'was convinced he was being plotted against and excluded from decisions.'

Prefacing questions with 'Do I not live in this house?' or 'Why am I not informed?' he would concern himself with petty issues such as 'Why does my wife have two people to look after her clothes, but I only have one [at that time, an Italian butler-cum-valet] to look after mine?' There were times when he was capable of reducing even the most experienced and resilient lady-in-waiting to tears. And on one occasion, in front of others, he attempted to humiliate one of the younger ladies, by asking her to spell a word she had misspelt in a letter she had typed for him.[12]

Lonely and desperately unhappy, Princess Margaret now drank too much, smoked even more, put on weight and spent tearful hours on the telephone to sympathetic and supportive friends. If, before it came to this, she and Tony had needed company because they couldn't bear to be alone with one another, the Princess now needed company simply because she couldn't bear to be alone. 'Much talk of Princess Margaret at the moment', Roy Strong noted in his diary, 'who now sits at home on her own in the evenings, with no one ringing her.'[13]

If he was at home during the day, Tony would remain closeted in his study – since converted into the Princess's Library – only to go out at night. If they met in passing, in the hall or on the stairs, there would be scarcely an acknowledgement, perhaps a grunt, but little else. Though lasting personal happiness would elude them both, there would at least be new 'lights' to help them out of the darkness that their marriage had become.

In 1972, Tony met Lucy Lindsay-Hogg, the tall and attractive divorcee he would marry six years later. Twenty years further on in May 1998, the couple separated. About seventeen months earlier, journalist Ann Hills, with whom he had been having an affair since 1977, had committed suicide. And in April 1998 Melanie Cable-Alexander, an editor with *Country Life* magazine, gave birth to Tony's baby, his second son, whom she called Jasper.

A year after Lord Snowdon and Lucy Lindsay-Hogg became involved with each other, Princess Margaret was introduced to Roderic Llewellyn, another young Welshman with more than a passing resemblance to the youthful Tony Armstrong-Jones. To some, it was as though the Princess was trying to recapture the lost years.

Not quite twenty-six when he and the Princess first met,

Roddy was a spontaneous and exuberant character who, at least to begin with, sported a gold earring long before so-called 'body-piercing' of any description became *de rigueur* among the young. Softly-spoken with a natural charm, he was unfailingly well-mannered and fun to be with. Seventeen years younger than Princess Margaret, Roddy had been born in October 1947, the second son of Cambridge-educated Harry Llewellyn, the celebrated steeplechaser, Olympic showjumper and eventer. With his famous horse Foxhunter, Sir Harry won nearly every grand prix in Europe during the late 1940s and early '50s. In fact, from 1947 to 1952, horse and rider enjoyed no fewer than seventy-eight successes, including winning the King George V Gold Cup an unprecedented three times.

Having shared a small studio flat with interior decorator Nicky Haslam whom, ironically, he had met through Jacqueline Rufus-Isaacs, Roddy, who had had a somewhat chequered life, was attracted in many ways to the same sort of people that Tony had known in his Pimlico days. During the mid-1970s, Roddy was invited to join a handful of friends in what was once described as an 'artistic and aristocratic' commune – of which for a time the young Helen Mirren was a member – at Surrendell, an abandoned farm in Wiltshire. On one occasion, much publicized after the event, Princess Margaret had spent the weekend there with Roddy and his friends. Later on, he would flirt with the idea of a singing career, release an album called *Roddy*, that was launched in a puff of media hype and appear on French television in a best-forgotten duet with a simpering Petula Clark, whose husband, Claude Wolff, had been a driving force behind the plan to turn Roddy into a pop star. Towards the end of the decade he finally found his level and, having studied at the Merrist Wood Agricultural College in Worplesdon, Surrey, embarked on what was to become a successful career as a landscape gardener and designer.

When he and Princess Margaret were first introduced by Colin and Anne Tennant, at the Café Royal in Edinburgh, in

September 1973, however, he was none of these things. He was simply an acceptable young man who, although he was unknown to his hosts, had been recommended by one of Colin's elderly relations when they suddenly needed another man to balance numbers during the final week of their house party at Glen, their estate near Innerleithen. That he and the Princess got on right from the start was as much a relief to Colin and Anne as it was a pleasure to Princess Margaret herself.

'She has got the most beautiful eyes,' he is supposed to have said to Anne Tennant, who replied, 'Don't tell me, tell her.' Five months later, in February 1974, the Princess invited Roddy to be her guest for the first time at Les Jolies Eaux, the 4- eventually extended to 7-bedroom house – complete with small swimming pool, thatched gazebo, and breathtaking ocean view – that Oliver Messel designed and Colin Tennant had built for her on Mustique. By this time, Tennant had tamed and developed his rough island paradise, where the rich and sybaritic now came to play in an exclusive setting of rustling palm trees, secluded coves and white sand beaches.

'Part of the attraction for Princess Margaret and others who had houses on the island,' said writer Robin Macwhirter, who knew the Tennants and who spent two or three days as a house guest of the Princess, playing Scrabble to the sound of Rachmaninov or helping to fit the pieces of a giant jig-saw puzzle, 'was the thrill of being part of "village" life, catching up with the tittle-tattle and enjoying the gossip and everyday stuff that was almost a normality to them.' Even though the houses, some more opulent than others, were no great distance apart, one feature of island life, in addition to the constant round of lunch parties, drinks parties and dinner parties, was taking it in turn to stay the night as one another's house guests. 'There was never much by way of intellectual stimulation,' said Robin.[14] In later years, when the facility came to the island, it was perhaps one of the reasons why Princess Margaret had an enlarged photocopy of *The Times* crossword faxed to her every day from her office. Used to doing, and most often completing it, at home on a daily basis, she and Sir Mark Weinberg, who with his wife, the former Anouska Hempel, were part of her circle of friends, indulged a friendly rivalry in seeing who could complete it first.[15]

Entertaining Roddy Llewellyn at Kensington Palace in the early days of their relationship was more of a problem. Tony, at least to all intents and purposes, was still in residence and, though perversely, objected to what was going on. 'Tell your friend to keep out of my house', he is said to have thundered on one occasion. Princess Margaret would one day describe the feelings she and Roddy shared as 'a loving friendship'.[16] So it was, of course, and so, as an affectionate friendship, it continued to the end of her days, with the Princess spending the occasional weekend with Roddy, his wife and daughters at their house, a former inn, not far from Woodstock in Oxfordshire; and the Llewellyns accepting the Princess's hospitality, often as overnight guests, at Kensington Palace.

In the autumn of 1997, almost a quarter of a century after they first met, Princess Margaret hosted a fiftieth birthday lunch party for Roddy, in her rose-pink Garden Room, at which guests sat at a series of round tables draped with white cloths and decorated with floral centrepieces.

In the early days, however, the nature of their relationship was yet more intimate. Physical, of course. Intense, certainly, but intensely physical – not for long. All the same, though the affair was not yet public knowledge, the pressure it put Roddy under and the conflicting emotions it caused him, especially during that first year, were enough to make him pack a bag and jump on a plane, to where didn't much matter so long as he could get away. In the event, he flew first to Guernsey and then, as impulsively, to Turkey.

While he was away, the Princess, who had recently asked Tony to move out – which he did two years later – suffered what some have described as a nervous breakdown and others attempted suicide. Although she had taken a handful of Mogadon tablets and had been difficult to rouse, no one who knew her believed she had suicide in mind. In her own words, 'I was so exhausted because of everything that all I wanted to do was sleep . . . and I did, right through to the following afternoon.'[17]

While Princess Margaret was in bed sleepily recovering, two of her ladies-in-waiting, Anne Tennant and Jean Wills, took it in turns to sit outside her bedroom door to keep Tony out. 'We had to say, "Sorry, Tony, you are not going in. She needs rest." He didn't like it very much, but he would only have let off another tirade.'[18] Instead, he got into his car and drove round and round Clock Court, the cobble-stone courtyard at the front of the house, blasting the horn, 'just to let her know he was still there.'

Not two years later, Princess Margaret's on-going relationship with Roddy Llewellyn finally became front page news. Ever since Les Jolies Eaux had been built, the Princess was accustomed to visiting twice a year, invariably in February and usually in November. For years her visits met a hostile reaction at home, though for just as many years it had been perfectly acceptable for the Kents to take to the ski slopes at much the same time as Princess Margaret was on her way to Barbados, there to take the island-hopper to Mustique. And for as long as she could manage it, the Queen's elderly great-aunt, Princess Alice, Countess of Athlone, was quietly admired for taking her customary annual voyage, literally by banana boat, out to the Caribbean. Yet there was, for some reason a definite resentment at Princess Margaret's winter holidays. Was it because she was newsier and had a higher profile than her more junior cousins, or was perceived to move in a racier, more hedonistic set?

Whatever the reason, while she and Roddy were on Mustique in February 1976, Ross Waby, a New Zealander who worked for Rupert Murdoch's News International Group in New York, had arrived on an up-market package to the island posing as a schoolteacher. As a way of supporting the island's 'economy' Colin Tennant was certainly not averse to that kind of tourism, though he usually did his best to discourage journalists. This time he failed. Biding his time, Waby got what he was after; an apparently compromising photograph of the Princess and her young friend sharing a private moment in a romantic setting.

As 'compromising' photographs go, it was tame stuff indeed. Published on the front page of the *News of the World*, the image was indistinct and shadowy. It was clear, however, that far from wearing 'a skimpy bikini', as one tabloid journalist put it, the Princess was wearing one of her usual bone-bodiced, all-in-one bathing costumes, with modesty-preserving peplum. It was also clear that she and Roddy, daringly bare-chested, were doing nothing more than sitting side by side at a wooden table with the ocean in the background. What the picture editor had done for maximum effect, however, was to crop the photograph, thus losing the figure of Viscount Coke, prominent in the left foreground, who was sitting on the opposite side of the table with his wife, Valeria.

Still, the picture served its purpose. Notwithstanding his own burgeoning relationship with Lucy Lindsay-Hogg, Tony – claiming public humiliation – adopted the moral high ground. The Queen, who had often urged them to try to resolve their difficulties, and who was deeply saddened that the marriage had not worked, finally acknowledged that the time for pretence was over. The press, meanwhile, and its more prurient subscribers, went into overdrive. Righteous indignation was all but palpable.

Though long overdue, an official statement issued from Kensington Palace on Friday, 19 March, announced that the Snowdons had finally recognized the need for a formal separation. There was at this time no talk of divorce. While it would come soon enough at Tony's request, it was not something Princess Margaret wanted, not least because it ran contrary to her views as a committed Christian. Indeed, she had said as much in her formal statement renouncing Peter Townsend more than twenty years earlier.

Under the terms of the agreement negotiated by the royal family's solicitors, Farrer & Co, and Lord Goodman acting on Tony's behalf, Princess Margaret had agreed to a settlement of £100,000 – at that time, a very considerable sum – in order that her estranged husband could buy a house and finally move out of Apartment 1A.

Roddy, meanwhile, though no shrinking violet when it came to the press, issued a well-intentioned, if ill-advised, statement of his own. Instead of remaining silent – one of Princess Margaret's friends was to say that 'Part of him enjoyed the publicity and the fame it brought him'[19] – Roddy said via the Press Association: 'I very much regret any embarrassment caused to Her Majesty The Queen and the Royal Family for whom I wish to express the greatest respect, admiration and loyalty. I thank my own family for their confidence and support and I am very grateful for the help of my friends . . . Could we please be permitted by the media, who have besieged us, to carry on with our work and private lives without further interference.' It was a vain hope and Roddy must have realized it. For as long as he was involved with Princess Margaret, he would never be entirely free of press 'interference'.

In 1978, the year in which Princess Margaret and Lord Snowdon were finally divorced, media-led public opinion, for one reason or another, seemed to be in an almost permanent state of frenzy. The year had begun with the Princess's usual departure for Mustique at the end of February. Though to all intents and purposes now free of the marriage bond, a widely-published photograph of the Princess and Roddy arriving together in her metallic red Rolls-Royce at Heathrow Airport, both of them avoiding eye contact with waiting photographers, was neither wise nor popular.

While many social barriers had been demolished and prejudices subdued, the idea of an older woman having an affair with a much younger man was, even then, a psychological obstacle too far. The age difference may not have worried her – 'You must meet young people, or else', she would advise an older friend. ' "The others are going or gone" '[20] – but publicly parading her 'toyboy' as people saw it, resulted in a fall from grace from which she would never entirely recover.

Public sensibilities weren't the only ones she would startle if not offend. To many of her friends, despite the fact that he gave her back her confidence, was entertaining, attentive and kind, not the sort of things she had had a lot of in recent years, Roddy was considered acceptable only because of what he meant to her. 'Roddy,' said one of the Princess's circle in a matter of fact way, 'was a lightweight, not in Princess Margaret's league. At least Tony was known and had been around.'[21] Other friends and observers formed their own opinions.

Roy Strong and his wife, the designer Julia Trevelyan Oman, were among the guests at a dinner party the Princess gave for the Marchioness of Cholmondeley one evening during the spring of 1978. 'It was a funny line up', noted Sir Roy in his diary, 'the actor Paul Scofield and his wife, David and Rachel Cecil, Rose Cecil and some other young ones that HRH was match-making with – and Roddy. Roddy sits opposite her at table in the role of host, which is rather unnerving. Lady Cholmondeley was very intrigued and rather shocked by it . . .'[22]

Nor were matters of public opinion much helped when, during their visit to Mustique, Roddy was taken ill with an upper gastro-intestinal haemorrhage and rushed to hospital in Barbados where the Princess visited him. Not long afterwards, though again perhaps unwisely, he allowed himself to be photographed by the press sitting beside his bed, smiling broadly and looking the picture of health.

At home, republican MPs, though admittedly with no discernible knowledge of the Civil List or its origins, again took a decidedly dim view of it all. Denis Canavan stood up in the House to object to 'the £1,000 a week pocket money we are giving to a royal parasite like Princess Margaret.' Willie Hamilton, whose tough Labour origins among the coal mines of northern England, had confirmed his belief, inculcated by his parents, that monarchy 'was the very apex of something evil', needed no excuse to denounce the Princess as a 'floosie', an 'expensive, kept woman' and 'a monstrous charge on the public purse.' 'If she thumbs her nose at taxpayers by flying off to Mustique to see this pop singer chap', he said, 'she shouldn't expect the workers of the country to pay for it.'

Criticism of Civil List annuities received by members of the royal family was nothing new. More than a century before, in November 1871, Sir Charles Dilke, the radical MP for Chelsea, had said that the royal family, a 'cumbersome fiction', as he put it, cost too much and weren't worth it. In April 1978, however, a poll conducted by the Opinion Research Centre (ORC), revealed that seventy-three per cent of the public believed Princess Margaret's relationship had damaged her standing as a member of the royal family.[23]

That month, criticism of the Princess struck deeper than ever before. The Queen, comfortable within her own family, content with her dogs and her horses, who loved and cared deeply for her only sister, but who thought her 'a total enigma',[24] neither liked nor approved of her involvement with Roddy. 'She thought the Princess was behaving badly', said Lord Charteris,[25] and wondered what could be done about her sister's 'gutter-snipe life.' Such was the concern, indeed, that the matter was discussed between the Queen and her Prime Minister James Callaghan who, on one occasion, also had an informal talk about the Princess's situation with one of her ladies-in-waiting.[26] There were even discussions in Downing Street, and a Whitehall paper drawn up 'about the options, including the suggestion that Princess Margaret should be taken off the Civil List and allowed to lead a private life – in effect the ultimatum issued to her over Townsend in the 1950s.'[27] It was not something the Queen liked the sound of.

Then, not long before the matter started to resolve itself, ill-health drew the sting. In April, Princess Margaret went to bed with flu so virulent that she had to miss her daughter Sarah's confirmation in St George's Chapel. Later that month, following a day's engagements in Manchester from where she returned 'feeling like death,' she was admitted to the King Edward VII's Hospital for Officers in Marylebone suffering not from gastro-entiritis as her doctors first suspected, but hepatitis with all its long-term implications. After a prolonged period of total absti-nence, the Princess was eventually allowed a glass of her favourite Famous Grouse – two parts water, one part whisky, with ice – as had always been the case. At all other times, Robinson's Barley Water – the genuine article not, as the *Daily Mail*'s royal writers misinformed readers, a euphemism for yet more Famous Grouse – was the drink she faithfully stuck to.

Discharged from hospital in the second week of May, the Princess's divorce petition was submitted as one of a batch of twenty-eight, that were heard and rubber-stamped by Judge Roger Willis at the London Divorce Court on the morning of the 24th. Six weeks later, decree nisi became decree absolute. That day Lord Snowdon was at Clock House, Kensington Palace, opposite Apartment 1A, photographing Princess Alice, Countess of Athlone, who at ninety-five, was the last surviving grandchild of Queen Victoria. Catching up with him, Princess Margaret mentioned that they were no longer married. Whereupon, in the kind of spontaneous moment recognizable to many couples in their situation, she recalled that, 'We danced a jig then and there in the courtyard – to the amazement of the children.'[28]

That August, Princess Margaret spent her forty-eighth birth-day at Balmoral, an annual visit that was invariably part of her summer holiday travels, which invariably included Italy – that year she stayed with Mario d'Urso in Amalfi – Corfu and, in more recent years, Turkey. There she was the guest of Haldun Simavi, business tycoon and owner of *Günaydin*, ('*Good Morning*'), one of Turkey's leading newspapers, and his wife Çidam, aboard their yacht, the *Hallas*. After her birthday cele-bration, the Princess drove from Balmoral to the Tennants' 10,000-acre estate, Glen House, some thirty miles from Edinburgh, where Roddy joined her.

The highlight of the Glen summer house party was invariably the evening of amateur theatricals staged on the last night. On this occasion Roddy, in whom, said a friend of Colin Tennant, the Princess had found 'the perfect playmate',[29] was the driving force behind the frivolities. Together, Princess Margaret and he decided on the sketches to be performed, while Tennant and a friend or two took care of the production side of things, such as the running order, sound, lighting and so on.

It also meant driving the Princess and Roddy to Moultrie's, the famous theatrical costumiers in Edinburgh. There, with the help of staff quite used to eminent figures dropping in, Princess Margaret, who was to appear in two sketches before an audience of about a hundred that evening, not only needed a horned-helmet, together with a suitable robe, spear and shield, for her role as the Valkyrie, but also a sequinned gown, feather boa and long blonde wig, for her impersonation of the legendary 'Red Hot Momma,' Sophie Tucker.

The following month, having flown out to the South Pacific where she was to represent the Queen at the independence celebrations of Tuvalu, then the Ellice islands, Princess Margaret was again taken ill, this time with viral pneumonia. With a temperature of 105°F, she was flown in a converted Hercules tank carrier, fully equipped and fitted out as a hospital plane, to Sydney nine hours away. As she herself said in disbelief, 'No sooner had I recovered from one [illness] than I was knocked down by another!'

What had been one of the most turbulent years in Princess Margaret's entire life ended on a relatively quiet note, save for one last surprise. With her return to London, Tony told the Princess that he was going to marry Lucy. What he did not tell her, for whatever reason, was when. That, too, came as something of a surprise just a few weeks later. At Kensington Register Office on the morning of 15 December, in a low-key ceremony witnessed by four friends and a crowd of waiting press photographers, the former Mrs Lindsay-Hogg became the second Countess of Snowdon. It was only now, with Tony's remarriage, that the Queen Mother finally acknowledged the fact that her younger daughter and he were no longer married.

In 1931, when Princess Margaret was only a few months old, Irish-born Edris Stannus, who would become famous as Dame Ninette de Valois, created two ballet companies and a ballet school: the Sadler's Wells Ballet, the Sadler's Wells Theatre Ballet, and the Sadler's Wells Ballet School. A quarter of a century later, in October 1956, the Queen granted them a Royal Charter. At a stroke, both ballet companies were transformed into The Royal Ballet and the Sadler's Wells Ballet School became The Royal Ballet School. Less than a year later, Princess Margaret accepted an invitation to become President of the Royal Ballet. From then on, through the 'golden years' of Frederick Ashton and Kenneth Macmillan, of Fonteyn and Nureyev, Dowell, Sibley, Park and Baryshnikov to Bintley, Bussell and Guillem of the present day, Princess Margaret was an astute and enthusiastic supporter of both the Company itself and the Ballet School.

Kept constantly in touch with what was going on, Sir Anthony Dowell, who became Director in 1986, said, 'The Princess is always sent rehearsal calls for the week, which she studies very closely. She has absolutely no hesitation in ringing up if there is a new ballet in rehearsal, or a new dancer, or anything with which she isn't familiar.'[30] Forthright in her comments about difficult or unmelodic scores – her own favourites included Ashton's *La Fille Mal Gardée* and Balanchine's *Symphony in C* with music by Bizet – the Princess, said Sir Anthony, proved herself 'a great champion' of productions which she felt had been unfairly criticized. Among them was his own 1986 production of *Swan Lake*, the American première of which Princess Margaret made a point of attending in Washington DC in April 1994, with President Bill Clinton and his wife Hillary.

Since she became President, the Princess always paid at least two official visits to the Royal Ballet School at White Lodge in

Richmond Park each year. But what she relished even more were her frequent informal and completely private visits to the eleven- to sixteen-year-olds at Richmond, and to the older students at Baron's Court in West London, to watch dance classes and rehearsals.

At White Lodge, where she sometimes stayed all day, the Princess, said former principal ballerina Dame Merle Park who became Director of the Royal Ballet School in 1983, took a thorough interest in visiting the classrooms to sit in on lessons and to watch the creative energies of the young students at work. 'She has always loved the choreographics', said Dame Merle, 'which is when the children make up their own ballets and choose their own music.'[31]

As President of the Royal Ballet, Princess Margaret regards her extensive experience of fund-raising, as much at home as on her many visits to the United States, as one of her most positive and constructive contributions. At White Lodge where there was nowhere for the younger students to put on performances other than three studios that were never big enough even to seat audiences made up of parents, Princess Margaret inaugurated the *Buy A Brick* campaign. Laying the first of them herself, she personally did much to raise the £3 million that a new Theatre Studio was going to cost. Having also made a point of following the progress of building work through frequent on-site visits, she finally opened the Ballet School's Margot Fonteyn Theatre Studio in 1991.

By the end of the decade, an even more ambitious £15 million scheme had been launched with the aim of moving the Upper School from Baron's Court to the Royal Opera House at Covent Garden. Again with Princess Margaret's active involvement, which included personal appeals to wealthy individuals as well as to companies, almost half the amount needed had been raised by the start of the new millennium.

As a guest on the BBC radio programme *Desert Island Discs*, the Princess joked that, alone on a desert island, she might have danced like a ballerina and, unseen by the world, 'would probably have been beautiful.' Instead, the performer in her, which was never far from the surface, agreed on one memorable occasion in 1982 to open a cabaret-like entertainment for the Friends of Covent Garden. Following drinks in the Crush Bar, the audience took their seats for a show in which Margot Fonteyn and Merle Park appeared as film legends Jane Russell and Marilyn Monroe singing a duet from *Gentlemen Prefer Blondes*. In similar fashion, though some years later, Diana, Princess of Wales and Wayne Sleep, a former principal with the Royal Ballet, would surprise Prince Charles and the special Friends audience with their now famous dance routine.

On this occasion, however, it was Princess Margaret who stole the show. As eight principal boys – formed rather like a corps de ballet – danced to the music of a waltz, the curtains parted to reveal the Princess standing centre stage in the chariot from Handel's opera *Semele*. As the dancers swirled around her, one produced a scroll from which she read a brief speech of welcome to the Friends. As she ended with the words, 'Now I must fly', the chariot – to which she had been safely harnessed – was whisked heavenward up to the flies.[32]

Officially apolitical, Princess Margaret was always conscientious about not involving herself in anything that might be seen as political. In October 1979, however, only weeks after the IRA (Irish Republican Army) assassinated Earl Mountbatten while he was sailing at his holiday home in County Sligo, the Princess found herself at the centre of a not only potentially dangerous, but also politically sensitive, situation.

It happened during a tour of Chicago, Texas, Los Angeles, San Francisco and Cleveland on behalf of the Royal Opera House, which at that time was raising funds for new and urgently required dressing rooms, as part of a £7-million development scheme. On her last night in Chicago, the Princess attended a reception and dinner given in her penthouse apartment at the Drake Hotel by Abra Anderson, who wrote a newspaper column called *Click*. As 100 guests seated at ten round tables were served dinner against the usual hubbub of chattering voices and music, the Mayor of Chicago, Jane Byrne, who was sitting with Princess Margaret and Mrs Anderson, said she had recently been in London for the funeral of Lord Mountbatten. In response, the Princess mentioned how touched the royal family and the Mountbattens had been by the number of letters they had received from ordinary Irish people. Towards the end of the evening, having already said her farewells to the Mayor, who had left at 11 o'clock to prepare for President Jimmy Carter's imminent arrival in the city, Princess Margaret retired without the slightest notion of what was about to erupt as they travelled on to Houston in Texas, the next destination on the itinerary.

In the press the day after Abra Anderson's soirée, a rival journalist named Kupsinek, who wrote something called *Kup's Kolumn* for the *Chicago Sun-Times*, claimed that the Princess had referred to the Irish as 'pigs' – and went on, 'suffice it to say, the Mayor departed the party as soon as possible.' A firm and immediate denial was issued on behalf of an incredulous Princess; Mayor Byrne 'in discussion with reporters at City Hall, stated categorically "She [Princess Margaret] did not say that the Irish are pigs" ', while Abra Anderson wrote in her own column, 'Mayor Byrne . . . did not leave in a huff because of an Irish slur made by the Princess [but] at 11pm (hardly as soon as possible) because of a busy schedule.'

Despite alarming repercussions, the tour continued. In Los Angeles, where, according to police intelligence received from London (via Washington), an IRA plot to assassinate Princess Margaret had been uncovered, the number of secret service agents was immediately doubled. Meanwhile, her arrival at the Mark Hopkins Hotel in San Francisco, where VIP guests were housed in an exclusive tower wing, was accompanied by jeering, placard-waving Irish-American demonstrators.

Having arrived at the hotel in the second or third car of the convoy that took them into the city, the Princess's lady-in-waiting, Annabel Whitehead, was not only spat at as she stepped on to the sidewalk, but once inside, was prevented from following the Princess and her burly American bodyguards into the lift. Stranded in the foyer, where she was frustrated by receptionists denying all knowledge of a guest called 'Princess Margaret', Annabel protested to one immovable officer, who had also seen her before, that the security agents knew perfectly well who she was. Eventually allowed up to the Princess's suite, one agent told her with throw-away nonchalance that had anybody followed her into the lift with the aim of using her as a shield to get to the Princess, they 'would have tried to shoot' her in some 'non-vital' part of her body.

In San Francisco, one of the Princess's evening engagements was a formal dinner with the British Consul. Having been warned that protestors intended to throw buckets of blood at her, one detective asked Annabel Whitehead if she and the Princess could wear something inexpensive that could be thrown away if the worst happened. 'I had to tell him,' she said, 'that it was a formal dinner for which we had to dress accordingly.' With missile-throwing demonstrators and television camera teams waiting at the main entrance, evasive measures were called for. With Princess Margaret – now driven everywhere in a bullet-proof limousine – and her party all in full evening dress, it was decided to stop a street or two away from the Consulate and, on foot, climb a steep and necessarily unlit path to the kitchen entrance. Guided by vigilant security agents talking up their sleeves, they made it to the top of the seemingly endless pathway and swept in through the back door. As soon as the television crews realized there was going to be nothing to see, they turned off their lights and, like the crowd, faded away into the night.

After all the drama elsewhere, Cleveland, at the end of the tour, unintentionally provided light relief when one venue, in which the Princess was to attend a dinner, turned out to have been double-booked. The result was that two separate dinner-dances took place simultaneously. For twenty minutes, the Princess shook hands with those she was designated to meet, including one elderly woman eager to tell her that she had once had lunch with Queen Mary in London thirty years earlier. By the time the same old lady with the same story had turned up to shake the Princess's hand for the third time, it finally dawned that she had been getting back into the presentation line to come round again. Later, when the Princess and Annabel Whitehead retired to the ladies' room – unusually, no private facility had been provided on this occasion – some of the women powdering their noses or waiting in line, pushed pieces of paper under the cubicle door in the hope of getting a royal autograph. By now, one old lady with a familiar voice had joined the line just outside the door and, to the amusement of the Princess and her lady-in-waiting, was loudly telling anyone who hadn't heard the story how she had once had lunch with Queen Mary in London thirty years earlier.[33]

1980 was to be the last full year of Princess Margaret's 'loving' friendship with Roddy Llewellyn. Not that anybody would have known it that July, when the Princess flew out to Canada on an official ten-day visit to Saskatchewan and Alberta, then celebrating the seventy-fifth anniversary of their entry into the Canadian Confederation. As she left London on 18 July, Roddy told a friend, that he wanted to look after her 'for as long as she lives.'

By then, though there had never been any likelihood of their marrying – 'The Princess never had any intention of taking the relationship beyond what it was'[34] said one source – their friendship had long since mellowed into one of everyday familiarity. Because of it, there were times when Roddy wasn't always at his most thoughtful. There had been occasions, for example, when he hadn't turned up for dinner when expected. At other times, with uncanny echoes of Elizabeth Cavendish's caution about Tony so many years earlier, he would simply not be around and would not make contact, leaving a distressed Princess to wonder why, and a member of her personal staff trying to locate him.

Three weeks after her return from Canada, Princess

Margaret quietly celebrated her fiftieth birthday with her family. A party, to be held at the Ritz on 4 November, the most convenient date in both royal and non-royal diaries for such an event, was organized by a group of friends as a belated birthday present.

One, albeit extremely delicate issue concerned Roddy's participation in it all. Sharing the sense of unease felt by a number of Princess Margaret's friends, the Queen, who did not 'receive' him until May 1999 when she entertained her indisposed sister's usual guests to dinner after a preview of the Chelsea Flower Show, was determined not to be seen to condone his relationship with the Princess and at first didn't want him there at all. Yet, if Princess Margaret minded her sister's attitude, she took exception to Dominic Elliot, one of her closest and most loyal friends, speaking his mind. 'Dommie was concerned that she was making a fool of herself', said one source, 'and they had a major falling out.'[35]

With arrangements for the evening still unclear, it was finally agreed that Roddy might be allowed to join the party at 10.30 with the rest of the after-dinner guests. Taken care of by Colin and Anne Tennant, whose friend he had become, and through whom he had met the Princess in the first place, he had dinner elsewhere.

If the Queen was never enamoured of her sister's liaison with Llewellyn, neither were the Princess's two children, David and Sarah. Now nineteen and the mirror-image of his father, David Linley – who would soon start to make his name as a furniture maker and designer of international renown – had left Bedales, the progressive co-educational school in Hampshire that both he and his sister attended, and was now at the John Makepiece School for Craftsmen at Parnham in Dorset. When she, too, left Bedales, the equally talented but completely unassuming Lady Sarah, or 'Ya Ya' as she was called after her earliest attempts at pronouncing her name, won a place at the prestigious Camberwell Art School, where she took a foundation course. From there, before embarking on a career as a professional painter, she took a Printed Textiles course at Middlesex Polytechnic and studied at the Royal Academy's schools in Piccadilly.

Though never overtly maternal, Princess Margaret was, said friends, 'Very good with her children, very fair and very disciplined. She always talked to them like adults.' Another source said, 'Her attitude was similar to that of Princess Anne, who would speak to her children rather like the dogs. When they came into a room she would say "Now *sit*." She was very matter of fact with them, but they, too, couldn't be nicer.'[36]

Despite the animosity between Princess Margaret and himself, Lord Snowdon was a strict, but on the whole, no less caring or affectionate father. Speaking of his childhood on one occasion, David Linley recalled times shared with his parents and sister as a family. 'We had my father's carpentry workshop in the cellar', he said. 'I was his assistant. We never watched television, so the whole family used to gather in the cellar. I remember the vivid smell of wood chippings, Gauloise [French] cigarettes and red wine . . .' Princess Margaret, Linley went on, 'was wonderful. She used to take us to a museum to view one painting at a time. Knowing that there were many more to see left us looking forward to the next visit.'[37]

The one person of whom David and Sarah inevitably saw most in their earliest years was their nanny, Miss Verona Sumner. One of a type who seemed to give the impression that they were never young, she was grey-haired, almost too precisely spoken and, said one of the Princess's ladies-in-waiting, 'frightfully grand.' With ideas above her station and, for that matter, above her charges, Nanny Sumner taught hauteur instead of humility. When the two daily ladies greeted them by their first names, as they always did, Nanny not only reminded them of the children's titles, but told them they did not speak to domestic staff. Suppliers of children's shoes and clothing had to come to them, rather than the other way round, and though they always travelled first class, she would complain about having to take a train instead of a car. Taxis were also to be disregarded as a means of transport, because, as she mysteriously put it, 'one hears of things happening.'

At the age of fourteen, David was deeply embarrassed when Nanny insisted on collecting him from school, while the very idea that Sarah should become a boarder anywhere was anathema to her. 'My Sarah's knickers being washed with everybody else's!' seemed a matter of paramount concern, leading to who could say what?[38] Such was Miss Sumner's character, however, that her tongue was all too frequently as sharp as it was malicious. Her elderly assistant, Jane, known as the 'nursery maid,' a misnomer if ever there was one, was usually reduced to tears by Nanny's demandingly autocratic manner. But then nobody was spared. After the retirement of Princess Margaret's dresser and personal maid, Miss Mathieson, otherwise known as 'Mattie' – a wizened little Scot to whom the butler would quietly slip a jugful of gin every day – Nanny Sumner complained about the number of telephone calls her successor received. 'That woman and the *men* who call her!' she once hissed disparagingly. The 'men' turned out to be the new employee's son.[39]

During Nanny Sumner's time there was an occasion when she ran to the Princess with a tale about one of her butlers. She [Nanny Sumner] had just seen him, so the story goes, take three uniformed sailors up to his top-floor room. To have seen it at all, she could only have been lurking behind the door with its one round window, which led from the nursery suite on to the back stairs.

Though Princess Margaret's official views were sometimes at odds with her personal views on such matters, few members of the royal family have been quite as broad-minded or tolerant. 'What are you trying to tell me, Nanny?' the Princess is said to have asked, knowing full well. 'Sailors in uniform, Your Royal Highness,' insisted Miss Sumner, 'walking past my children's door.' The matter was resolved when the Princess asked the butler if he would like a staff apartment elsewhere in the Kensington Palace complex, where he could live his private life, albeit discreetly, away from prying eyes.[40]

Though as teenagers, David and Sarah's need for a nanny was no greater than Princess Margaret's was for a governess at much the same age, Nanny Sumner, just like Crawfie, was kept on longer than was strictly necessary.

Though she formally retired from full-time employment at the start of 1977, after almost fifteen years, she remained on a weekend and holiday basis for two years after that. Despite her narrow ways, Miss Sumner did at least act as a buffer between the children when they were at home from school and the misery that their parents' marriage had become in its death throes. She was also there through much of Princess Margaret's relationship with Roddy Llewellyn. In its own way, that was just as problematic for them and perhaps their dislike of the situation, even though they were unfailingly polite and courteous to Roddy, was succinctly illustrated in just one instance.

For her fiftieth birthday, Roddy had given the Princess an attractive vase-like object in the same turquoise blue opaque glass, sometimes called lustre, that she collected. To distinguish it, he commissioned a gold lid surmounted by a carefully crafted representation of the Princess's personal cypher. It was given pride of place in the centre of other pieces on the mantelshelf above the dining room fireplace. Before lunch one day, however, shortly before the Princess joined them, David looked at Roddy's gift and said to his sister, 'I'm sick of looking at that thing.' Without further ado, he removed it and put it inside a jardinière on a nearby sideboard. Noticing its absence the moment she came in, Princess Margaret demanded, '*Who* has moved that piece?' The then butler, who was just about to serve lunch, saved the moment by saying, 'I'm sorry, Your Royal Highness, I moved it this morning to clean it and forgot to put it back.'[41]

Early in 1981, not long after the Princess's birthday party at the Ritz, Roddy asked a friend, 'What would you say if I said I wanted to get married?' 'To you know who?' 'No', he replied, 'not to you know who. To someone else.' For somebody who had only recently said that he wanted to 'look after' Princess Margaret for the rest of her life, and who had always claimed he was too selfish to marry, it seemed the most extraordinary *volte-face.*

Two or three weeks later, having gone with her again to Mustique, Roddy was forced to tell the Princess that he wanted to marry somebody he had known for ten years, but whom he had been seeing for only two or three months. Her name, he said, was Tatiana Soskin. Better known as Tania, she was variously described in the press as a fashion designer, a travel writer and even an heiress. Though there can be no doubt that Roddy's news shocked her, 'I had absolutely no idea it had been going on', she is reported to have said, the Princess put a brave face on her own feelings, urged him to propose and, stoically facing the inevitable, gave them her blessing.

Had they married in late June as they originally hoped, Princess Margaret would almost certainly have been among the guests at the Llewellyns' wedding. The logistics of planning the occasion at a small church near the family home at Llanvair, near Abergavenny, however, evidently proved more complex than anticipated; and the wedding was arranged to take place in Marlow, Buckinghamshire, where Tania's uncle had a house, on 11 July. Although several of her friends, including two of her ladies-in-waiting, Davina Woodhouse and Elizabeth Paget, were there, it was a date the Princess herself could not make. In her capacity as President of the Royal Ballet, she was making her fifth official visit to Canada.

At the end of the month, one wedding Princess Margaret did attend was that of her eldest nephew Charles, Prince of Wales, to the twenty-year-old Diana Spencer, third and youngest daughter of the 8th Earl Spencer who, as Viscount Althorp had served as equerry first to King George VI for the last two years of his life and then, for the first two years of her reign, including the six-month Coronation tour, to the present Queen.

From the time of her marriage Diana, Princess of Wales, wittingly and unwittingly dominated the news media, by and large eclipsing the rest of the royal family. Above all, she had, if only for a younger generation with a different perspective of monarchy, succeeded Princess Margaret in the gallery of royal icons. The Princess was still there, however, active in her support both of the Queen, always her prime objective, and in her work, done publicly but – as with other members of the royal family – generally unpublicized, for the charities, regiments and official bodies with which she has long been associated.

'In my twenty years with the Society,' said Giles Pegram, Appeals Director of the NSPCC (National Society for the Prevention of Cruelty to Children), I can't think of anything she hasn't done when we have asked.' Yet unlike Diana, who tended to ensure that the press were tipped off about her private visits to hostels, hospices and hospitals, Princess Margaret always insisted that private should be exactly that.

'On visits to Protection Units,' said Giles Pegram speaking in October 1999, 'Princess Margaret always meets the people who work on the ground, the staff and the social workers. What she asks is extremely intelligent and searching. She is very analytical and will doggedly pursue a point; you really can't get away with a superficial answer. She isn't interested in that. Her questions are incisive and they sometimes come at you from a direction you would not have thought about.

'With team leaders, the Princess will talk privately and in confidence to the parents and to the children themselves. She goes in to ask what "her" society is doing to help them. And she asks questions not out of politeness, but because she wants to understand. She is very hands on.'

As with the Royal Ballet, or any of her organizations for that matter, fund raising for the NSPCC was something to which Princess Margaret was wholly committed. 'She isn't in the "rent-a-royal" business', Giles Pegram went on, 'so before she considers going to an event, she always asks what added value there would be by her being there. Once she has said yes, she throws herself into it whole-heartedly.

'People', said Pegram, 'can sometimes make assumptions about her "grandeur". On one occasion, it was thought that, as a member of the royal family, she wouldn't want to take part in a quiz. Quite wrong. She asked for a card and got stuck in. I also remember one dinner in the north of England, at which I thought some of the jokes were inappropriate. But on the flight back to London, the Princess repeated a lot of them, including some of the bluest jokes. It proves it isn't wise to make assumptions.'[42]

Not since 1978, when viral pneumonia followed hard on the heels of hepatitis, had ill-health been a matter of serious concern in Princess Margaret's life. Though it was true that she was less robust than either her mother or sister, she had never been as susceptible to illness as some, particularly in the press, seemed to insist. On 6 January 1985, however, when the Princess underwent surgery for the removal of part of her left lung, during which an incision was made from her shoulder to her waist, it looked as if history was about to repeat itself. It was certainly true that the spectre of her father's final illness, and his operation at much the same age for the removal of a cancerous left lung, was uppermost in many people's minds.

The Princess was given the all clear when surgeons at the Royal Brompton Hospital in Chelsea, pronounced the removed lung section 'innocent.' It would be another eight years, however, before she finally conquered the habit of smoking around sixty cigarettes a day. Caught out once more by Britain's damp winter weather, she was admitted to the King Edward VII's Hospital for Officers on 3 January 1993 suffering from pneumonia. If it hadn't been a serious attack, for the Princess was able to go home only five days later, it was enough to make her find the will and the determination to give up smoking once and for all.

For the Queen, her sister's latest illness had been a further anxiety after a year in which a series of family events had, by turns, been upsetting, infuriating, shocking and highly embarrassing. On 24 November, speaking with a husky, cold-laden, voice at a formal Guildhall luncheon, held belatedly by the Lord Mayor of London to commemorate the fortieth anniversary of her accession to the throne, the Queen said that 1992 had not

been a year on which she would look back with 'undiluted pleasure.' It had, in fact, been an '*annus horribilis.*'

The marriage of the Prince and Princess of Wales that had
started amid such high hopes and in so great a blaze of glory
had, within five years, started to disintegrate with dramatic
consequences. 'Neither of them had understood enough about
themselves or each other to be confident of climbing the
foothills of such a public marriage', wrote the Prince's authorized biographer, Jonathan Dimbleby. 'Both needed the support
from the other that neither was competent to provide.'[43] It had
become a familiar refrain in royal marriages.

Charles and Diana would finally separate in December 1992,
but at the start of the year, as the Prince left Sandringham
Church with his two sons, William and Harry, a voice from the
crowd shouted, 'Where's Di?' 'She's not here today,' replied
Charles with undisguised irritation, 'so you can get your money
back!' The Prince and Princess divorced four years later.
Princess Margaret, though no advocate of divorce – she had not
even wanted her own – was among those who urged the Waleses
along that path; though to begin with her relationship with
Diana couldn't have been warmer.

When the young Princess returned home from hospital with
her first baby, for example, Princess Margaret had rounded up
her staff and rushed outside with them to wave handkerchiefs
and tea towels, as mother and baby drove by. When Diana had a
new jacuzzi installed, 'Margot' was among the first to be invited
to look and admire. Suitably impressed, Princess Margaret jetti-
soned her old bath to have one too. Almost the same age as
Diana, Sarah Armstrong-Jones, who had been her chief bridesmaid, became one of her closest friends. Such was the tone of
the relationship. When, however, things started to go wrong
between the Wales's and Diana distanced herself from her royal
in-laws, all except the Queen, Princess Margaret also drew back,
not least from a sense of personal loyalty that told her Diana had
let the Queen down.

She felt the same way about Sarah Ferguson, whom the late

Lord Charteris had once called, 'vulgar, vulgar, vulgar.' Making her own contribution to the Queen's *annus horribilis*, Sarah Ferguson had also discredited the title of Duchess of York, held previously by Queen Mary and Queen Elizabeth The Queen Mother, by her much publicized antics with Texan playboy Steve Wyatt and, not six months later, with his fellow American John Bryan. Allegedly without realizing it, a topless Sarah was photographed with Bryan, while on one of her many holidays, this time in the South of France, kissing, canoodling and, famously, toe-sucking.

The final disaster for the Queen and her family was the Great Fire at Windsor Castle that began in the Private Chapel, now the Lantern Lobby, at 11.37 on the morning of Friday, 20 November – the Queen's forty-fifth wedding anniversary. Fifteen hours later, at 2.30am the following day when it was finally put out, the fire – which some held up as a metaphor for the then state of the monarchy itself – had devastated several major rooms in the north-east range of State Apartments; among them St George's Hall, the Crimson Drawing Room, where Peter Townsend had once proposed to Princess Margaret, the State Dining Room, the smaller Octagon Dining Room in the Brunswick Tower, which had literally acted as a chimney during the blaze, and the Grand Reception Room, all of which, over the next five years, were to be spectacularly restored. When, during the same period, a new Private Chapel was designed for the royal family by Giles Downes, David Linley was commissioned to provide a new altar table.

For Princess Margaret, her ninth official visit to the United States early in October 1992 also provided an opportunity to indulge her love of Country and Western music. While in New York for two days attending fund raising events for the Royal Academy and the British Museum, the Princess extended her visit by a further two days and, arranged by Peter Duchin, a New York theatrical agent, flew down to Nashville in Tennessee to visit the Grand Ol' 'Opree. Loving every moment, Princess Margaret sat, and sang, through a regular programme of folk singers before some of Country and Western's most famous names, among them Emmylou Harris and Chet Atkins, who gave her a guitar for David, came on stage to perform for her. The undoubted highlight, however, was an appearance by Dolly Parton, of whom the Princess had long been a huge fan, and with whom there was a 'wildly exciting' meeting afterwards. 'I met Dolly Parton', she proudly told friends back at home.

At home, musical evenings were still a feature of the Princess's life whether at Kensington Palace, Royal Lodge, Windsor, or at the homes of friends. On one occasion, while visiting friends in Wales with Colin and Charmian Campbell, the Princess and three of her girlfriends started singing songs that ranged from Scottish airs to Cole Porter and Rogers and Hart. 'We sound just like the Spice Girls', said Charmian Campbell, 'and you, Ma'am, are "Posh Spice." ' The Princess cried with laughter.[44]

If during the early 1990s their royal cousins were heading for the divorce courts, David Linley and his sister Sarah both had marriage on their minds. On 8 October 1993, David's wedding to Viscount Petersham's only daughter Serena Stanhope looked rather like a pastiche of his parents' Westminster Abbey wedding, thirty-three years earlier. Staged at 'high society' St Margaret's, Westminster, standing within the very precincts of the Abbey itself, the entire length of the pathway from bustling Parliament Square to the church's west door – festooned with a massive arch of flowers – was covered in blue carpet. Just as the Abbey's nave had been in 1960. In 'silhouette' Serena paid unmistakable tribute to Princess Margaret, with her V-necked, full-skirted wedding dress. Her hair, though piled higher than the chignon favoured by Princess Margaret as a bride, was clasped not by the Poltimore diadem, but by the Princess's 'second-best' diamond tiara. Even the bridal bouquet of the Princess's favourite lilies-of-the-valley resembled the brides-maids' posies at that earlier wedding. Leaving the church after the ceremony with hands clasped in the same way that David's parents' had been, the Linleys drove off in a vintage car to a reception at St James's Palace. There the official photographs were taken in the white and gold Throne Room, posed against the deep red velvet drapes of the throne canopy emblazoned with the royal coat-of-arms and the initials 'VR,' representing the cypher of the younger Queen Victoria.

The contrast with Sarah's much simpler wedding to Westminster- and Oxford-educated Daniel Chatto, on 14 July the following year, could not have been clearer. Nor, indeed, could it have better illustrated the contrasting characters of Princess Margaret's offspring: David, conspicuously high-living and publicity loving; Sarah, intensely private, charmingly natural, and anxious to avoid the media spotlight.

While the royal family were again out in force for Sarah and Daniel's wedding, their choice of the church of St Stephen Walbrook, in the City of London – where they were married by the Rector, Prebendary Dr Chad Varah, better known as the founder of the Samaritans – meant that it would be an altogether more intimate occasion. Widely considered to be the finest of the fifty-two City churches Wren built after the Great Fire of London, St Stephen's seats a modest 200. That consideration alone gave Sarah and Daniel the freedom to plan the kind of wedding they wanted, without any sense of official obligation. Indeed, with a reception afterwards at Clarence House, the home of Sarah's 'Grannie', the emphasis would be placed very firmly on family rather than on society.

In what was almost a country wedding in a city setting, Sarah had chosen three teenaged bridesmaids to attend her. Dressed in white pre-Raphaelite style dresses with roses in their hair, they were her half-sister Frances Armstrong-Jones, her cousin Zara Phillips, and a friend, Tara Noble Singh. The thirty-year-old bride, simply but stunningly dressed by Jasper Conran, wore a gown of white silk georgette and organza, which one writer described as an 'exercise in perfection.' Worn with a tiara of diamond flowers specially constructed from 'wedding brooches' that had been given to her mother, Sarah's hair was also dressed with a circlet of rosebuds and ivy leaves, just visible under her veil.

Watching her daughter marry beneath Wren's deep, coffered dome, and in front of Henry Moore's massive, almost circular, altar of polished white stone, was an occasion that, for all her other emotions, also appealed to Princess Margaret's theatrical side. For among the guests, some on the bride's list, others invited by Daniel's mother, the theatrical agent Ros Chatto, were a number of friends from film, theatre and television, including the actors Paul Scofield, who read a poem during the service, Alan Bates, Susan Hampshire, Felicity Kendal, and Angus Deayton, together with the distinguished playwright Tom Stoppard.

Friends and friendship always mattered very deeply to Princess Margaret, not least because those with whom she was able to be herself, entirely at ease and totally natural, were relatively few in number. Yet there were times when even her closest friends found her exasperating. 'She can be difficult. We all know that', said one source, 'and it can sometimes make you wonder why we love her. But we do.'[45]

In the Princess's position, being difficult was also about exercising power; though whether she recognized it as such is open to question. Few, however, were brave enough to tackle her about it head on, partly because they accepted it was how she was and partly because they feared falling from grace. Nevertheless, it has to be said that Princess Margaret attracted to her friends who were entertaining, interesting, and thoroughly likeable. To her credit, she was very much aware of it and so, indeed, was the Queen who, especially at times when her sister needed support, remarked how pleased she was that the Princess had such good friends around her.[46]

In return, to quote Sarah's godmother, Lady (Pru) Penn, Princess Margaret was 'A kind, loyal, thoughtful and generous friend.'[47] Anouska Weinberg is yet more succinct, summing up the Princess as 'Witty, Wicked and Wonderful.'[48] Imaginative in friendship she was, said one who knew her well, 'always thinking up treats', visits to art galleries, museum exhibitions, theatre parties, picnics in memorable settings and so on. Such was her untrumpeted generosity, that she was no less quick to show her appreciation for something that might have been done for her, or on her behalf, by somebody she scarcely knew. When that happened, a discreet telephone call to ask about the interests or needs of the person concerned would be followed up by a carefully chosen gift, accompanied by a handwritten note of thanks from the Princess herself.

The caring side of Princess Margaret, perhaps partly from her own need to be wanted, meant that she was always there to help friends at a time of need. 'On the day my husband died', recalled Prue Penn, 'Princess Margaret was the first friend to call and offer her condolences. She asked, "What are you doing this evening?" I said I didn't know. She said, "Then you are going to have dinner here with me. I will send my car for you." I said I didn't think I would be very good company and the Princess said that didn't matter. She didn't want me to be on my own. That is an example of her kindness.'[49]

Another was her support for Anne and Colin Tennant (now Glenconner). Of their three sons the eldest, Charlie, was a confirmed drug addict. To help fund his addiction, he had sold private photographs of Princess Margaret in costume on the night of the Glen theatricals in 1978 to a national tabloid newspaper. If such monies helped to pay for heroin, they also helped to pay for his death. Diagnosed as HIV-positive, Charlie also contracted hepatitis C. He died in 1986. Four years later, his brother Henry who, despite marrying, realized he was gay, died of AIDS. Anne and Colin's youngest son, Christopher, was to survive his brothers, but only just. On Belize in 1987, he was involved in a motorcycle accident and left for dead at the side of the road.

'Princess Margaret was absolutely wonderful,' Anne Glenconner recalled. 'I was desperate. When I rang her, she said we must get Christopher to the British Garrison on Belize, and due to her and the Foreign Office, medical attention was provided and he was airlifted to the garrison. As luck would have it, the surgeon, who wasn't there all the time, was visiting that day and he operated straight away.' Despite brain damage and the fact that he was in a coma for months, Christopher's condition gradually improved. 'Princess Margaret helped to save his life,' said Anne, in the same way that, while others shunned Henry at a time when very little was known about AIDS and how it was contracted, the Princess, 'Always hugged him whenever they met and brought the children to stay when Henry was there. She would also ring up if she'd heard about something that she thought might help. That's friendship.'[50]

Some years earlier, when Diane, Countess Beatty, a young widow she had befriended in Sardinia in the late 1960s, told her she was going to remarry, she, her fiancé John Nutting, a QC, and Princess Margaret talked about the sort of wedding they would like. 'We said we'd like a church wedding', Diane Nutting recalled, 'but a quiet church wedding.' Telling them to 'Leave it to me,' the Princess spoke to her old friend, Eric Abbott, the Dean of Westminster, who suggested they marry in the Henry VII Chapel at Westminster Abbey. All but master-minding the arrangements, the Princess advised John and Diane to have a morning wedding, followed by lunch at Claridge's and an afternoon departure for Mustique where, as a wedding present, she put her house at their disposal for their honeymoon.[51]

On 28 July 1996, at the Portland Hospital in London, exactly two weeks after their second wedding anniversary, Lady Sarah Chatto, as she now was, gave birth to her first baby; a son for Daniel, a first grandchild for Princess Margaret and Lord Snowdon. Though they both visited separately the following day, the Princess and Tony, who for the past nine or ten years had been on much friendlier terms, were both keen to see Sarah and to meet their infant grandson, Samuel. Ever the photographer, the delighted grandfather took his camera with him and, with the baby cradled in his mother's arms, took the earliest photographs of the newest addition to the family.

One month later, on 28 August, though it had little impact on the royal family in its broadest sense, the Prince and Princess of Wales were finally divorced. By way of settlement, Diana received £17 million as a lump sum, and retained her apartments at Kensington Palace, in other words, houses 8 and 9, that had originally been the marital home. She had, in addition, retained her two butlers, at least for as long as she felt the services of both were required, and the staff of her private office, paid for out of a separate allowance. With the divorce, though she had told the world in her famous *Panorama* television interview on 20 November 1995, the Queen's forty-eighth wedding anniversary, that she wanted to be a 'Queen of Hearts', Diana immediately dropped all but half a dozen of her charities. 'Not', said a member of the royal family, 'the way we do things.' By her own choice, she was also to drop the title of Royal Highness. Asked by the Queen, during negotiations of the divorce settlement, whether she would like to retain the title, Diana said it was not a matter of importance to her and therefore she would not. It was only afterwards that she claimed the title had been taken away.[52]

Almost a year to the day after the Wales's marriage officially ended, the final tragic act in Diana's brief, but troubled life, unfolded in Paris during the very early hours of Sunday, 31 August 1997. Fatally injured in that indescribably horrific accident in the underpass at the Place de L'Alma beside the Seine, the Princess, despite the valiant attempts of surgeons who fought to save her, died at the Hôpital Pitié Salpétrière at 4am (3am British time).

At Balmoral, where a shocked royal family received the news, the Prince of Wales had the unenviable task of telling his sons of their mother's death. Later, the Princes, 'looking sombre, but remarkably composed,' as *The Times* described them, went with their father, the Queen and Prince Philip, the Queen Mother and the Duke of York, to morning service at Crathie Church. The following day, as a prelude to what can only be likened to near mob-rule, instigated and led yet again by the tabloid press, headline writers claimed that it had been 'heartless' for the young Princes to appear in public at such a time.

'The press,' said one of the Queen Mother's ladies-in-waiting, 'made it sound as though William and Harry had been *made* to go to church that morning. In fact, the Prince of Wales said they [the family] were going and asked if they also wanted to go. If they didn't, he said he would stay behind with them. *They* said they wanted to go.'[53]

Over the next few days, while the royal family remained at Balmoral and the Princess's body lay in the Chapel Royal at St James's Palace in London, the tabloids' impatience with the fact that the family hadn't immediately travelled south led to headlines which, to quote the former MP Chris Patten's description of Earl Spencer's funeral oration, amounted to 'populist impertinence.' Nevertheless, they inflamed the already heightened emotions of a public grieving, not so much for the Diana few of them knew personally, as for the death of a popular perception, of an image; for the death of a young and beautiful icon. Another Marilyn. Another Elvis. Another James Dean.

Anxious that 'the boys', as she called her great-nephews, should be given time and space in which to grieve, Princess Margaret wondered that anybody would expect their immediate return to London, when they were safe in the greater privacy of Balmoral, away from the press cameras and prying eyes that the royal family had just been accused of thrusting them into.

At Balmoral, protected by those they loved, including Tiggy Legge-Bourke, who was almost a big-sister figure to them and to whom they were both devoted, William and Harry had the freedom to do whatever they wanted in their attempt to comprehend their mother's sudden and shocking loss. 'Terrible to lose your mother at that age', said Princess Margaret, 'and with little Harry's birthday only a few days away.'[54]

'It is not easy to express a sense of loss,' said the Queen in her live television broadcast to the nation on 5 September, the day before Diana's funeral, 'since the initial shock is often

succeeded by a mixture of other feelings: disbelief, incomprehension, anger and concern for those who remain. We have all
felt those emotions in these last few days . . . . At Balmoral we
have all been trying to help William and Harry come to terms
with the devastating loss that they and the rest of us have
suffered. No one who knew Diana will ever forget her. Millions
of others who never met her, but felt they knew her, will remember her.'

If, as the Queen went on to say, there were 'lessons to be
drawn' from Diana's life and 'the extraordinary and moving
reaction to her death', her passing first brought to a close one
of the most turbulent, misunderstood and divisive chapters in
the late twentieth century history of the monarchy.

Since the days when Princess Margaret was berated for her
Caribbean holidays, the march of consumerism and the growth
of long-haul travel had been such that the Princess had long
been able to visit Mustique without arousing comment or criticism. In early 1998, however, her stay on the island, although
nearing its end, was brought to an unexpectedly dramatic
conclusion.

After her usual three-week visit, the Princess was scheduled to
leave on 24 February. With the Glenconners, she was then to
have flown to Grand Cayman to join Colin and Charmian
Campbell as guests of Blanche Blackwell, a former lover of Ian
Fleming, and a friend and one-time neighbour in Jamaica of
Noël Coward. On the night of Monday, 23 February, Princess
Margaret attended a dinner party given at their Palladian-style
house by Harding Lawrence, former head of Braniff Airways,
and his wife Mary Wells.

Around the dining-room table, buzzing with animated
conversation, the Lawrence's other guests included Mark and
Anouska Weinberg, Patrick Lichfield and Annunziata Asquith,
and Ned Ryan, a friend of the Princess since Lady Weinberg had
introduced them in the early '70s.

At one point during the evening, Ned Ryan's attention was

drawn across the table by his neighbour who, indicating Princess Margaret, asked anxiously, 'Is she all right?' Without warning, the Princess had slumped to one side in her chair, her mouth twisted to the left. Realizing that she had suffered a stroke and acting with a swiftness that was later thought to have helped prevent anything more serious, Anouska Weinberg and the Lawrences helped the Princess to a sofa in the drawing room. There she was given two aspirins in water which, as a blood-thinning agent, Anouska had immediately prepared. Oxygen, which for reasons of their own health and indeed, that of their two King Charles spaniels, the Lawrences always kept in the house, was also administered. Shortly afterwards, the Princess was taken to the local surgery where she was seen by the island's resident GP, Dr Bunbry. Although the stroke had affected her left side, causing an almost imperceptible drag of her left foot as she walked, there was no paralysis. Since the Princess was also aware of all that was happening, it was decided she should return to her own house to rest overnight. Her condition would then be assessed the following morning and arrangements made for her to be flown that afternoon to Barbados. There, having first been seen at the Woodside Clinic, she would be transferred to the Bayview Hospital, near Bridgetown.

News of the Princess's stroke was immediately telephoned through to the Queen, to David and Sarah and to Lord Snowdon. A call was also made to Blanche Blackwell on Grand Cayman. Although it was by now three o'clock in the morning, she ensured the airstrip was open so that Princess Margaret's detective, who had already arrived on the island with the special blood supply that is always carried on such visits, could fly to Miami, then on to Barbados. Among the calls made to members of the royal family, one had been to the Queen Mother asking her to telephone the Princess. She did the following morning, so that when Anne Glenconner asked if she had received any telephone calls, the Princess replied, 'Yes. Mummie rang,' then added, 'She usually thinks we have no telephones here.'[55]

From the hospital in Barbados where, despite her private

anxieties, she was, said Anouska Weinberg, 'So charming, beautifully mannered and appreciative of all the doctors and nurses,' Princess Margaret took an overnight flight back to England. With her arrival on the morning of Thursday, the 26th, she was driven to London and admitted, once again, to the King Edward VII's Hospital for Officers. It was there that, only four weeks before, looking the very picture of health and vitality, she had visited her mother who, at the age of ninety-seven, had undergone a hip replacement operation after a fall at Sandringham.

During her two week stay at the hospital undergoing tests and treatment, Princess Margaret, who had escaped physical disability, still 'had to learn to do things' as one close friend put it. 'To begin with she couldn't smile, which meant that if she was telling a funny story, it looked deadly serious. And because she spoke slowly you had to listen carefully to what she was saying.'[56]

Visited by her immediate family, her mother, the Queen and Prince Charles, Princess Margaret was reported to have made good and steady progress. By the time she returned home on 13 March, the stroke's most noticeable legacy was a tendency for her to tire more easily and more quickly. By mid- to late-afternoon, for example, particularly if she had had guests for lunch or visitors during the day, there was a danger that tiredness would leave her confused and forgetful. Otherwise, and certainly to all outward appearances, she was active and mentally alert with scarcely a sign that anything untoward had happened.

If during the months that followed, official engagements in her own right were necessarily restricted, the Princess while continuing to make 'slow but steady progress', began a gradual, albeit more general, return to public life, attending a reception given by the Queen at Windsor Castle for those involved in the Arts; visiting the Chelsea Flower Show in the grounds of the Royal Hospital; and, to the cheers of the crowds on a damp and chilly June morning, riding to and from Horse Guards with the Queen Mother in an open barouche – a small, elegant horse-drawn carriage, popular throughout the nineteenth century – to attend the Queen's Birthday Parade, the ceremony otherwise known as Trooping the Colour.

Though Princess Margaret was not much given to looking back, there were times when friends thought they detected moments of reflection, not least when, as frequently happened that year, she privately attended sung Eucharist on a Sunday morning at St George's Chapel, Windsor. With friends or entirely alone, she would drive down from the Royal Lodge and, unobtrusively entering through the Chancel door, take her usual seat on the north side of the Choir aisle.

It was often while listening to the choir – whom she particularly enjoyed hearing perform the Langlais *Messe Solenele* on special occasions – that friends sometimes noticed a distant, almost contemplative, look in her eyes. None will know what her private thoughts might have been as she looked round at the familiar architectural and heraldic features of 'the family chapel,' as she always called St George's. But since she was not by nature a pessimist, there can be little doubt that whatever her innermost feelings at that time, her view of the future was one of optimism.

By Christmas, her daughter-in-law Serena had discovered that she and David, who had now been married for five years, were expecting their first baby the following summer, while Sarah was due to give birth to her second child early in the New Year. In the wider context of family events, there was to be the June wedding of the Queen's youngest son Edward to Public Relations consultant Sophie Rhys-Jones, whose engagement was to be formally announced on 6 January. At much the same time, the Princess herself surprised many by planning to return to Mustique as usual in February.

Like his brother, Sarah and Daniel's second son, Arthur, was born at the Portland Hospital, on 5 February 1999. Just over two weeks later, Princess Margaret, accompanied by Serena Linley, who were to be joined by Janie Stevens and Ned Ryan a few days later, left London for Mustique and Les Jolies Eaux. The only house she had ever owned in her own right, the Princess had transferred it to David on his twenty-seventh birthday on 3 November 1988. Even so, twenty-five years after she first stepped foot inside its newly-built walls, the Princess still retained an almost proprietorial manner, unconsciously indicated by the fact that she re-arranged the furniture to her own liking whenever she arrived.

Intending to stay until mid-March, it must have seemed to her the cruellest of ironies that, no more than a week after her arrival, and just a year since her stroke, a second – and in many ways even more damaging – misfortune should have befallen her. 'At least the stroke happened at the end of the holiday', the Princess was to say, 'but this time the accident happened at the beginning and ruined everything.'[57]

At home when it was announced three weeks after the event that Princess Margaret had accidentally scalded her feet, the press immediately came up with various scenarios, each one as speculative as the last. While one claimed she had 'plunged' her legs into boiling water, another had her 'collapsing' into it. 'Unaware just how hot the water was', the story ran, 'she sat on the side of the bath and swivelled sideways to lower both her legs. The shock caused her to collapse . . .'[58]

The truth of the matter was that with the intention of washing her hair, the Princess had stepped into an *empty* bath. Standing under the shower head, she inadvertently turned the wrong set of controls, those of the bath taps instead of the shower, with the result that, while her lower legs and soles escaped injury, scalding water – the consequence of a faulty thermostat, said the Princess – poured over the tops of her feet.[59]

It is believed that because she has long suffered from bad circulation – and in particular from Raynaud's Disease, which affects the peripheral circulation primarily in the hands, but also the feet – coupled with a loss of skin sensitivity and lowered reaction time caused by her stroke, the burns were far more severe than might otherwise have been the case.

Although Princess Margaret was to tell a friend that she screamed and nobody heard her, it was the maid who first suspected that something was wrong. Working outside, she became aware of the persistent sound of running water. When she then noticed that the bathroom window had steamed up, she ran inside to alert Janie Stevens, who found the dazed Princess sitting on the edge of the bath, the tops of both feet very severely burned and her right leg badly swollen. In fact, her right foot proved the most difficult to heal and was still doing so a year later.

Attended once again by Dr Bunbry, who treated the burns and gave her antibiotics, the Princess, who was in intense pain and feeling extremely unwell, soon found herself having to vacate Les Jolies Eaux because David, who had recently arrived to join Serena, had let the house. In fact, only one hour before the new tenants were due to arrive, Princess Margaret, who with Janie Stevens' return to London had been joined by Anne Glenconner, was moved by the island's 'bone-shaker' ambulance to the house of an American neighbour.

There, in a darkened room, its shutters closed uncharacteristically at her request, a single light on in a corner, the Princess remained until she felt up to making the journey back to London. Returning by Concorde to minimize flying time and the consequent effect on her already painfully swollen feet, Princess Margaret was at first confined to bed, a cradle over her lower legs, where she now received proper specialist treatment and daily visits by the Royal Household nursing sister. One method of treatment was age-old, well tried and tested. 'I bet you can't guess what I've got on my feet,' the Princess said to Anne Glenconner when she rang on one occasion, '*maggots!*'[60]

With her feet bandaged and unable to walk, Princess Margaret spent much of her time in her bedroom, in bed to begin with or sitting in a wheelchair. In April, at the Queen's invitation, she was at Windsor for two or three weeks where, because she wasn't able to attend the Easter Day service at St George's Chapel, the Dean visited the Princess in her room to give Holy Communion. A few weeks later, though continuing to experience considerable discomfort and not a little anxiety about attempting to walk, one friend is reported to have said that only 'a bomb would get Princess Margaret out of her wheelchair.' That, in the event, is virtually what did move her.

During the early hours of Saturday, 5 June, the police had received a coded bomb warning which, because of a serious attack on the nearby Israeli Embassy some time before, led to a major security alert and the command that Kensington Palace was to be completely evacuated.

Roused from their beds at around 1am, royalty and staff alike headed for the safety of Buckingham Palace, where one of the rooms was opened up for them. Leaving Apartment No. 1, the Duke of Gloucester, with his Danish-born wife Birgitte, drove his confused and uncomprehending ninety-seven-year-old mother, Princess Alice, away from the potential danger zone; followed from Wren House by the Duke of Kent at the wheel of his Jaguar, and the Duchess and her two dogs travelling in a police van.

At an hour when her chauffeur, like her Scotland Yard Protection Officers, was off duty, Princess Margaret's butler brought a car from the garage and with her dresser, helped the Princess from her wheelchair. Accompanied by a uniformed officer who had been on duty in the police lodge, they drove off to the Palace where, said Princess Margaret, making herself comfortable on a sofa, 'It's just like the war.' The 'All Clear' was given just over two hours later when the evacuees were able to wend their way back to 'KP' as it is familiarly known.[61]

For much of that summer, there was a good deal of press talk about David Linley's sale of Les Jolies Eaux, and the allegedly devastating effect it had on Princess Margaret's frame of mind. Such was her unhappiness, so it was said, that she had been plunged into a profound depression. It was the sort of thing that, although without foundation, wasn't much helped when her old friend, Colin Glenconner, from far away St Lucia, was quoted as saying that the Princess was going through a 'sense of inner turmoil and despair.'

There can be no doubt that, while she put a brave face on it,

Princess Margaret was unhappy about the potential sale of Les Jolies Eaux. However, since it had already been on the market for a year, the Princess could scarcely be said to have been taken by surprise. Indeed, there was even the suggestion that Viscount Linley might negotiate a clause in the conditions of sale that would permit the Princess to stay at the house for her customary three-week winter holiday each year.

What most certainly did keep Princess Margaret on an emotional see-saw of highs and lows throughout this time, sometimes in excellent form, at others, discouraged and despondent, was the condition of her feet. It had, after all, been an extremely difficult year, first recovering from a stroke, now a prolonged period of inactivity forced upon her while her feet healed.

There was also the fact that, despite Sarah's twice-weekly visits and the presence in the house of David and Serena, who had sold their apartment in once exclusively working-class Battersea, and were now leisurely house hunting, Princess Margaret had nobody at home specifically for her. As one of her friends put it, 'She has not had fulfilment in her middle and later years. She has suffered the deprivation of not having someone with whom to share her life. And in a public life, that is a particular loss.'[62] It was also a particular loss in somebody with so great a capacity to love.

By the end of summer, the Princess, with the encouragement of the Queen and her family, was again walking, albeit with the aid of a stick; first in slippers that resembled ballet shoes known as 'flats' then, because she was still unable to wear heels, she had specially made flat walking shoes with velcro straps that fastened over the instep. With greater mobility and less discomfort, Princess Margaret made a tentative return to public duties.

Yet if, as the journalist Fiametta Rocco wrote at the time of David's marriage, Princess Margaret's life today is centred on 'Her children, her friends, her memories, her loyalty to her Sovereign',[63] then a family event in December 1999 drew on most of those elements. David and Serena's first child, a third grandson for Princess Margaret and her former husband, a ninth great-grandson for the Queen Mother, had like his cousins Samuel and Arthur Chatto, been born at the Portland Hospital, on 2 July. His christening, during which he received the names Charles Patrick Inigo, took place five months later at the Queen's Chapel, St James's Palace, followed by a reception at Clarence House. Attended by the Queen and the Queen Mother, both sets of grandparents, and six godparents, it was a tea and champagne celebration. Tea for Princess Margaret, who otherwise preferred a ginger-based soft drink prepared by her chef in place of alcohol; champagne for those who preferred to toast the health of the Honourable Charles Armstrong-Jones in something stronger.

At the end of the month, on New Year's Eve, while the Queen and Prince Philip with the Princess Royal and her husband, naval Commodore Timothy Laurence, attended Millennium celebrations and the inauguration of the controversial Dome at Greenwich in South-East London, Princess Margaret and her mother were together at Sandringham. Joined for dinner by Sir Michael Oswald, the Queen's Stud Manager, and his wife Angela, a lady-in-waiting to the Queen Mother, it was a quiet beginning to a new century. It was also a quiet beginning to the year of Queen Elizabeth's centenary, and the year in which Princess Margaret celebrated her seventieth birthday.

Although she returned from the Christmas and New Year holiday at Sandringham in high spirits, it was not long before concerns were again expressed about the Princess's low energy levels and, though rather more candidly, what again seemed to be an absence of incentive or motivation on her part. There was no doubt that the recovery from her accident had been a long and frequently uphill struggle, or that it had taken a very considerable toll, both physical and psychological. In fact, the cumulative effect of the stroke only a year earlier, which those close to her were beginning to feel had had a greater effect than originally thought, together with her accident, led one of her friends to ask if she had now 'turned her face to the wall.' If at one point it was beginning to look that way, the prospect of a four-week Caribbean holiday, first in St Lucia and then back on Mustique, gave her renewed impetus.

When she returned in mid-March, looking tanned and relaxed, her recalcitrant right foot all but healed at long last, it was as though she had found a renewed sense of wellbeing.

THE FINAL CHAPTER

The hope that Princess Margaret's newly found sense of invigoration would survive her return from the West Indies in March 2000, sadly proved to be short lived. Within a matter of weeks a familiar pattern had started to re-emerge. Highs, that were rarely very high, were matched by lows that again triggered bouts of depression; not, it has to be said, the 'manic' depression of some of the more imaginative, though wholly inaccurate news items, but the more usual 'reactive' kind, brought on by and in reaction to the unpredictable nature of her health which, like her father, made old before his time, had noticeably aged her.

Low energy levels were again evident as were occasional recurrences of trouble with her right foot, proving, to the Princess's chagrin, that the long healing process was not as yet complete.

Of the final year or two of Princess Margaret's life, the first year of the new millennium, though scarcely easy for her, was the most active and in hindsight, perhaps the most satisfactory. Though nobody would know it for certain at the time, it was also to be the last year of her official life, carrying out as she did a number of engagements that were connected with the Worshipful Company of Haberdashers; the St John Ambulance Association and Brigade; the Guide Association, through which she had been associated as a Brownie, a Guide and as President, for most of her life; and the Zebra Trust, an organization that concerned itself with African students in the United Kingdom and with which, through a friend, Jeannine Bartosik, she had long been associated as patron.

The year 2000 was also memorable as the year in which Queen Elizabeth the Queen Mother reached the age of 100 and Princess Margaret herself attained that biblical milestone, three score years and ten. It was to some of the official events celebrating her centenary that Queen Elizabeth was accompanied by her younger daughter, beginning in late June with a lunch party attended by 500 guests, which the Lord Mayor of London and the Corporation of the City hosted in the splendid setting of London's medieval Guildhall. Much more private was the unique one-off event that took the form of a reception and dance held in the State Apartments at Windsor Castle on 21 June, to celebrate what the formal invitation referred to as 'the Decade Birthdays' of the Queen Mother, Princess Margaret, Anne, the Princess Royal, who was fifty that August, and Andrew, Duke of York, forty the previous February. Following a family dinner party in the Castle's State Dining Room – to which the kings and queens of Sweden and Spain, the former king and queen of the Hellenes and a veritable *Almanac de Gotha* of German, Belgian, Dutch, Greek and Spanish princes, princesses and infantas were also invited – the reception for some 900 guests, specially asked by the Queen and Prince Philip as hosts, and those celebrating their 'decade' birthdays, began. That night, with dancing in the subtly-lit Waterloo Chamber, arranged as a ballroom, and less traditional choreographic activity happening in the Queen's Presence Chamber, rigged up as a disco with red and green flashing lights, the celebrations inside the floodlit castle went on into the early hours.

Dressed in cream silk, a ruby and diamond brooch loaned by her mother at her shoulder, and her hair – which for some time and for whatever reason she had not wanted anyone to touch – freshly and elegantly styled, the Princess was on animated form. Having taken to a wheelchair for the latter part of the evening to ease the pressure on her right foot, she was wheeled through the flower-filled State Rooms, stopping to greet and talk to friends, among them singers, actors, dancers, writers, musicians, designers, art dealers and financiers. Talking enthusiastically about the evening afterwards, the Princess said, 'I couldn't have enjoyed myself more,'[1] and one was immediately reminded of how things used to be. All the same, the evening was not without a downside, in that it drained the Princess's easily depleted energy levels and took her a full forty-eight hours to recover.

Four months later on 25 October another, smaller, seventieth birthday party, arranged by her son David and daughter Sarah, and attended by the Queen and Prince Philip and some of the Princess's oldest friends, was given in her honour at the Ritz. Dinner that evening was served at tables garlanded with pink roses and set with silver candelabra for which the Princess's butler, Harold Brown, had made parchment shades stencilled with the Princess's personal monogram. It was a touch she genuinely appreciated.

Another birthday tribute to Princess Margaret, who had by then been President of the Royal Ballet for more than forty years, was paid to her in what was described as 'a strikingly inclusive affair'[2] by all of Britain's major dance companies. Staged at Sadler's Wells on 22 October, the gala performance, which had been master-minded by Wayne Sleep, consisted of tributes from Sir Anthony Dowell, Dame Beryl Grey, Derek Deane and Sir Peter Wright, and a programme of dance that ranged from the *pas de deux* from the second Act of *Swan Lake,* danced by Darcey Bussell and Roberto Bolle of the Royal Ballet, to Balanchine's *Tarantella,* performed by Monica Perego of the English National Ballet and Irek Mukhamedov, to Christopher Hampson's specially-created *Homage to a Princess.* One of the most innovative and comic pieces of the entire evening, was an excerpt from Matthew Bourne's *Spitfire,* in which, to the audience's amusement, male dancers from 'Adventures in Motion Pictures' struck a series of mock heroic poses while dressed in nothing more than underwear.

With the approach of Christmas came renewed concern for Princess Margaret's health. At the beginning of December she returned to London from a weekend visit to Royal Lodge, Windsor and, because of the 'heavy tiredness' she spoke of to one or two old friends, and which, particularly in the last months of her life was often to envelop her, went straight to her bed. Though significant in relation to the Princess's overall, though gradual decline, alarm bells did not start to ring until a week or so later. When friends called, they were told that Princess Margaret was not taking telephone calls – invariably a sign that something was not right – and when one friend endeavoured to find out more, was told by a member of her staff that the Princess was feeling 'a little under the weather.' At that time, she herself put persistent feelings of listlessness down to some sort of virus,[3] but still intended to join her family at Sandringham for the Christmas holiday. Though doctors were twice called to her bedside on the royal estate at the end of December and unspecified tests were carried out, the diagnosis was that the Princess's condition might have been linked to the 'follow-on' effects of her first stroke, even though that had occurred almost two years before. As a precaution, Buckingham Palace issued a statement that said that, while there was cause for 'concern', there was none for 'alarm.' At the start of the New Year, however, fears for the Princess's deteriorating health had reached a point that when, despite her lack of appetite, she managed to eat a jam tart, a mood of celebration immediately lightened the atmosphere at the Queen's Norfolk residence. After visiting the Princess, Lady [Anne] Glenconner, one of her oldest friends, as well as an extra lady-in-waiting of many years' standing, remarked that while Princess Margaret was 'very frail indeed and rather depressed at being so ill,' she was still 'being very brave [and] very stoic.'[4]

Days later, on 4 January, it was announced that the Princess had suffered a second stroke. Though it was something she herself refuted, the down-turned mouth and eye, the slurred speech (which was to continue for almost three weeks) and the need to use her walking stick once more for support, strongly contradicted any suggestion that it was nothing more than the 'circulatory' problem she claimed, perhaps even wanted to believe it to be; or even a Transient Ischaemic Attack (TIA) which, while giving every indication of a stroke – 'headache, visual disturbance, dizziness, slurred or loss of speech, paralysis and trouble swallowing'[5] – normally lasts no more than a day.

Almost a week later, anxiety about the Princess's 'extreme loss of appetite', led to her being admitted to the King Edward VII's Hospital for Officers in London. Contrary to media speculation, however, Princess Margaret did not have problems swallowing nor, by her own testimony, was she being tube-fed. Once again, it was during one of Anne Glenconner's visits to her bedside that she was tempted to eat something. A chocolate cake, 'the size of an Ascot hat, and decorated with roses', was brought in, said Lady Glenconner, and though 'she was feeling very tired', the Princess managed to 'polish off a piece.'[6]

On this occasion, Princess Margaret's stay in hospital lasted ten days and on 20 January she delayed her departure until she had had her hair done so that, although still frail and perhaps some-what bemused by quite so much media attention, she should at least look her best for the press and television news cameras, massed behind crowd barriers opposite the hospital's main entrance.

Over the next several weeks, in addition to the physiotherapy and hydrotherapy treatment she received, Princess Margaret had consultations with two specialists. Between them – if only, it would transpire, for a relatively short time – their combined efforts were able to bring about a significant improvement in the Princess. At the suggestion of her daughter Sarah and one or two other friends, Princess Margaret first saw Dr Mark Collins of the Priory Clinic, who specialized in addictive and mood disorders. A little later, this time at the recommendation of her nephew, the Prince of Wales, the Princess was visited at Kensington Palace by Dr Mosaraf Ali, an Indian-born holistic healer and nutritionist whom Prince Charles himself consulted. Explaining his treat-ment, Dr Ali – who established the Integrated Medical Centre in London's Harley Street in 1999 – said, 'We start off with treating the neck. There are a pair of arteries called the vertebral arteries that supply blood to the base of the brain. So I stimulate those arteries and that irrigates the brain and reactivates all the centres such as appetite, emotions, mood swings. Sleep is better and the panic or anxiety is less.'[7]

By early March, Princess Margaret seemed to be well established on the road to recovery. Not only was she looking well, eating properly and again walking largely unaided, but her outlook was also much more positive. She had even consigned the grey and khaki suits and dresses that she had taken to wearing to the back of her wardrobe and instead favoured positive and vibrant colours, particularly red or red and gold, that reflected her newly invigorated frame of mind. At this time, Princess Margaret was also seeing more visitors and, on 14 March, was on particularly good form when she went out to dinner, joining her old friend Ned Ryan – who described the Princess as 'fifty times better than she was' – and her cousin, Lady Elizabeth Shakerley, at the famous Le Caprice restaurant.

The Princess's marked improvement also came as a great relief to the Queen, who had dinner with her sister at Kensington Palace the next day, and her mother, who came to lunch the day after. Both the Queen and the Queen Mother had, said Lady Elizabeth, been 'worried sick'[8] about the Princess.

Like Princess Margaret herself, whose fragile progress was at the mercy of a frightening and unpredictable condition, so feelings of relief and optimism among those around her could so easily suffer grave setbacks. Indeed, in what soon appeared to be one of fate's crueller tricks, Princess Margaret suffered a further stroke. On Tuesday, 27 March, shortly before she was due to host a lunch at home, and not two weeks since she had delighted Elizabeth Shakerley and Ned Ryan over dinner, the Princess complained of feeling unwell and went to her room.

This time the stroke she sustained not only caused paralysis of her left arm and leg (though physiotherapy would in time restore a little movement to both limbs), but it also, albeit fleetingly, affected her eyesight. She nevertheless remained in an optimistic and positive frame of mind, which would surely have lasted had she not suffered yet another 'blip' (or TIA) at Windsor Castle on Easter Monday. This, though it did not blind her, is thought to have robbed her of the sight in her left eye, while causing that in her right eye to blur. Once again, specialists when asked by the media explained that while up to 30 per cent of people who suffer strokes have problems with eyesight, about three-quarters of them do recover their vision to some extent. This, over the next few months, is precisely what happened in Princess Margaret's case. Though reading and writing were no longer possible, and her vision remained restricted, especially where the middle distance and anything on her left-hand side were concerned, she could nevertheless make out certain things, and even watch a little television.[9] When she felt well enough, she would also make occasional private visits to places that had always interested her. On 21 May, for instance, just a month after the latest 'blip' had impaired her vision, the Princess took everybody by surprise when, despite being confined to her wheelchair, a pair of dark glasses shielding her eyes, she more or less insisted that she was going to visit the Chelsea Flower Show as she always had.

In June, she was no less determined to attend Prince Philip's eightieth birthday thanksgiving service at St George's Chapel, Windsor. Not the least of her reasons for going was to see the birthday 'gift' she had carefully planned for her brother-in-law delivered. Having said a few words in tribute to her husband during the reception in St George's Hall that followed the thanksgiving service, the Queen said, 'And now, my sister has something for you.' Moments later, as the sound of a lone whistle grew nearer, a boy dancer from the Royal Ballet School entered, followed by twenty of his fellow students. To Prince Philip's amusement, Princess Margaret had arranged a specially choreographed version of the 'Hornpipe' to be performed for him.

That afternoon, again feeling extremely tired, Princess Margaret returned to Kensington Palace and after lunch was asleep within minutes of being settled in her bed.[10] Save for a private visit one month later to the Great Court at the British Museum, the opening of which ill health had prevented her from attending, Princess Margaret spent much of her time in her room. Every day, her lady-in-waiting would bring the post across from the office to be read to her, and most often she or perhaps another female friend from among the handful who visited (telephone calls and male visitors were by now a thing of the past), would sit in her often dimly-lit room and read to her. At one point, the novels of Charles Dickens had become a particular favourite.

Although there would still be a few occasions in the coming months that she was able to enjoy, though she again paid the price for them in terms of expended energy, the Princess's quality of life was now non-existent. Even having to be helped to do some of the simplest things was an affront to her independence and her dignity. 'All her life she has been the sparkling one,' her cousin Margaret Rhodes was quoted as saying, 'but since her [first] stroke three years ago, she has lost that particular facility to sparkle.'

Rarely seen in public by now, the change in Princess Margaret, even in the two months since she had attended Prince Philip's birthday celebration at Windsor, shocked those who saw her at Clarence House on 4 August, the day of her mother's 101st birthday. Yet, despite her appearance – wheelchair-bound, her face made puffy by medication, her left arm in a sling and heavy, wrap-around dark glasses shielding her eyes from glare – the Princess saw no good reason why she should not join her mother, as she invariably had, on her birthday.

As the end of the year approached, Princess Margaret – her appearance on this occasion far less dramatic – joined the Queen and other members of the royal family at the neighbouring Kensington Palace apartments of the Duke and Duchess of Gloucester. The family gathering on 12 December, was held to celebrate the 100th birthday on Christmas Day of Princess Alice, Duchess of Gloucester, widow of George V's third son, Prince Henry and, albeit by marriage, the Queen and Princess Margaret's only surviving aunt.

Ten days later, a helicopter flew Princess Margaret and her

mother, who was already suffering from the worrying 'flu like cough that would put her out of action for several weeks, to Sandringham for the Christmas and New Year holiday. While the Queen Mother's ill health kept her in Norfolk far longer than usual, Princess Margaret returned home on 6 January. Already pencilled in her diary for the end of the month was a visit to the Victoria & Albert Museum in London to see the new British Galleries, a £31 million project recently opened by Prince Charles; and a party for her middle grandson, Arthur Chatto, three years old on 5 February. On both occasions, the Princess was said by a friend to have been on extremely good form; even returning from Arthur's party with a helium-filled balloon tied to her wheelchair.

Wednesday, 6 February was a day of mixed emotions for Princess Margaret. That date always was. For while, in 2002, it marked the 50th anniversary of the Queen's accession to the throne, her Golden Jubilee, it also marked the 50th anniversary of the death of King George VI. Anne Glenconner, who visited that day, said she had found the Princess in reflective mood, but that by the time she left, she was feeling more cheerful.

Three days later, at 6.30 on the morning of Saturday, 9 February, with her son David and daughter Sarah at her bedside, Princess Margaret herself died, passing away peacefully in her sleep, as her father had done and just as, she recently told a friend, she hoped she might.[11]

It was during the Thursday night/Friday morning of 7/8 February that the Princess had suffered yet another stroke. As her condition worsened with the development of cardiac complications, not helped perhaps by the heart aneurysm her doctors had discovered some time before, and of which the Princess herself was aware,[12] it was decided to move her to the King Edward VII's Hospital for Officers and an ambulance was summoned at 2.30am on the day she died.

Whether by stroke or heart condition, Princess Margaret's death was almost inevitably going to be sudden. All the same, there was a palpable sense of shock when, at 8.30am on

9 February, Buckingham Palace released an unexpected statement on behalf of the Queen announcing the death of 'Her
beloved sister'. Almost immediately tributes from politicians, religious leaders and world figures began to arrive, while in what was
seen as a spontaneous and wholly unprecedented tribute to his
aunt, Prince Charles told television and radio audiences that
Princess Margaret would be 'terribly missed' by all her family and
friends. 'My darling aunt,' he said, 'had such a dreadful time the
last few years with her awful illness and it was hard for her to deal
with, particularly as she was such a wonderfully vibrant woman....
She loved life and lived it to the full ... and as dreadfully sad as
death is at times like this, in a way it must have been a merciful
release for somebody who was such a vital and free spirit.'

From the King Edward VII's Hospital that morning, the
Princess's son and daughter drove first to Buckingham Palace to
be with their aunt, 'Lilibet' as they, too, always called her, before
returning to Kensington Palace to await the arrival later that
afternoon of Princess Margaret's oak coffin draped with her
personal standard of crimson, blue and gold. Carried not into
her Drawing Room as might have been expected, but along the
hall and up the main staircase, past the full-length portrait of
King Leopold of the Belgians, resplendent in order-bedecked
military uniform, that dominates the half-landing, the Princess's
coffin was taken into her bedroom. There it would lie for two
days before being transferred to St James's Palace. Not, however,
to the Chapel Royal (where the coffin of Diana, Princess of
Wales, had lain) which was currently closed for refurbishment,
but to The Queen's Chapel, standing in the precincts of nearby
Marlborough House. Designed by Inigo Jones in the style of
Palladio, and commissioned in 1623, the chapel was completed
four years later for Charles I's queen, Henrietta Maria. It was
here in 1761 that King George III married Sophia Charlotte of
Mecklenburg-Strelitz and here in our own time that Princess
Margaret's youngest grandson, Charles Armstrong-Jones, was
christened in December 1999.

Having lain for a further two days within the pale grey and

gold panelled walls of The Queen's Chapel, flanked by unbleached funerary candles and enormous pedestal arrangements of roses, lilies and hydrangeas, the Princess's coffin, still draped with her personal standard and covered with white and cream roses, lilies, tuba roses and white lilac, was moved from its place before the altar, from above which Annibale Caracci's *The Virgin and Child with Saints Joseph, John the Baptist and Catherine* looks down, and on the evening of 14 February, was taken by road to Windsor. There, as the hearse drove through the King Henry VIII Gate, entering the castle precincts at 6.45pm, a member of the Corps of Drums from the Household Division beat out a royal salute.

Through the night, in accordance with her wishes, Princess Margaret lay beneath the soaring fan-vaulted roof in the nave of St George's Chapel. The following afternoon, fifty years to the very day since the funeral of King George VI took place there, the coffin of his younger daughter was carried by a Bearer Party of the Royal Highland Fusiliers (Princess Margaret's Own Glasgow and Ayrshire Regiment) to a catafalque beneath the banners of the Knights of the Most Noble Order of the Garter in the Quire where, until the service began, two Military Knights of Windsor in scarlet swallow-tailed coats and black cockaded hats, stood with heads bowed, one at the head and one at the foot of the Princess's coffin.

Always a great planner, Princess Margaret had given very considerable thought to the music, prayers and hymns that were to be included in what she specifically wanted to be a private funeral, attended only by her family and friends. It was also typical of a woman who liked surprises that she should spring one final surprise herself by choosing to be cremated rather than buried. It was a decision that was no doubt influenced by a number of considerations, among them the Princess's dislike of the royal family's private burial ground at Frogmore, about a mile through the park from Windsor Castle itself, which she always said was 'gloomy'; a conviction that in our more conservation conscious times cremation is a space-saving alternative to burial, and no doubt most important of all, a wish to be interred beside her adored father within the limited confines of the King George VI Memorial Chapel.

As sunshine poured through the stained glass windows of St George's Chapel and the muffled bells of the Curfew Tower tolled out over Windsor, so the congregation of some 450 mourners began to take their seats in the nave. Included among them and reflecting the Princess's life-long love of the arts were Dame Judi Dench, Felicity Kendal, Bryan Forbes and Nanette Newman, and Dame Cleo Laine and John Dankworth. Music from *Swan Lake*, played on the organ immediately before the service began, was an equally poignant reminder of Princess Margaret's love of the ballet.

By 3pm the scene was set. The Queen and Prince Philip, Princess Margaret's son and daughter, her son-in-law, Daniel Chatto and daughter-in-law, Serena Linley, and almost every member of the royal family – including the Queen Mother, whose presence because of her frailty and recent ill health had been a matter of debate – had all arrived; and the Ecclesiastical Procession including the Dean of Windsor, the Right Reverend David Connor, the sub-Dean of Her Majesty's Chapels Royal, the Reverend Prebendary William Booth and the Archbishop of Canterbury, Dr George Carey, had taken their places in the Quire.

To music by William Croft, the choir sang The Sentences, *I am the resurrection and the life, saith the Lord: he that believeth in me, though he were dead, yet shall he live: and whosoever liveth and believeth in me shall never die.* The Dean then opened the service, during which the choir sang Psalm 23, Lord Linley read the Lesson from Romans 8, and the congregation sang the hymns Princess Margaret had chosen, first *Immortal, Invisible, God Only Wise* and then, following the Collects, *Nunc Dimittis* (with words from the second chapter of St Luke's Gospel), and the Prayers, the second hymn, *When I Survey the Wondrous Cross*.

Following the Commendation, the Archbishop of Canterbury recited the Princess's favourite prayer: 'Enter my heart, O Holy

Spirit, come in blessed mercy and set me free. Throw open, O Lord, the locked doors of my mind; cleanse the chambers of my thought for thy dwelling: light there the fires of thine own holy brightness in new understandings of truth, O Holy Spirit, very God, whose presence is liberty, grant me the perfect freedom to be thy servant today, tomorrow, evermore.'

After the Archbishop had pronounced the Blessing, trumpeters of the Hussars and Light Dragoons (Princess Margaret had been Colonel-in-Chief of the latter) under the direction of Trumpet Major Ted Ashworth, sounded The Last Post and Reveille. As the sound echoed through the chapel and faded away, the Bearer Party lifted the Princess's coffin onto their shoulders and, followed by her family, slowly made their way along the blue-carpeted nave to the West Door. There a piper of the Royal Highland Fusiliers began to play a lament called, appropriately, *The Desperate Struggle of the Bird*, specially chosen by the Princess's daughter, Sarah, around whose waist the Queen placed a comforting arm as they watched the hearse bear Princess Margaret away from the castle precincts towards Slough Crematorium. The ceremonial aspect of her funeral over, the Princess, practical to the end, had directed that nobody should follow her on the last, purely functional part of her earthly remains' final journey.

Though it stands in its own right as a highly individual life well lived, Princess Margaret's story should also be seen in the wider context of the evolution of the monarchy itself. History remembers relatively few of its princes and princesses, but Princess Margaret is unlikely to be soon forgotten. Despite the popular image of her as a fast-living, party-loving socialite, she was wholly dedicated to and supportive of the monarchic ideal and, like other virtues that are today considered old-fashioned, a sense of duty was deeply ingrained in her character.

Though not, perhaps, without hubris, Princess Margaret's was, on balance, a happy and fulfilled existence. It is also true to say that because of the course her life followed, the Princess, probably without realizing it, played a significant part in helping to change attitudes and modernize the monarchy we know today.

As the Reverend Canon Barry Thompson said at her funeral service, it is for her 'loyalty and sense of duty; her faithfulness towards her family and her friends; her energy and enthusiasm; her quick wit and sound advice, and for her depth of knowledge and her love of life' that Princess Margaret should be remembered.

SOURCE NOTES

Chapter One

1   John W. Wheeler-Bennett, *King George VI His Life and Reign*, p 150
2   Sarah Bradford, *Elizabeth, A Biography of Her Majesty The Queen*, p 20
3   Sarah Bradford, *Elizabeth*, p 24
4   Conversation with Lady Mary Clayton
5   Grania Forbes, *My Darling Buffy*, p 149
6   John W. Wheeler-Bennett, *King George VI*, p 150
7   Grania Forbes, *My Darling Buffy*, p 168
8   (Cited) Christopher Warwick, *Queen Mary's Photograph Albums*, p 12
9   Grania Forbes, *My Darling Buffy*, pp 157–59
10 Conversation with Princess Margaret

Chapter Two

1   *The Scotsman*, 21 August 1930
2   John W. Wheeler-Bennett, *King George VI*, p 253
3   Conversation with Lady Mary Clayton
4   *Aberdeen Press & Journal*, 22 August 1930

5   *The Glasgow Herald,* 23 August 1930

6   *The Bulletin,* 28 August 1930

7   Conversation with Princess Margaret

8   Conversation with Princess Margaret

9   Conversation with Lady Mary Clayton

10 Grania Forbes, *My Darling Buffy,* pp 45–46

11 John W. Wheeler-Bennett, *King George VI,* p 258

12 HRH The Duke of Windsor, *A King's Story,* pp 254–55

13 Conversation with Princess Margaret

14 Sarah Bradford, *Elizabeth,* pp 151–52

15 Conversation with Lady Mary Clayton

16 Conversation with Princess Margaret

Chapter Three

1   Marion Crawford, *The Little Princesses,* p 18

2   Conversation with Lady Mary Clayton

3   Conversation with Princess Margaret

4   Conversation with Princess Margaret

5   Conversation with Lady Mary Clayton

6   Confidential source

7   Confidential source

8   Kenneth Rose, *Kings, Queens & Courtiers,* p 186

9   Gore Vidal, *Palimpsest,* p 194

10 Private conversation

11 Kenneth Rose, *Sunday Telegraph,* 1 March 1998

12 Conversation with Princess Margaret

13 Ben Pimlott, *The Queen,* p 26

14 *Ibid,* p 24

15 *Ibid,* p 25

16 Conversation with Lady Mary Clayton

17 Conversation with Princess Margaret

18 Private conversation

19 Conversation with Princess Margaret

20 Conversation with Princess Margaret

21 Marion Crawford, *The Little Princesses*, p 26
22 Conversation with Princess Margaret
23 Conversation with Lady Mary Clayton
24 Conversation with Colin Campbell
25 Private conversation
26 HRH The Duke of Windsor, *A King's Story*, pp 187–88
27 The Duchess of Windsor, *The Heart Has Its Reasons*, p 205
28 John W. Wheeler-Bennett, *King George VI*, p 265

Chapter Four

1 HRH The Duke of Windsor, *A King's Story*, p 267
2 The Duchess of Windsor, *The Heart Has Its Reasons*, pp 224–25
3 Graham Turner, 'The Real Queen Mother', *The Daily Telegraph* 6 July 1999
4 HRH The Duke of Windsor, *A King's Story*, p 258
5 Graham Turner, 'The Real Queen Mother', *The Daily Telegraph*, 6 July 1999
6 John W. Wheeler-Bennett, *King George VI*, p 286
7 *George VI: The Reluctant King*, Blakeway Productions, BBC 2 *Reputations* series, May 1999
8 Conversation with Princess Margaret
9 Conversation with Princess Margaret
10 Private conversation
11 Ralph Selby to Christopher Warwick for *Abdication* 1985
12 Conversation with Princess Margaret
13 Ronald Allison & Sarah Riddell, *The Royal Encyclopedia*, p 461
14 Sarah Bradford, *Elizabeth*, p 68
15 Conversation with Lady Mary Clayton

Chapter Five

1 Private information

2 Private conversation
3 Private conversation
4 Conversation with Princess Margaret
5 Sarah Bradford, *Elizabeth*, p 77
6 John W. Wheeler-Bennett, *King George VI*, p 343
7 Conversation with Princess Margaret
8 Conversation with Princess Margaret
9 Sir John W. Wheeler-Bennett, *King George VI*, p 749
10 Conversation with Princess Margaret
11 Quoted in Christopher Warwick's *Queen Mary's Photograph Albums*, p 121

Chapter Six

1 Sarah Bradford, *Elizabeth*, pp 90–91
2 Edna Healey, *The Queen's House*, p 305
3 *Ibid*, pp 302–3
4 Conversation with Princess Margaret
5 Conversation with Princess Margaret
6 Marion Crawford, *The Little Princesses*, p 81
7 Conversation with the Hon. Mrs Rhodes
8 Conversation with Princess Margaret
9 The late Lord Adeane to Christopher Warwick (in 1982) for *Princess Margaret*
10 Conversation with Kenneth Rose
11 Private Information
12 Conversation with Princess Margaret
13 Conversation with Princess Margaret
14 Kenneth Rose, *Sunday Telegraph*, 1 March 1998
15 Private conversation
16 Christopher Warwick, *King George VI & Queen Elizabeth*, p 115
17 The Hon. Mrs Rhodes
18 Anne Edwards, *Royal Sisters*, p 88
19 Conversation with Princess Margaret
20 Private information

21   Private conversation
22   Christopher Warwick, *Princess Margaret*, p 30
23   Ben Pimlott, *The Queen*, p 65
24   Roy Strong, *Cecil Beaton: The Royal Portraits*, p 90
25   John W. Wheeler-Bennett, *King George VI*, p 741
26   Sarah Bradford, *Elizabeth*, p 101
27   Private conversation
28   Roy Strong, *Cecil Beaton: The Royal Portraits*, p 92
29   Conversation with Princess Margaret
30   *HRH The Princess Margaret: Memories of VE Day*, SSCV Production, BBC Television, 8 May 1995

Chapter Seven

1   Royal College of Arms, Vol. I 81, p 104
2   The late Audrey Russell to Christopher Warwick for *Princess Margaret* (1983)
3   Ben Pimlott, *The Queen*, p 111
4   John W. Wheeler-Bennett, *King George VI*, p 687
5   *Ibid*, p 692
6   Private information
7   Marion Crawford, *The Little Princesses*, p 99
8   John Colville, *The Fringes of Power*, p 620
9   G. Payn & S. Morley, *The Noël Coward Diaries*, p 136
10   John Colville, *The Fringes of Power*, p 621
11   Private conversation
12   Private conversation
13   Private information
14   Conversation with Princess Margaret
15   Conversation with the Hon. Dominic Elliot
16   Private conversation
17   Conversation with the Hon. Mrs Rhodes
18   Joanna Chase, *HRH Princess Margaret*, 1948
19   Roy Strong, *Cecil Beaton: The Royal Portraits*, p 147
20   Conversation with Princess Margaret

21 John Hearsey, *Marie Antoinette*, p 53
22 Conversation with Lady Mary Clayton
23 Gwen Robyns, *HRH The Princess Margaret 21st Birthday Album*
24 Conversation with Princess Margaret
25 Conversation with Lady Mary Clayton
26 John Colville, *The Fringes of Power*, p 621
27 Norman Barrymaine, *The Story of Peter Townsend*, p 40
28 *The Times Magazine*, 15 April 1995
29 Conversation with Mrs Derek Lawson
30 Sarah Bradford, *Elizabeth*, p 198
31 Private conversation
32 Private conversation
33 Norman Barrymaine, *The Story of Peter Townsend*, p 68

Chapter Eight

1 Robert Rhodes James in *George VI: The Reluctant King*, Blakeway Productions, BBC 2, May, 1999
2 Conversation with Princess Margaret
3 Conversations with Princess Margaret, and Lady Lowther
4 *The Star*, 7 March 1949
5 Miles Jebb (Ed.) *The Diaries of Cynthia Gladwyn*, pp 96–7
6 Conversation with Princess Margaret
7 Private conversation
8 Private conversation
9 Vivien Batchelor, *HRH The Princess Margaret Gift Book*
10 Lady Lowther - private album
11 Private information
12 Anne Edwards, *Royal Sisters*, p 199
13 Conversation with Lady Mary Clayton
14 Conversation with Janie Stevens
15 Conversation with Alexander McEwen
16 Suzy Menkes, *The Royal Jewels*, p 112
17 Peter Townsend, *Time and Chance*, p 189
18 Vivien Batchelor, *HRH The Princess Margaret Gift Book*, p 44

19 John W. Wheeler-Bennett, *King George VI*, p 801
20 Conversation with Princess Margaret
21 Private information
22 Graham Turner, 'The Real Queen Mother', *The Daily Telegraph*, 6 July 1999
23 Ben Pimlott, *The Queen*, p 199
24 Christopher Warwick, *King George VI & Queen Elizabeth*, p 142; from the collection of Dr Wayne Swift, New York

Chapter Nine

1 Graham Turner, 'The Real Queen Mother', *The Daily Telegraph*, 6 July 1999
2 Private information
3 Ben Pimlott, *The Queen*, p 187
4 Conversation with Princess Margaret
5 Private conversation
6 Conversation with Lady Mary Clayton
7 Conversation with Lady Mary Clayton
8 Private conversation
9 Conversation with Janie Stevens
10 Conversation with Marigold Bridgeman
11 Conversation with Marigold Bridgeman
12 Conversation with Lady Elizabeth Cavendish
13 Private conversation
14 Conversation with Marigold Bridgeman
15 Sarah Bradford, *Elizabeth*, p 201
16 Norman Barrymaine, *The Story of Peter Townsend*, p 50
17 Conversation with the late Lord Charteris
18 Chrissey Iley, *Style* Magazine
19 Private information
20 Conversation with Princess Margaret
21 Private information
22 Conversation with the late Lord Charteris
23 Sarah Bradford, *Elizabeth*, p 194

24   Conversation with Princess Margaret
25   Conversation with Princess Margaret
26   Conversation with the late Lord Charteris
27   Conversation with Princess Margaret
28   Conversation with Princess Margaret
29   Conversation with the late Lord Charteris
30   Private conversation
31   Anne Edwards, Royal Sisters, p 246
32   Jean Rook, Majesty magazine, August 1990
33   Conversation with the late Lord Charteris
34   Norman Barrymaine, The Story of Peter Townsend, p 131
35   G. Payn & S. Morley, The Noël Coward Diaries, p 215
36   Sarah Bradford, Elizabeth, p 205
37   G. Payn & S. Morley, The Noël Coward Diaries, pp 222–3

Chapter Ten

1   Conversation with Lady Elizabeth Cavendish
2   Conversation with Lady Elizabeth Cavendish
3   Ben Pimlott, The Queen, p 235
4   Norman Barrymaine, The Story of Peter Townsend, p 154
5   Ibid
6   Conversation with Princess Margaret
7   Sarah Bradford, Elizabeth, p 211
8   Ibid
9   Conversation with the late Lord Charteris
10   Jocelyn Stevens to Christopher Warwick (1981)
11   Norman Barrymaine, The Story of Peter Townsend, p 173
12   Conversation with Princess Margaret
13   Conversation with Princess Margaret
14   G. Payn & S. Morley, The Noël Coward Diaries, p 289
15   Christopher Warwick, George & Marina, p 93
16   Private conversation
17   National Archives file 1955 Royal Family Eden Archive
Notes AP20/30/2

18 to 20 Ibid
21   Conversation with Princess Margaret
22   Conversation with Princess Margaret
23   Private conversation
24   Conversation with the Hon. Dominic Elliot
25   Conversation with Princess Margaret
26   Carl Toms, Photographs of Snowdon, p 11
27   R Glenton & S King, Once Upon A Time, p 24
28   Conversation with Lady Elizabeth Cavendish
29   Conversation with Princess Margaret
30   Sunday Telegraph Magazine, 18 April 1999
31   Hugo Vickers, Cecil Beaton, p 435
32   Ibid
33   Private information
34   Private conversation
35   Conversation with Alexander McEwen
36   Bill Glenton
37   Christopher Warwick, Princess Margaret, p 92
38   Conversation with Princess Margaret

Chapter Eleven

1   Private conversation
2   Gore Vidal, Palimpsest, p 194
3   Daily Mail (Woodrow Wyatt Diaries), 5 October 1998
4   Kenneth Rose, Sunday Telegraph, 1 March 1998
5 to 6   Private conversation
7   Private information
8 to 10   Private conversation
11   Miles Jebb (Ed.), Diaries of Cynthia Gladwyn, pp 235–40
12   Conversation with Princess Margaret
13   Christopher Warwick, Princess Margaret, pp 95–6
14   Private information
15   Conversation with Lady Elizabeth Cavendish
16   Sarah Bradford, Elizabeth, p 291

17   Conversation with Princess Margaret
18 to 22   Contemporary diary notes: Private source
23   Conversation with Princess Margaret
24   Private information
25   Conversation with Princess Margaret
26   Christopher Warwick, *Princess Margaret*, p 107
27   *Ibid*
28   Kenneth Rose
29   Kenneth Rose, unpublished diary entry
30   Conversation with Princess Margaret
31   Conversation with Princess Margaret
32   Conversation with Colin Campbell
33   Miles Jebb (Ed), *Diaries of Cynthia Gladwyn*, p 296
34   Kathleen Tynan, *The Life of Kenneth Tynan*, p 270
35   Interviewed on *The Windsors*, Channel 4 series
36   Private conversation
37   Private information
38   Private conversation
39   Private conversation
40   R. Glenton & S. King, *Once Upon A Time*, p 21
41   Sarah Bradford, *Elizabeth*, p 200
42   Private conversation
43   Christopher Warwick, *Princess Margaret*, p 120
44   Christopher Warwick, *Princess Margaret*, p 121

Chapter Twelve

1   Private conversation
2   Nigel Dempster, *HRH The Princess Margaret*, p 67
3   Roger Lewis, *The Life and Death of Peter Sellers*, p 356
4   *Daily Mail*, (quote from Michael Sellers' story) 25 January 1999
5   Private conversation
6   Private information

7 Conversation with Princess Margaret
8 Private information
9 Private conversation
10 Private conversation
11 Private conversation
12 Private conversation
13 Roy Strong, *The Roy Strong Diaries 1967–1987*, p 89
14 Conversation with Robin Macwhirter
15 Conversation with Lady Weinberg
16 Conversation with Princess Margaret
17 Conversation with Princess Margaret
18 Private conversation
19 Private conversation
20 Gore Vidal, *Palimpsest*, p 193
21 Private conversation
22 Roy Strong, *The Roy Strong Diaries*, p 214
23 Ben Pimlott, *The Queen*, p 439
24 Conversation with the Hon. Mrs Rhodes
25 Conversation with the late Lord Charteris
26 Private information
27 Ben Pimlott, *The Queen*, p 441
28 Conversation with Princess Margaret
29 Conversation with Robin Macwhirter
30 Conversation with Sir Anthony Dowell
31 Conversation with Dame Merle Park
32 Conversation with Princess Margaret
33 Conversation with the Hon. Mrs Whitehead
34 Private conversation
35 Private conversation
36 Private conversation
37 *Daily Mail*, 4 April 1996
38 Private information
39 Private information
40 Private information
41 Private information
42 Conversation with Giles Pegram, NSPCC

43   Jonathan Dimbleby, *The Prince of Wales*, p 394
44   Conversation with Colin and Charmian Campbell
45   Private conversation
46   Private information
47   Conversation with Lady Penn
48   Conversation with Lady Weinberg
49   Conversation with Lady Penn
50   Conversation with Lady Glenconner
51   Conversation with Sir John and Lady Nutting
52   Private conversation
53   Private conversation
54   Private information
55   Private conversation
56   Private conversation
57   Conversations with Princess Margaret
58   *Daily Mail*, 12 April 1999
59   Conversations with Princess Margaret and Lady Glenconner
60   Conversation with Lady Glenconner
61   Private information
62   Private conversation
63   *Independent on Sunday*, 3 October 1993

The Final Chapter

1   Conversation with Princess Margaret
2   *Ballet* Magazine, December 2000
3   Conversation with Princess Margaret
4   BBC Television News interview, January 2001
5   *The Times Medical Guide*, 15 February 2002
6   Conversation with Lady Glenconner
7   BBC Television News interview, April 2001
8   Conversation with Lady Elizabeth Shakerley
9   Private conversation
10   Private information
11   Private conversation
12   Private information

BIBLIOGRAPHY

Allison, R & Riddell, S, *The Royal Encyclopedia*, Macmillan (1991)

Batchelor, Vivien, *HRH The Princess Margaret Gift Book*, Pitkin (1951)

Barrymaine, Norman, *The Story of Peter Townsend*, Peter Davies (1958)

Bradford, Sarah, *Elizabeth: A Biography of HM The Queen*, William Heinemann (1996)

Chance, Michael, *Our Princesses and Their Dogs*, John Murray (1936)

Chase, Joanna, *HRH Princess Margaret*, Pitkin (1948)

Colville, John, *The Fringes of Power: Downing Street Diaries 1939–1955*, Hodder & Stoughton (1985)

Cornforth, John, *Queen Elizabeth The Queen Mother at Clarence House*, Michael Joseph (1996)

Crawford, Marion, *The Little Princesses*, Cassell & Co (1950)

Dempster, Nigel, *HRH The Princess Margaret*, Quartet (1981)

Dimbleby, Jonathan, *The Prince of Wales*, Little, Brown (1994)

Edwards, Anne, *Royal Sisters*, Collins (1990)

Forbes, Grania, *My Darling Buffy*, Richard Cohen (1997)

Glenton, R & King, S, *Once Upon A Time*, Anthony Blond (1960)

Healey, Edna, *The Queen's House*, Michael Joseph (1997)

Hearsey, John, *Marie Antoinette*, Constable (1974)

Jebb, Miles, *The Diaries of Cynthia Gladwyn*, Constable (1995)

Lacey, Robert, *Majesty*, Hutchinson (1977)

Lacey, Robert, *God Bless Her!* Century Hutchinson (1987)

Lea, Christopher, *This Sceptred Isle*, BBC (1997)

Lewis, Roger, *The Life and Death of Peter Sellers*, Century (1994)

Menkes, Suzy, *The Royal Jewels*, Grafton (1985)

National Portrait Gallery Publications, *Photographs by Snowdon – A Retrospective*, NPG (2000)

Payn, G & Morley, S, *The Noël Coward Diaries*, Weidenfeld & Nicolson (1982)

Pimlott, Ben, *The Queen*, HarperCollins(1996)

Roberts, Jane, *Royal Landscape*, Yale (1997)

Robyns, Gwen, *Her Royal Highness The Princess Margaret 21st Birthday Album*, Pitkin (1951)

Rose, Kenneth, *Kings, Queens & Courtiers*, Weidenfeld & Nicolson (1985)

Strong, Roy, *The Roy Strong Diaries*, Weidenfeld & Nicolson (1997)

Strong, Roy, *The Royal Portraits*, Thames & Hudson (1988)

Townsend, Peter, *Time and Chance*, Collins (1978)

Tynan, Kathleen, *The Life of Kenneth Tynan*, Weidenfeld & Nicolson (1987)

Vickers, Hugo, *Cecil Beaton*, Weidenfeld & Nicolson (1985)

Vidal, Gore, *Palimpsest*, André Deutsch (1995)

Warwick, Christopher, *Princess Margaret*, Weidenfeld & Nicolson (1983)

Warwick, Christopher, *King George VI & Queen Elizabeth*, Sidgwick & Jackson (1985)

Warwick, Christopher, *Abdication*, Sidgwick & Jackson (1986)

Warwick, Christopher, *George and Marina, Duke and Duchess of Kent*, Weidenfeld & Nicolson (1988)

Warwick, Christopher, *Queen Mary's Photograph Albums*, Sidgwick & Jackson (1989)

Wheeler-Bennett, John W., *King George VI: His Life & Reign*, Macmillan (1958)

Windsor, The Duchess of, *The Heart Has Its Reasons*, Michael Joseph (1956)

Windsor, HRH The Duke of, *A King's Story*, Cassell (1951)

Newspapers and Magazines include:

Waltham, Claude, *Windelsora, Issue No 12*, (1993)

Aberdeen Press & Journal, 25 August 1930

Bulletin & Scots Pictorial, 23–28 August, & 1, 23 September 1930

The Daily Telegraph, 'The British Century Part One 1900–45', John Keegan, 1999

The Daily Telegraph, 'The Real Queen Mother', Graham Turner, 6 July 1999

Evening Times, 22 & 28 August 1930

Glasgow Herald, August/September 1930

Majesty Magazine. *The Golden Years,* Jean Rook, August 1990

Style Magazine, *Relationship of the Week,* Chrissey Iley, 25 June 1995

Sunday Telegraph Magazine, The View from Snowdon, Lucy Cavendish, 18 April 1999

Sunday Telegraph, 1 March 1998

The Presidencies, Patronages and Service Appointments held by H.R.H. The Princess Margaret

Presidencies:

The Royal Ballet
British Museum 250th Anniversary Development Appeal
 (Honorary President)
Commonwealth Trust
English Folk Dance and Song Society
Friends of the Elderly and Gentlefolk's Help
The Guide Association
Horder Centre for Arthritis
Invalid Children's Aid Nationwide
Lowland Brigade Club (Joint President)
National Society for the Prevention of Cruelty to Children
Scottish Children's League
Scottish Society for the Prevention of Cruelty to Children
St John Ambulance Association and Brigade (Grand President)
Victoria League for Commonwealth Friendship

Patronages:

The Royal Anglian Regimental Association (Vice Patron)
Architects' Benevolent Society
Association of Anaesthetists of Great Britain and Ireland
Barristers' Benevolent Association

Bristol Royal Society for the Blind
British and International Sailors' Society (Ladies' Guilds)
Clarence House Restoration Trust (Antigua)
The Royal College of Nursing
Combined Theatrical Charities Appeals Council
English Harbour Repair Fund (Patron in Chief)
Friends of Southwark Cathedral
Friends of St John's Smith Square
Friends of the Iveagh Bequest, Kenwood
Grand Antiquity Society of Glasgow
Halle Concert Society
Heart Disease and Diabetes Research Trust
HMS Illustrious (Sponsor)
HMS Norfolk (Sponsor)
League of Friends of the Royal London Hospital
Light Infantry Club
London Lighthouse
Maria Callas Society
Mary Hare Grammar School for the Deaf
Mathilda and Terence Kennedy Institute of Rheumatology
Migraine Trust
Mustique Educational Trust
National Pony Society
Northern Ballet Theatre
Pottery and Glass Trades' Benevolent Institution
Purine Research Laboratory
Queen Alexandra's Royal Army Nursing Corps Association
Scottish Community Drama Association
Services Sound and Vision Corporation
St Margaret's Chapel Guild, Edinburgh Castle
St Pancras Housing Association in Camden
Suffolk Regimental Association
Tenovus and Tenovus Scotland
Union of Schools for Social Service
University of London Chorus
Winnipeg Art Gallery (Honorary Patron)

Youth Clubs Scotland
Zebra Trust

Service Appointments:

Honorary Air Commodore - Royal Air Force Coningsby
Deputy Colonel in Chief - The Royal Anglian Regiment
Colonel in Chief - The Bermuda Regiment
Colonel in Chief - The Royal Highland Fusiliers (Princess Margaret's Own Glasgow and Ayrshire Regiment)
Colonel in Chief - The Highland Fusiliers of Canada
Colonel in Chief - Light Dragoons
Colonel in Chief - The Princess Louise Fusiliers
Colonel in Chief - Queen Alexandra's Royal Army Nursing Corps

Other Honours:

Honorary Life Member – Royal Air Force Club
Honorary Life Member – Automobile Association
Honorary Member – The Royal Automobile Club
Freeman – Borough of Queensferry (Lothian, Scotland)
Life Member – Royal British Legion Women's Section
Honorary Life Member – Century House Association
Honorary Freeman – City of London
Honorary Fellow – Royal College of Obstetricians and Gynaecologists
Honorary Fellow – Royal College of Surgeons of England
Royal Master of the Bench – The Honourable Society of Lincoln's Inn
Honorary Fellow – Royal Institute of British Architects
Visitor – King George VI and Queen Elizabeth Foundation of St Catharine's
Founder Member – Olave Baden-Powell Society

Member – The Order of the Road

Honorary Fellow – The Royal Photographic Society of Great Britain

Honorary Member – Sealyham Terrier Breeders' Association

Honorary Fellow – Royal Society of Medicine

Member of the Court of Assistants – The Worshipful Company of Haberdashers

Honorary Life Fellow – The Zoological Society of London

Official Overseas Visits Undertaken by H.R.H. The Princess Margaret

1947   South Africa   (with King George VI, Queen Elizabeth and Princess Elizabeth)

1948   The Netherlands

1949   Italy, Switzerland and France

1950   Malta and Tripoli

1951   France (Paris)

1953   Norway

Southern Rhodesia (with the Queen Mother)

1954   Germany

1955   West Indies

1956   Sweden

East Africa and Indian Ocean Dependencies

1958   Germany

West Indies

Canada

Belgium

1959   Portugal

1960   Belgium (Brussels for the marriage of King Baudoin)

1961   Norway

1962   Jamaica (Independence celebrations)

1963   Germany (Münster)

        Germany (Westphalia and Brüggen)

1964   Denmark

1965   Uganda

        Netherlands

        United States of America

1966   Hong Kong

        France

1967   Belgium

1968   USA

        France

1969   Tour of Japan, Cambodia, Thailand and Iran

1970   Yugoslavia

1971   France

        Canada

1972   British Virgin Islands

        Italy

        Germany

        Seychelles

        Western Australia

        Singapore

1973   Barbados

        Germany

1974   Cyprus

        USA

        Canada

1975 Germany

      Australia

      Bermuda

1976 Morocco

      Tunisia

      Cyprus

1977 Italy

      USA

1978 Tuvalu

      Japan

      Dominica

1979 USA

1980 Germany

      Philippines

      Singapore

      Malaysia

      Canada

1981 Greece

      Germany

      Canada

      Swaziland

      Antigua

      St Vincent

1982 USA

      Germany

      Italy (Venice)

1983 St Christopher and Nevis

1984   Bermuda

      USA

1985   Hungary

      Denmark and Sweden

1986   Netherlands

1987   China and Hong Kong

1988   Canada

      Egypt

1990   Bermuda

1991   USA

1992   Netherlands

      USA

      Belgium (Brussels)

1993   USA

      France (Paris)

      Canada

1994   USA (April - Washington DC

               July – New York)

1995   USA (San Francisco)

1996   USA (Los Angeles)

      Russia (St Petersburg)

      Canada

1997   Antigua

      Italy (Milan)

      USA (New York)

INDEX

Footnotes are indicated by 'n' immediately after the number. Subheadings are in alphabetical or page order, as appropriate.